Nature Walks
in Connecticut

- South of Chaplin on 198

- CT state Forest off rt 6. west of rt 97

- Nautaug 198 into Castford CT state forest

- LAUREL LANE ORCHARD
    74 TOWARD 44 just outside of Willington

- Holman - CT State Forest just past 84 ramps on 74

Nature Walks
in Connecticut

René Laubach
Charles W. G. Smith

APPALACHIAN MOUNTAIN CLUB BOOKS
BOSTON, MASSACHUSETTS

Cover Photograph: René Laubach
All photographs by the authors unless otherwise noted
Cover Design: Elisabeth Leydon Brady
Book & Map Design: Carol Bast Tyler

Distributed by The Globe Pequot Press, Inc., Old Saybrook, CT

Library of Congress Cataloging-in-Publication Data
Laubach, René.
Nature walks in Connecticut: explore mountains, forest, caves, and coastline throughout the State / René Laubach, Charles W. G. Smith.
p. cm.
Includes bibliographical references and index.
ISBN 1 878239 69-4 (alk. paper)
1. Nature trails—Connecticut—Guidebooks. 2. Natural history—Connecticut—Guidebooks. 3. Walking—Connecticut—Guidbeooks. 4. Connecticut—Guidebooks. I. Smith, Charles W. G. II. Title.
QH105.C8L28 1999
508.746—dc21   98-54592
                                                               CIP

The paper used in this publication meets the minimum requirements of the American National Standard for Information Sciences—Permanence of Paper for Printed Library Materials, ANSI Z39.48–1984.∞

**Due to changes in conditions,
use of the information in this book
is at the sole risk of the user.**

Printed on recycled paper using soy-based inks.
Printed in the United States of America.

10 9 8 7 6 5 4 3 2 1   98 99 00 01 02 03

Contents

For my brother Rainer, with love and admiration.
René Laubach

To my mother and father, may they rest in peace;
to my brothers and sisters; and to the generations that follow us:
Nathaniel, Lisa, Joseph Jr., Ashley, Joseph III, Debbie, Joshua, Kimber-
ly, Rick, Christen, Lindsay, Nate, Parker, Conner, Ernie, and Kyle.
Charles W. G. Smith

Acknowledgments

Thanks to the gentleman at White Memorial Foundation whose name we never learned but who took the time to share his favorite paths with us; to Laura Rogers-Castro of the Connecticut Department of Environmental Protection's Wildlife Division for telling me about Sessions Woods Wildlife Management Area; to Elaine La Bara of the Housatonic Valley Association; to Annie Guion of Trail Wood Sanctuary; and to the late Edwin Way Teale for his inspirational writing.

My collaboration with Charly Smith has been a great pleasure and I thank him for his partnership.

Also a note of appreciation to publisher Gordon Hardy for enabling us to bring this book to fruition, and to our editor, Mark Russell, for helping us to improve the final product.

Finally, thanks to my wife, Christyna, for wonderful companionship and assistance in the field.

René Laubach

The first two decades of my life were spent in Connecticut. When I left for other places, the paths I chose to follow always seemed to bring me back to the place of my birth. The idea of this book came from René, who is always thinking of new things. When he asked me to join in the journey I was all too happy to follow the path back home.

As I walked the Connecticut trails over the last year, I visited favorite places of my youth and discovered many more that were new and charming. Along the way I bumped into many people who were more than willing to stop and chat for a bit. Thanks for the happy faces and pleasant conversation.

In addition to those I met on the trail were those I sought out off the trail. These people, from librarians at the Curtis Memorial Library to rangers at Mount Misery, were very helpful and generous with their knowledge.

Another group who were with me in spirit as I wandered about were the friends and family with whom I first hiked some of these trails many years ago. Since then many have scattered like milkweed seeds on the breeze, but their absence does not diminish the value of their contribution. As I revisited the Meremere cliffs or paused to admire the cascades of Wentworth Falls, the fun we shared in the Connecticut hills long ago came back tenfold.

Thank you, Nathaniel, for being such a wonderful person and for climbing all those mountains with me. Thank you, Christine, for being a companion and partner in the woods and out. And thank you to the rest of my family for your support and love.

I also extend my appreciation to all the folks, professional and volunteer, who preserve and maintain the trail systems of Connecticut. And a special thanks to those at the Appalachian Mountain Club and its chapters in Connecticut and the Berkshires. Finally, thanks to everyone at Appalachian Mountain Club Books for assembling all the pieces, maps, pictures, and words into a book to be proud of.

Charles W. G. Smith

Introduction

An old proverb says, "Where you walk is where you are. Where you have walked is who you are."

This is a book of 45 walks across the hills, shoreline, and woodlands of Connecticut. The trails described will lead you to a variety of places: mountaintops with gorgeous views, windy ridges that pulse with energy, and shoreline marshes alive with birds. There are paths to waterfalls that are slender veils of lacy mist, and powerful cataracts with drumbeat crescendos. You will walk by ponds and lakes where geese, swans, and ducks paddle across the water and beaver ferry sticks to their sinuous dams. And you will tramp to the marshes and swamps where egrets, great blue heron, bobcat, and bear live. Some are trails that follow the courses of big rivers as they wind through wide valleys; some are paths where wildflowers bend on slender stems beneath the shade of the maidenhair and cinnamon ferns.

Everything along the trails—each stone and flower, every view, cellar hole, field, and tree—has a story to tell. The stone may be a bit of traprock that began as a subterranean reservoir of molten magma millions of years ago, and the flower may be Dutchman's-breeches clinging to the traprock cliffs. The views may show you valleys carved by glaciers or shorelines caressed by the unerring pulse of the tide. There are miles of stone walls that once separated pasture from forest or roadway from wilderness. There are Indian legends of giants and stories of a chestnut grove that is helping to save the chestnut tree from extinction.

Homer wrote that the value of a voyage lay not in the destination, but in the journey. This is a book of 45 journeys that will take the curious and the patient to unforgettable places. We hope you enjoy them as much as we have.

How to Use This Book

Each walk begins with a listing of important facts which includes the **names of the trails**, the **total length** of the walk in miles, the **elevation gain** or change along the hike, an approximate **time** range needed to complete the walk, and a **rating of the terrain** covered.

Of these criteria the last two are subjective. The time ratings for completing each walk are based on a very relaxed pace that allows for plenty of observation and hanging out. Most people can finish the hikes in less time than we have allowed, but we hope they won't want to. The faster the pace, the less is learned and observed.

The ratings for the type of terrain covered include **easy, moderate,** and **difficult**. In general the terrain rating is a reflection of the total length of the walk, the elevation gain, and any unique features—such as scrambles or very steep sections—of that walk. Remember that a faster pace will make any walk more difficult and that it is possible to encounter poor footing on all trails, regardless of rating.

The second section of each walk consists of a short summary of that walk as well as a description of how the trails are marked. This introduction is followed by a *Look Forward To* list of that walk's highlights.

The Trail is a guided tour of the entire walk. Landmarks are used as reference points, so you can know where you are along the walk at almost any given time. Plants, rock formations, animal burrows, and the like are described in the text in relation to where they appear along the trail, which makes it easier to find these things as you walk along. At the end of each trail section is an essay that explores a relevant topic in greater detail.

Getting There gives directions to the trailhead by the most traveled routes.

What to Bring

Walking or hiking in Connecticut often will take you away from the conveniences many of us have grown dependent on. We are, to be blunt, a wimpy bunch of folks when compared with the animals of the woods that thrive all by themselves through storms and snows. It takes many years to become as self-reliant as nature originally intended us to be, so in the meantime it is prudent to bring our technological crutches with us where we walk.

Every time you go for a hike you should have a day pack with you to carry the ten essentials. The ten essentials are the ten commandments of hikers and will go a long way to making you more self-reliant in the woods. They are:

1) *Extra clothing.* What you bring depends on the season of the year and where you are going. Some of the staples include rain gear, hats and gloves, fleece or wool sweaters, and socks. Bring clothes made of fibers that retain their insulating value when wet, such as fleece and wool, instead of those that lose it, such as cotton.

2) *Food and water.* High-energy food such as cereal bars or gorp (a blend of chocolate, raisins, and nuts), along with at least one quart of water or sports drink per person (on long hikes you can easily need twice this much). These items help replace what hiking depletes from your body. Bring more than you think you will need.

3) *Sunglasses and whistle.* Sunglasses are needed in the winter when the combination of snow and sun can bring on snow blindness. The whistle is used in case you get lost and need to communicate with rescuers. The sound carries farther than a yell. Whistles are used only in emergencies.

4) *Tools-All.* This wonderful invention combines folding pliers with a knife blade, screwdrivers, awl, and other goodies. The Swiss army knife was its inspiration but the Tools-All is even more versatile.

5) *Fire starter.* Campfires are not a part of the wilderness experience anymore, but they do have a place in some emergencies. The simplest fire starter to bring with you is a small candle.

6) *Matches.* It doesn't do much good to have a candle if you can't light it.

7) *First-aid kit.* Pick up a hiker's first-aid kit (specifically designed for treating the troubles encountered in the woods) from a good outdoor-recreation store.

8) *Flashlight.* Sometimes it gets dark a lot faster than you thought it was going to. A flashlight will go a long way to helping you find your way back in the dark.

9) *Map.* Know where you are and where you are going. Never go anywhere without one.

10) *Compass.* Learn how to use it and don't go anywhere without this either.

Footwear

You can wear hiking boots to play tennis or wear sneakers to hike the Appalachian Trail, but why would you? Woodland trails are best negotiated in a pair of hiking boots. They give good footing and protect your ankles from twisting. Today you can get hiking boots that are hybrids between cross-trainers and sturdy leather boots. They are light and versatile and usually meet the challenges of the Connecticut trails quite well. Under the boots should be a good pair of hiking socks made of a fabric other than cotton.

Lyme Disease

Named after Lyme, the Connecticut coastal town where it was originally identified in 1975, Lyme disease is by far the best known of several diseases borne by ticks. It is apparently one of the fastest-spread infectious diseases in this country, with cases reported in all states except Alaska. Lyme disease is caused by a bacterium and borne by the black-legged tick. The hosts of this tiny tick, formerly known as the deer tick, are white-tailed deer and white-footed mice. This tick is very much smaller than the American dog tick and the wood tick. Black-legged ticks may be active any time the temperature is above 32°F.

Black-legged ticks have a three-stage, two-year life cycle. At each stage the ticks require a blood meal. Larvae are most active from late July to early September, peaking in mid-August. Some years there is a secondary peak from mid-June to early July. Larvae molt into nymphs over the winter. Nymphs are most active from May through August. In late summer nymphs molt into adults that are about 2 mm in length.

The classic symptoms of the disease include a red, circular rash at the site of the bite. Early symptoms may resemble those caused by the flu. Later symptoms may include arthritis and heart and neurological problems.

Lyme disease can be successfully treated with antibiotics. A new vaccine to combat the disease is under development.

How to Protect Yourself

- Wear light-colored clothing.

- Tuck shirts into pants and pants into socks. Wear closed shoes.

- Spray pants with a commercial tick/insect spray that contains no more than 33 percent DEET, being careful not to get the repellent directly on your skin.

- Stay on trails and away from branches, brush, and tall grass.

- Check your clothing for ticks periodically. The black-legged tick larva may be no larger than the period at the end of this sentence.

- Conduct a thorough tick check after you return home. Be sure to examine your scalp, back of the neck, armpits, groin, and behind the knees. Also check beneath elastic bands.

If you find an attached tick, remove it carefully by grasping it with very fine tweezers by the head and gently pulling it straight out. Be careful not to break off its mouthparts. Wash the site with an antiseptic. Watch for signs of a rash. You may want to save the tick for later identification by your physician if symptoms appear.

Note that dogs can also contract Lyme disease.

With all that said, do not let the fear of contracting Lyme disease keep you out of the woods. Do take the sensible precautions listed above and be alert for signs of potential symptoms of the disease.

Walking in Connecticut

Western Connecticut

The northwest hills are home to the Connecticut section of the Appalachian Trail (AT), which weaves through about fifty miles of beautiful woodlands and mountains from the New York border to the Massachusetts state line in the southern Berkshires. Along the way many walks show you some of the best sections of the Connecticut AT, from the easy stroll along the Housatonic River outside Kent to the views from Lion's Head and the stone pyramid atop Bear Mountain. If this touch of wilderness isn't quite wild enough, you can even ascend a rugged trail through three states to a lonely perch of rock that marks the highest elevation in the state. The walks in western Connecticut also include the oasis-like sanctuaries of Greenwich Audubon, and Weir Preserve in and around the southwest panhandle and the unforgettable forests and wildlife of White Memorial and Sharon Audubon. To top it off, you can visit a grove of ancient pines pillaged by a tornado, and the spooky stone remains of Connecticut's most infamous ghost town. Whichever walk you choose, in whatever season, the western region of this beautiful state is a fascinating place to explore.

The Central Region

The central section of Connecticut is sandwiched between the metamorphic mountains and highlands of the west and east. This area is home to the state's signature river, the Connecticut, with its broad valleys of fertile soil and ridges of traprock and sandstone that loom over the fields and towns below. The walks in this region explore the fascinating traprock mountains, from Sleeping Giant and Bluff Head in the south to Mount Higby, the Hanging Hills, and Talcott Mountain to the north. Here Indian legends still live on, and wildlife, from copperheads to bobcats, still survives. The windy crests of the traprock ridges preserve unique ecosystems where hardy northern species overlap with more-southern ones, and endangered plants and animals still hold on.

The central region also contains walks that take you to caves to explore, from the overhang of Coginchaug to the deep recesses of Indian Council Caves. In addition to these attractions are beautiful walks through the McLean Game Refuge, Sessions Woods, and West Woods, where majestic rock formations mingle with the water birds and mysterious rock carvings of Lost Lake. You will be surprised that in this region of cities, suburbs, and thoroughfares so many lovely, private locations await your visit.

Eastern Connecticut

The eastern region is a largely quiet area of fishing villages and rural towns. It holds some of the most enchanting areas of shoreline in the state, from Hammonasset to Bluff Point and Barn Island. Here along sandy beaches horseshoe crabs still congregate in spring, as do flocks of seabirds. In fall the thickets of beach rose harbor scores of songbirds waiting to begin their long, hectic flight south.

North of the shore are walks that take you through the haunting atmosphere of Chatfield Caves and Devil's Hopyard. In spring the display of mountain laurel along Laurel Loop and rosebay rhododendron in the Rhododendron Sanctuary is spellbinding.

But this region has even more in store, for in the northeast corner of the state are walks through Trail Wood Sanctuary and one of the most beautiful spots in the state, Rock Spring Wildlife Refuge.

Locator Map

WESTERN

CENTRAL

TORRINGTON

HARTFORD

MANCHEST

BRISTOL

WATERBURY

MERIDEN

MIDDLETOWN

DANBURY

NEW HAVEN

BRIDGEPORT

STAMFORD

Walks and Highlights

WALK	PAGE	DIFFICULTY LEVEL	DISTANCE (MILES-RT)
Barn Island Wildlife Management Area	311	moderate	5.3
Bear Mountain	7	difficult	6.5
Bear Rock	177	easy/moderate	1.1
Bluff Head	198	easy/moderate	1.8
Bluff Point Coastal Reserve	295	easy	4.5
Breakneck Pond	215	mod./difficult	6.7
Burnham Brook Preserve	260	easy/moderate	1.7
Burr Pond	46	easy	2.5
Candlewood Mountain	67	mod./difficult	3.0
Cat-Hole Pass and East Peak	153	mod./difficult	4.2
Cathedral Pines and Mohawk Mountain	40	mod./difficult	3.7
Chatfield Trail Caves	277	mod./difficult	2.6
Chauncey Peak	159	mod./difficult	2.0
Coginchaug Cave	193	easy/moderate	1.5

Waterfalls	Scenic Vista	Bogs & Marshes	Ponds, Lakes & Rivers	History	Fields	Forest	Wildlife	Plants & Wildflowers	Geology	Seacoast
✔	✔	✔			✔	✔	✔	✔	✔	
✔	✔	✔	✔			✔	✔	✔	✔	
✔	✔	✔				✔	✔	✔		
✔						✔	✔	✔		
✔	✔	✔	✔		✔	✔	✔	✔	✔	✔
	✔	✔				✔	✔	✔	✔	
		✔			✔	✔	✔	✔	✔	
✔		✔	✔			✔	✔	✔	✔	
✔		✔			✔	✔	✔	✔	✔	
✔	✔	✔	✔			✔	✔	✔	✔	
✔		✔	✔		✔	✔	✔	✔		
✔						✔	✔	✔	✔	
✔		✔			✔	✔	✔	✔		
		✔	✔			✔	✔	✔	✔	

Waterfalls	Scenic Vista	Bogs & Marshes	Ponds, Lakes & Rivers	History	Fields	Forest	Wildlife	Plants & Wildflowers	Geology	Seacoast
		✓	✓		✓	✓	✓	✓	✓	
	✓	✓	✓	✓	✓	✓	✓	✓		
✓	✓		✓	✓	✓	✓	✓	✓		
	✓		✓	✓	✓	✓	✓	✓		
			✓		✓	✓	✓	✓	✓	
✓	✓	✓			✓		✓	✓	✓	✓
	✓			✓		✓	✓	✓	✓	
	✓	✓	✓	✓		✓	✓	✓	✓	
		✓	✓	✓	✓	✓	✓	✓	✓	
	✓	✓	✓		✓	✓	✓	✓		
	✓	✓	✓			✓	✓	✓	✓	
	✓	✓	✓		✓	✓	✓	✓	✓	
			✓			✓	✓	✓	✓	
	✓	✓	✓	✓	✓	✓	✓	✓	✓	
	✓					✓	✓	✓	✓	

WALK	PAGE	DIFFICULTY LEVEL	DISTANCE (MILES-RT)
Mount Misery	249	moderate	1.7
People's Forest	110	difficult	4.5
Pine Knob	29	mod./difficult	2.6
Rhododendron Sanctuary	244	easy	0.5
River Road	54	easy	2.9
Rock Spring Wildlife Refuge	235	moderate	3.6
Sessions Woods Wildlife Management Area	129	easy/moderate	3.0
Sharon Audubon Center	20	moderate	2.8
Sleeping Giant	182	difficult	3.2
Sunny Valley Preserve	75	moderate	3.4
Talcott Mountain	147	moderate	3.1
Trail Wood Sanctuary	225	easy	2.3
Wadsworth Falls	171	easy/moderate	3.3
Weir Nature Preserve	93	easy	1.1
West Woods	204	mod./difficult	3.3
White Memorial Conservation Center	59	easy	4.7

WATERFALLS	SCENIC VISTA	BOGS & MARSHES	PONDS, LAKES & RIVERS	HISTORY	FIELDS	FOREST	WILDLIFE	PLANTS & WILDFLOWERS	GEOLOGY	SEACOAST
	✔		✔			✔	✔	✔		
	✔	✔	✔	✔		✔	✔	✔	✔	
	✔		✔			✔	✔	✔		
		✔	✔	✔		✔	✔	✔		
			✔	✔	✔	✔	✔	✔		
	✔	✔	✔			✔	✔	✔	✔	
✔	✔	✔	✔		✔	✔	✔	✔	✔	
		✔	✔		✔	✔	✔	✔		
	✔		✔	✔		✔	✔	✔	✔	
	✔		✔			✔	✔	✔	✔	
	✔		✔	✔		✔	✔	✔		
		✔	✔	✔	✔	✔	✔	✔		
✔		✔	✔	✔		✔	✔	✔	✔	
			✔		✔	✔	✔	✔	✔	
		✔	✔			✔	✔	✔	✔	
		✔	✔		✔	✔	✔	✔		

10/14/01

Western Connecticut

 **1** Mount Frissell

Salisbury

- Brace Mountain Trail, South Taconic Trail, Mount Frissell Trail
- 4.6 miles
- 430-foot elevation gain
- 2.5–3.5 hours
- moderate

There is no other place in Connecticut as lofty or as wild as the forests of Mount Frissell. Here the highest elevation in the state hides among dense thickets of mountain laurel, and black bear and bobcat still stalk the woods. If you want to walk on the wild side, this walk is for you.

The walk to Mount Frissell passes through three states and offers unforgettable views from the most remote corner of Connecticut. The Brace Mountain Trail is unblazed but easy to follow. The South Taconic Trail is marked with small white blazes, and the Mount Frissell Trail is blazed in red.

Look Forward To

- the highest point in Connecticut
- spectacular views
- wild, remote forests

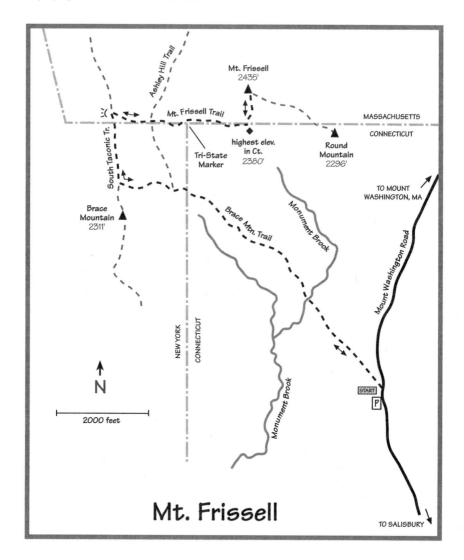

Mt. Frissell

The Trail

From the parking area on Mount Washington Road, set in a grove of oak and maple, the Mount Brace Trail heads northwest. The path is unblazed, but the wide, grassy treadway is easy to follow. The beginning of the trail is lined with mountain laurel and is quite attractive, following the roadbed of a long-abandoned logging road. Here and there, stump sprouts of American chestnut poke through the laurel, and pasture brake, a large fern that likes partly shaded spots, mingles with blueberries and wintergreen. Overhead is a verdant mosaic of oak, maple, and gray birch leaves.

The gentle terrain then begins to descend into the Monument Brook valley. The laurel gradually gives way to more-open woodlands covered with oceans of ferns beneath spreading boughs of hemlock.

The path then comes to Monument Brook. This small drainage flows through a series of marshy wetlands along its course, and one of these is visible through the trees to the right. Black bear comb this and other swamps for food around dawn and again at dusk on summer days. During the heat of the day they head back into the timber to rest.

From the brook the path ascends past thickets of ferns, laurel, blue-berries, and goldenrod. Look for deer and bear tracks along the trail through here. Other animals you may spot include coyote, raccoon, red squirrel, fox, fisher, marten, and chipmunks. In spring the wild apples bloom, followed by fragrant milkweed in early summer and goldenrod in late summer. Woodland butterflies drift by, including the mourning cloak, with black-brown wings edged in cream. Mourning cloaks pass the winter in a state of hibernation, more accurately called diapause, and begin to flutter by on the first warm breezes of spring.

At an intermittent stream near a small grassy clearing, the easy walk comes to an end and the climbing begins. The path becomes rocky as it ascends the eastern slope of Mount Brace. In late May the very fragrant blossoms of trailing arbutus appear and provide a welcome excuse to stop and smell the flowers. Trailing arbutus is a creeping plant that grows at the edge of the trail. Soon after beginning the climb, the trail passes into New York. A small rock cairn, placed to the right of the trail and high up the mountain, marks an unblazed shortcut to the Ashley-Hill Trail.

As you climb higher, species of trees that prefer cooler climates begin to dominate. Paper and gray birch, oak, and red maple are here, as is striped maple, a low-growing tree of the mountains.

After a fairly strenuous climb the Mount Brace Trail ends at the junction with the South Taconic Trail. The South Taconic Trail straddles the windy, largely open ridge crest of the Taconic Range and is one of the most lovely paths in the Northeast. The summit of Mount Brace is a short walk south (left), and makes a nice adventure all on its own. Its summit, marked by a stone cairn, is a great place to picnic. Continue straight ahead (north) along the white-blazed South Taconic Trail. Do not take the unmarked trail to the right. The path hugs the ridge crest, wandering through stands of oak, dwarf birch, and pitch pine to an incredibly beautiful open area with wonderful views.

The ridge is grassy, with plenty of places to rest and enjoy the sights. To the south is the grassy summit of Mount Brace, with Mount Frissell visible to the east. To the north are the Berkshires of Massachusetts. To the west the Taconic hills drop away and the broad sweep of the Harlem valley becomes prominent. The small cluster of homes to the west is Boston Corners, New York. If you are wondering how a town in New York acquired the name of a Massachusetts city, it is really quite simple. Generations ago Boston Corners was part of Massachusetts, but being on the west side of the Taconic Mountains, the town was essentially cut off from the rest of the Bay State. Consequently, with little or no law enforcement from Massachusetts, the town became a favorite place for entrepreneurs with a flair for the illegal. In desperation Massachusetts gave its western frontier, including Boston Corners, to New York. Just west of Boston Corners is Fox Hill, with the impressive profile of the Catskill Mountains beyond.

A cluster of signs at the overlook are well maintained and very helpful. From the trail signs take the red-blazed Mount Frissell Trail east into dense stands of bear oak, chokeberry, birch, and blueberry studded with rounded bedrock outcrops. The small white flowers of three-leafed cinquefoil, a subalpine wildflower, bloom here in early summer. This is a magnificent landscape and should not be hurried through. As the path gently descends toward the gap between Mount Frissell and Mount Brace, the forest of oaks become taller and more open.

After a short walk the Ashley-Hill Trail leaves left (north) and the unblazed, unmaintained shortcut between the Ashley-Hill Trail and the Mount Brace Trail enters right (south). Continue straight ahead (east) to a four-foot-tall granite pillar which marks the spot where Connecticut, Massachusetts, and New York meet.

The west side of the marker is engraved NEW YORK, while the north side is engraved MASS. CONN is feebly hand-scratched into the stone's south side. The reason Connecticut is not formally engraved into the rock monument has to do with the history of Connecticut itself. Since its founding centuries ago, Connecticut has had a long series of border disputes with its neighbors. Of these the troubles with Massachusetts and New York dragged on the longest. As folks who live in Connecticut know, a Connecticut Yankee is one of the most stubborn creatures alive. When this monument was erected in the late 1800s, Connecticut still thought the boundaries were unfair, and refused to allow its name on the marker. More than a century later the borders are still the same, and Connecticut's signature is still missing from the marker. Sometimes stubbornness can go too far; it took some folks with a sharp rock to scratch CONN into the stone many years later.

From the marker the trail follows the Connecticut-Massachusetts state line east through woods of oak and maple, laurel, pasture brake, wild sarsaparilla, wintergreen, and blue-bead lily. The terrain steepens as the path tackles the western slope of Mount Frissell, becoming briefly very

The view from a grassy field near the overlook on the South Taconic Trail.

steep as it scrambles up a bare rock ledge.

Wild azalea and very thick tangles of laurel line the trail as it reenters the woods, soon coming to a loose stone cairn and a United States Geological Survey marker at the highest point in Connecticut, 2,380 feet, 64 feet higher than the summit of Bear Mountain to the east (the highest summit in Connecticut).

Just east of the stone cairn is a good view of this wild, northwestern corner of Connecticut. Due east is the low contour of Round Mountain, with Bear Mountain just to its right. To the right of Bear Mountain is Gridley Mountain, while to the south is Riga Lake. The summit of Mount Frissell (2,453 feet) is a short walk on the Mount Frissell Trail. To return to the parking area, retrace your steps.

CLIMBING THE TACONIC KLIPPE

Sometimes as you hike up a seemingly endless rocky summit trail, you may not particularly care whether you're walking over igneous basalt or metamorphic schists. When you're climbing a steep slope, to paraphrase Freud, sometimes a rock is just a rock. Well, not always.

Rocks have more to tell us about the natural world than anything else we commonly bump into. Many of them are tens of millions of years old, and some are closer to a billion. You just can't get to be that old and not have a good story to tell. Such is the case with the rocks called the Taconic Klippe.

The Taconics are a narrow range of mountains that straddles the borders of Vermont, New York, Massachusetts, and Connecticut. Near the tristate boundary of Connecticut, Massachusetts, and New York the principal peaks are Mount Brace (2,311 feet), South Brace Mountain (2,304 feet), Round Mountain (2,296 feet), and Mount Frissell (2,453 feet).

The Taconics, like all of New England, are an incredibly old landscape. The mountain trails that lead to the highest point in Connecticut traverse rocks that took their present form during the Taconian mountain-building event which began 445 million years ago. At this time Europe and North America began to drift toward each other. The pressures that resulted caused volcanic islands to form off the coast and the Taconic Mountains to begin to rise. Around 435 million years ago the volcanic islands were pushed against the mainland and the Taconic Mountains reached their ultimate height, probably near 20,000 feet high.

Huge thrust faults formed across the Taconics, a product of the continuing drift of the European continent against North America. These pressures dislodged a gigantic section of the Earth's crust, called a *klippe*. This enormous section of land, which now reaches from the Hudson Highlands to Ticonderoga along Lake Champlain in Vermont, then slid westward in huge earthquake-induced landslides.

Hundreds of millions of years of erosion have worn down these impressive peaks to one-tenth their original height. The rock beneath your feet is mainly gneiss (pronounced *nice*), which formed miles beneath the Earth's surface after being subjected to intense heat and pressure.

Knowing all this does not take away the burning in the legs as you climb up the mountainside. But it does give you something to think about, while giving the view from the top even more meaning.

Getting There

Near the town hall in the center of Salisbury turn onto Factory Street (about 100 yards south of the junction of Routes 44 and 41). Proceed down Factory Street 0.7 mile, following signs to Mount Riga. At 1.3 miles the road becomes gravel. At 1.6 miles you pass through the gate of Mount Riga Forest Preserve. Continue on the road to a dam at the lake. From the dam a road turns right, becoming Mount Washington Road, which is rough and narrow. At 5.9 miles from Salisbury Center is a parking area on the left, with a gate marking the trailhead.

Note: The road to Mount Frissell is passable only during warm seasons of the year.

—C.S.

Bear Mountain

Salisbury

- Undermountain Trail, Appalachian Trail, Paradise Lane Trail
- 6.5 miles
- 1,560-foot elevation gain
- 3.5–4.5 hours
- difficult

Bear Mountain is one of the most popular hiking destinations in the state. A grand stone pyramid crowns its summit, offering unrestricted views which include broad valleys, shimmering lakes, and rugged mountains in three different states. In addition to the vistas this walk takes you on a long loop through ancient forests where animals such as fisher, deer, and coyote roam. There are ponds and bogs, songbirds and wildflowers, and much, much more.

The walk over Bear Mountain is on the Undermountain and Paradise Lane Trails, both blazed with pale blue markers, and the Appalachian Trail (AT), blazed in white. Turns are noted by two stacked blazes, the upper blaze offset in the direction of the turn. All trail junctions are signed. The Appalachian Trail in Connecticut is maintained by the Connecticut Chapter of the Appalachian Mountain Club and managed by the Appalachian Trail Conference.

Look Forward To

- the highest summit in the state
- views and more views
- beautiful forests

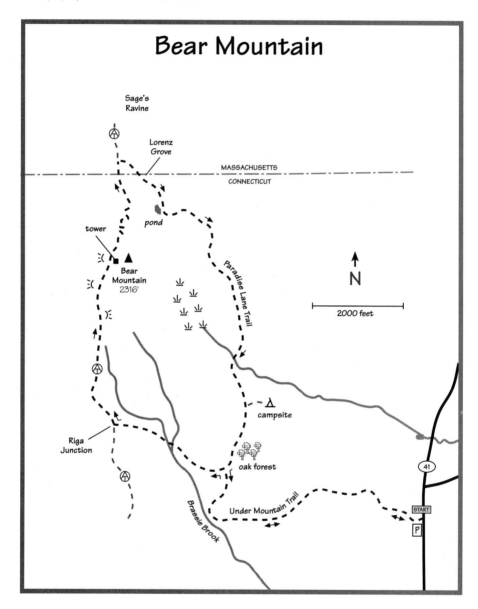

Bear Mountain

Sage's
Ravine

Lorenz
Grove

MASSACHUSETTS

CONNECTICUT

tower

pond

Bear
Mountain
2316'

Paradise Lane Trail

N

2000 feet

campsite

Riga
Junction

oak forest

41

Brassie Brook

Under Mountain Trail

START

P

The Trail

From the parking area on Route 41 in Salisbury the Undermountain Trail passes a kiosk where trail maps and other information are available. Near the kiosk a short path leads to a privy. The trail then begins a gentle westward climb into a forest of red and white oak, ash, and hickory that shade clumps of witch hazel, mountain laurel, wild azalea, and striped maple. Evergreen Christmas fern shares the forest floor with mats of partridgeberry, sprigs of wintergreen, and isolated specimens of rose twisted-stalk and wild sarsaparilla. Cardinals, blue jays, chickadees, and woodpeckers are common sights in the nearby trees, and the leafy summer homes of gray squirrels can be seen tucked into the limbs of tall oaks.

Rose twisted-stalk is a plant that favors the cool climates of mountain slopes from southern Canada south along the spine of the Appalachians. The one-foot-tall herbaceous stems grow in a pronounced zigzag pattern, with each zig and zag accented by a solitary deep-green leaf. In late spring through early summer, small deep-pink, pendant, bell-shaped flowers appear along the stems.

The moderate but relentless climb becomes steeper as the path traverses the eastern slope of Riga Ridge. Beside the trail are a number of interesting plants including selfheal, a member of the mint family with short, square stems and stubby spikes of lilac flowers in summer; aster; and spotted wintergreen, with lance-shaped green leaves decorated with a white central stripe. Look for spotted newts through here as well. These little amphibians look like salamanders and are colored bright orange.

After passing the sign welcoming you to Appalachian Trail lands, the trail swings past Brassie Brook, climbs a series of stone steps, and intersects with the Paradise Lane Trail at 1.1 miles. Continue on the Undermountain Trail through woods of birch, hemlock, beech, and maple. The path is level here and soon crosses Brassie Brook near a cluster of mossy boulders and small, quiet pools. On the low, easternmost boulder is a small bronze plaque which reads:

In memory of
Dave Gilman
a teacher and friend
as long as the mountain laurel
shall bloom your spirit and
wisdom will abide in us all

From Brassie Brook the path proceeds through areas dotted with hobblebush, laurel, wild azalea, wintergreen, and trailing arbutus. Hobblebush, like rose twisted-stalk, prefers cooler climates. This open-branched, rather gangly shrub has large leaves and wide, flat clusters of white, hydrangea-like blossoms in spring. The tall, open woods yield to moist thickets of summersweet, laurel, and striped maple. This wet area is crossed on two log bridges lined with tall ferns and clusters of blue-bead lily.

A short distance farther the path climbs a moderate slope to Riga Junction where the Undermountain Trail meets the Appalachian Trail. Turn right (north) on the AT and proceed through low, wind-stunted woods of maple, birch, and oak with an understory of laurel, honeysuckle, sassafras, and chestnut. For a short way the terrain is level. After passing an unmarked woods road to the left that leads to Mount Washington Road, the treadway steepens as it ascends the southern slope of Bear Mountain. The thin, boulder-strewn landscape can no longer support the trees of lower elevations. In their place red maple, bear oak, chokeberry, blueberries, and pitch pine become increasingly common.

The trail winds up the mountain, passing a large boulder on the left that, for a little effort, offers a fine view to the south, west, and east. You don't need to climb it, however, because a short way farther bedrock outcrops grow more common, each one with a nice view enough to stop and celebrate. Ravens make frequent flybys, and in fall the stunning foliage serves as a backdrop to a steady stream of migrating hawks.

The path now becomes more rock than soil, with a beautiful southern view a nearly constant companion. Reindeer moss, named for its antler-shaped stems, grows in the sheltered crevices of rocks as does three-leafed cinquefoil, a subalpine wildflower with small white summer blossoms and crimson autumn leaves. As the path levels out the low thickets of oak and pine are dwarfed by the stone pyramid topping the mountain's wooded summit.

The flat top of the stone monument offers a spectacular view. To the north are the rounded profiles of Mount Race (2,365 feet) and Mount Everett (2,602 feet), crowned by a now unused fire tower. The pure-blue bodies of water to the east are Washinee and Washining Lakes, together called Twin Lakes, some 1,500 feet below. To the west-northwest are the summits of Round Mountain (2,296 feet) and Mount Frissell (2,453 feet). The closest mountain to the southwest is Gridley Mountain (2,211 feet), while due west is Brace Mountain (2,311 feet). On clear days the Catskills are visible far beyond the profile of Brace Mountain.

At the base of the stone monument is a stone plaque which proudly proclaims the summit of Bear Mountain as the highest point in Connecticut. This plaque has been a source of misunderstanding for most of the century. In 1885, when the plaque was carved, the summit of Bear Mountain was indeed the highest surveyed point in the state. Unfortunately not all of the state was surveyed in 1885. Years later it was determined that the

Hikers perch atop the stone pyramid on the summit of Bear Mountain.

highest ground in the state actually lay on the south slope of Mount Frissell (see chapter one) a short distance to the west.

From the summit continue north along the AT, which quickly begins a steep 600-foot descent of Bear Mountain's northern slope.

The path winds around many rock outcrops and windfalls on its way to the level col far below. When the trail does level out, it passes the unmarked Northwest Road on the left and heads gently downhill. Soon a tree, faintly marked with the letters MA, marks the boundary of Massachusetts and Connecticut. Continue north into Massachusetts to a sign welcoming you to Sage's Ravine and the intersection with the Paradise Lane Trail.

Turn right onto the Paradise Lane Trail and into a stand of hemlock and white pine called the Lorenz Grove. A short way farther is a bronze plaque honoring Edward Lorenz for his work in protecting this land and his dedication to the Connecticut Chapter of the Appalachian Mountain Club. Many of the trees in this grove have the sinuous scars of lightning strikes on their trunks. On sunny days this is a pleasant place to linger. If dark clouds are on the western horizon, however, it is best to move along.

From the grove the trail enters a clearing of scrubby bear oak and blueberries, with a nice view of Bear Mountain to the southwest. Deer are frequent visitors here, most often passing through at twilight. The clearing yields to woods of red maple and serviceberry, also called shadblow, a small gray-barked tree covered with lacy white blossoms in early spring. The tasty fruit ripens in June and is sometimes used as a substitute for blueberries in pies.

A small pond is passed on the right, followed by a wet, boggy stretch where gray birch, pitch pine, and bear oak mingle with the long fronds of pasture brake. The path then proceeds through a series of long, fairly flat stretches where moist fields of ferns alternate with forested, rocky uplands. Near a large tree a side trail left leads to the Paradise Lane campsite, where overnight camping is permitted.

The path now comes to a broad, open forest of low, thick-trunked oak trees. These trees look no different from the hundreds of others along the trail, but they are far older, many being more than 120 years old. The grassy woods are home to turkey, coyote, deer, bobcat, red squirrels, porcupines, raccoons, deer mice, pileated woodpeckers, and fishers.

Fishers are not usually seen by humans because they prefer to be abroad at night. These large members of the weasel family are jet black, can reach nearly three feet in length, and can climb trees in the blink of an eye. They hunt a number of small animals but are best known for their ability to dispatch porcupines.

From the oak forest the path descends gently, crossing some stone walls before meeting the Undermountain Trail. To return to the parking area, turn left on the Undermountain Trail and continue downhill 1.1 miles to Route 41.

WOODPECKERS, LARGE AND SMALL

Most people become familiar with woodpeckers by supplying suet for the cute little black-and-white birds that visit backyard feeding stations. These birds, called downy woodpeckers, are fairly tame creatures and mingle freely in mixed winter flocks of chickadees, nuthatches, and titmice. Downy woodpeckers are the smallest of Connecticut's woodpeckers, reaching only six inches long. The birds have a small red patch on the back of the neck and a stubby bill. As they cling to trees or feeders, they often utter a soft *tik, tik* call. In spring they nest in a hole in a tree, where they lay a clutch of four to five white eggs.

At the opposite end of the size spectrum is the pileated woodpecker. This crow-sized bird reaches about seventeen inches in length, with jet-black plumage accented with splashes of white on the sides of the neck and a bright red head crest. It flies like a missile through the forest with deceptive speed. Pileated woodpeckers are shy birds and are not easily observed. If the surroundings get noisy, they find more-secluded places.

In past decades it was believed that pileated woodpeckers were declining in numbers throughout their range, including Connecticut. As the forests were chopped into smaller and smaller plots, the populations of the birds dropped. Studies showed that pileated woodpeckers need large acreages of unbroken forest to thrive. Woodlands of more than forty hectares, about 100 acres, were considered the minimum area needed for the birds to survive. In a tribute to their adaptability, recent observations have shown that pileated woodpeckers are beginning to be seen in areas previously considered unfavorable to them. Suburban parks and small forest reserves are noting the return of a small number of pileated woodpeckers.

Even if you are not fortunate enough to view these beautiful birds, their handiwork is easily found along most forest trails in the state. Pileated woodpeckers eat insects that live in trees. They pursue these tasty treats with great zeal, hammering away with their strong bills and tossing chips of wood everywhere. The resulting rectangular excavations can be quite large, about three inches wide, six inches long, and two to three inches deep. Often deer mice enlarge the holes further. Sometimes, in a demonstration of the versatility of nature, downy woodpeckers discover them and use them as nesting sites.

Getting There

From Salisbury take Route 41 north 3.5 miles to a parking area on the left. A blue sign for Undermountain Trail is near the large parking area.

—C.S.

Lion's Head and Bald Peak

Salisbury

- Lion's Head Trail, Appalachian Trail, Bald Peak Trail, Lion's Head Bypass Trail
- 4.1 miles
- 810-foot elevation gain
- 2.5–3.5 hours
- difficult

Lion's Head, named for its feline profile, is one of the more popular spots along the Connecticut section of the Appalachian Trail. It is a place of incomparable vistas and friendly hikers. Bald Peak also has excellent views but is more private and wild. This walk takes you to both on scenic trails populated by many species of songbirds and wonderful spring wildflowers.

The Lion's Head and Bald Peak Trails are marked with pale blue blazes, while the Appalchian Trail (AT) is blazed with white marks. Turns on all trails are noted with stacked double blazes. The Connecticut Chapter of the Appalachian Mountain Club maintains the AT in Connecticut.

Look Forward To

- mountaintop views
- lots of wildflowers
- songbirds

The Trail

From the parking area follow the dirt road north through a field of sensitive fern, goldenrod, and isolated islands of willow, alder, apple, and red cedar. Just beyond a signal-relay station the trail turns left (west) and follows a wide cart path lined with barberry and honeysuckle bushes beneath the

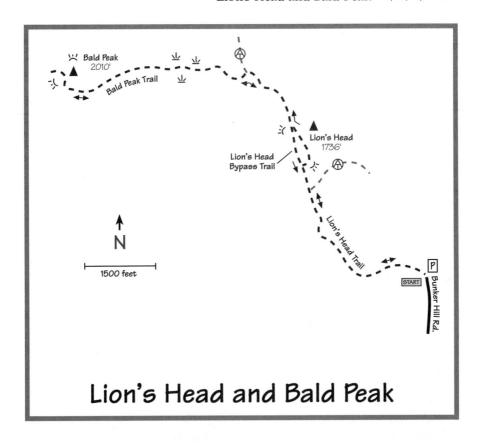

Lion's Head and Bald Peak

spreading boughs of wild apple, cherry, and ash trees. The apple trees are covered with blush-white, lightly fragrant flowers just after Mother's Day each year. The blossoms attract bumble- and honeybees as well as hummingbirds.

The cart path heads down a gentle grade and crosses a small brook where sweet violets bloom in spring and veeries and wood thrush sing on warm summer mornings. From the stream the trail ascends gradually near a stone wall, climbing through a young, mixed hardwood forest of red oak, cherry, red maple, apple, and black birch, with a scattered understory of striped maple. As the woods open into a fairyland of ferns, trillium, and Canada mayflower, the grade becomes moderate. Paper and gray birch begin to appear and yellow-throated vireos can be seen clinging to pliant branches of understory shrubs as the birds hunt for food.

Just after crossing a stone wall, the grade becomes a bit easier and the path wanders between a fence line on the right and a field of ragged boulders to the left. Soon the blue-blazed Lion's Head Trail intersects the white-blazed Appalachian Trail and the path becomes a bouquet of blue-above-white blazes. Continue uphill through thickets of mountain laurel, wild azalea, blueberries, and wintergreen. As you continue to gain elevation the character of the forest begins to change. Hemlock, oak, and white pine appear, shading boulders of metamorphic schist. The pale pink blossoms of wild azalea, which grow near the boulders, flower in late spring.

At a level spot high on the hillside, the Lion's Head Bypass Trail continues straight (north) while the combined Lion's Head/AT turns right (northeast) and tackles the very steep final scramble to Lion's Head lookout. At the top of the cobble the laurel and pine open into spectacular views to the south and east. From the smooth rock ledges Salisbury's famous Twin Lakes are to the east while Wetauwanchu Mountain and Red Mountain are to the southeast and south, respectively. It is a bit of a rugged climb to Lion's Head, so stay awhile and soak up the beautiful vistas as a reward before continuing on. Pleasant hideaways tucked beneath the pitch pines offer nice resting places, or you can scan the ridge in hopes of sighting some of the ravens that nest in the crags beneath the overlook.

Painted trillium on the Bald Peak Trail.

From Lion's Head the trail follows the rocky ridge through brushy stands of bear oak, pine, serviceberry, and blueberry. Before long the Lion's Head Bypass Trail enters left. Continue along the Appalachian Trail a short distance to a rounded rock shelf and another beautiful view, this one to the north. Bear Mountain lies straight ahead, with Mount Race just to the right. The peak with the fire tower on its crest is Mount Everett, the highest mountain in the southern Berkshires. On clear days, just to the right of Mount Race, the saddle-shaped form of Mount Greylock, the tallest peak in Massachusetts, is visible some seventy miles away.

The trail now drops down off the Lion's Head ridge through patches of scrubby oak and blueberry. In a pretty hardwood forest the path levels out. To some this stretch of woods may seem unremarkable, but in spring it is home to an enchanting little wildflower called gaywings. The blossoms are bright pink and shaped like a tiny, cheerful airplane, hence the name.

After a very pleasant walk the AT continues straight (northwest) while Bald Peak Trail enters left (west). Turn left onto Bald Peak Trail, which enters the Mount Riga Forest Preserve after crossing an intermittent stream. The path then traverses a rocky slope beneath red oak, maple, and yellow and gray birch above an understory of striped maple, laurel, and witch hazel before tackling a steep climb up a pair of ridges. At the crest of the second ridge the footway levels out, passing through an open hardwood forest. Bracken and sheep and mountain laurel grow beneath the tall trees, giving the place a tranquil, though magical atmosphere.

The trail then makes a brief, steep descent to a wetland carpeted with lacy ferns. In the center of the wetland is a small stream where skunk cabbage and the bright yellow flowers of marsh marigold bloom in early spring. Nearby the straggly stems of hobblebush grow near mountain laurel. Deer are frequent visitors here, as are coyotes, who use the deer trails to travel their large home ranges. The path continues through waves of hemlock and laurel alternating with open wetlands filled with wildflowers, including goldthread, trailing arbutus, painted trillium, wild oats, and dwarf ginseng.

Dwarf ginseng indeed looks like a miniature version of ginseng, with three to five small, toothed, dark green leaflets and a small sphere of little white flowers held above the foliage in late spring. It is not nearly as rare as its more vaunted relative, but is just as exciting to see in the wild.

The trail then crosses a small stream on a log bridge before intersecting a woods road. Continue on Bald Peak Trail (west), which begins to climb the wooded flank of Bald Peak. The trail climbs steeply through woods of beech, gray birch, and oak with mountain laurel beneath before coming to a rocky scramble that leads to the summit. The crest of Bald Peak is a mosaic of metamorphic rock, serviceberry, blueberry, and chokeberry, all framing a gorgeous 360° view. Bear Mountain, the highest summit in Connecticut, is to the north-northwest. To its left are Gridley Mountain followed by Round Mountain, Mount Frissell (the highest point in Connecticut), and Brace Mountain in New York. To the west are the Catskills. In fall this area is a great place to watch migrating hawks. In spring the mountaintop is covered with the white bouquets of serviceberry and chokeberry. Three-leafed cinquefoil, a subalpine wildflower, grows in the crevices between the rocks. It has small white summertime flowers, and in fall its green leaves turn a fiery scarlet.

Unlike Bear Mountain, Bald Peak isn't visited much, so you should have the mountain largely to yourself. It is a wonderful place to sit and enjoy a warm summer day, and it is especially inspiring in the fall when the woods are ablaze with color. To return to the parking area, simply retrace your steps.

HUMMINGBIRDS

There are few creatures as magical as hummingbirds. With plumage dyed in iridescent colors, they are like rainbows on the wing. There are about fourteen species of hummingbirds that breed in North America, yet only one, the ruby-throated hummingbird, breeds in the eastern United States.

Ruby-throated hummingbirds are not the most colorful of hummingbirds, but they are the flashiest dressers of any bird east of the Mississippi River. The males are decked out with sparkling green feathers on their back and sides that shimmer like rhinestones, a snow-white breast, and a bold ruby-red patch beneath the chin. The females, who don't need to wear neon to get a male's attention, are more modestly attired with yellow-green feathers on their back and a white breast and throat.

Hummingbirds are tiny things, reaching only three and a half inches when full grown. They are spectacular flyers and zip around forests and gardens with amazing speed. Hummingbirds can also hover and are the only birds that can fly backwards. All this hyperactivity burns a lot of calories, and hummingbirds seem in a constant search for food. For entrees hummingbirds like to nibble on small flying insects, which they grab and consume in the air. For dessert the birds visit flowers to sip the sweet nectar.

Hummingbirds are migrants, spending their summers up north and wintering in the tropics. Ruby-throated hummingbirds travel south in late summer or early fall, and fly to their wintering grounds in Mexico, Belize, and Guatemala. There these adaptable birds visit many habitats, and are one of the few species that seem to thrive in previously deforested areas in the first stages of regrowth.

In addition to viewing hummingbirds in the wild, you can attract these magnificent birds to your yard by planting some of their favorite flowers in the garden. These include bee balm, cardinal flower, blazing star, fuchsia, hollyhock, foxglove, scarlet sage, spider flower, and petunia.

Getting There

From the junction of Routes 41 and 44 in Salisbury, proceed south on Route 44 about 100 yards to the Salisbury Town Hall where Factory Street meets Route 44. Turn onto Factory Street and follow signs toward Mount Riga. Bear right onto Bunker Hill Road. Follow Bunker Hill Road to its end, about 0.95 mile. Park along the side of the road where signs indicate.

—C.S.

10/28/01

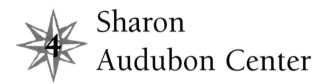

Sharon Audubon Center

Sharon

- Deer Trail, Fern Trail, Bog Meadow Trail, Hazelnut Trail, Ford Trail, Borland Trail
- 2.8-mile loop
- 210-foot elevation gain
- 3.0 hours
- moderate

Owned and operated by the National Audubon Society, this 758-acre wildlife sanctuary in northwestern Connecticut has twelve miles of well-marked and well-maintained trails which lead the walker through an interesting mix of natural communities. Ponds, streams, and associated wetlands are especially well represented. Boardwalks make the wet areas accessible and make exciting wildlife observations possible.

The property is large and rural enough that one can get at least a sense of what pre-colonial New England may have been like. If you visit during the week, you may be rewarded with a feeling of solitude as you gaze out over Bog Meadow Pond toward the rolling uplands beyond. The low, guttural croak of a passing raven will further enhance the wilderness atmosphere.

The grounds are open daily dawn to dusk. The center is closed on major holidays. The main building is open Monday through Saturday, 9:00 A.M. to 5:00 P.M. and Sunday, 1:00 to 5:00 P.M. The main building houses an exhibit center featuring seasonal displays and several species of live raptors and reptiles. Nonmembers pay an admissions fee. Dogs are not allowed.

Look Forward To

- scenic Bog Meadow Pond
- abundant wildlife
- teeming wetlands

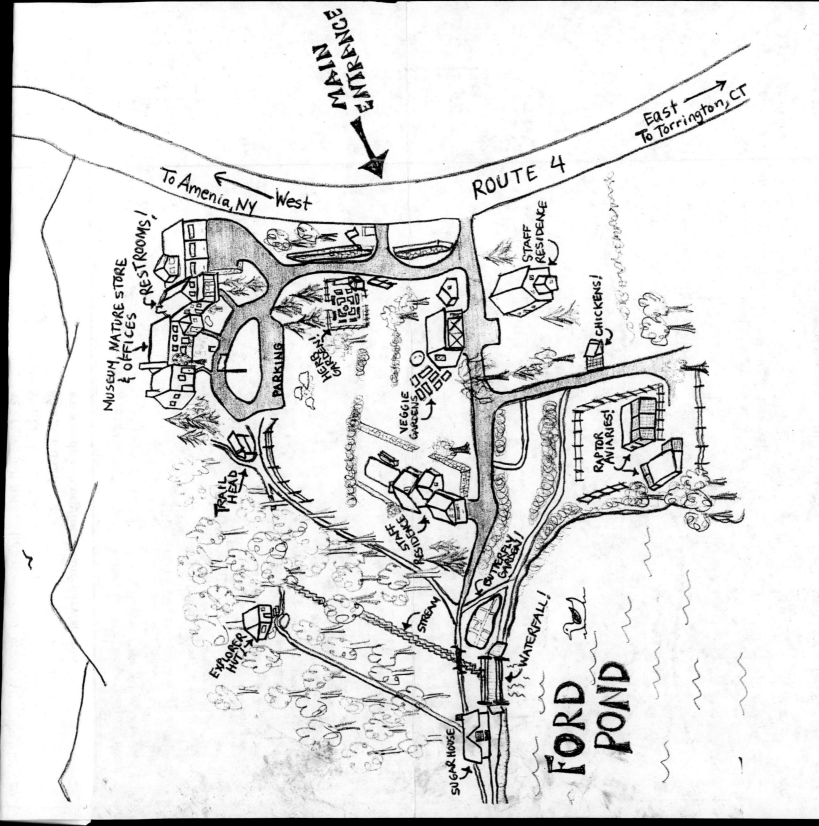

MAIN ENTRANCE

East → To Torrington, CT

To Amenia, NY ← West

ROUTE 4

RESTROOMS!

MUSEUM, NATURE STORE & OFFICES

STAFF RESIDENCE

CHICKENS!

PARKING

HERB GARDEN!

VEGGIE GARDENS!

RAPTOR AVIARIES!

TRAIL HEAD

STAFF RESIDENCE

BUTTERFLY GARDEN!

STREAM

EXPLORER HUT!

WATERFALL!

SUGAR HOUSE

FORD POND

ALL HIKING TRAILS BEGIN AT TRAILHEAD

ENJOY YOUR VISIT... PLEASE COME AGAIN!

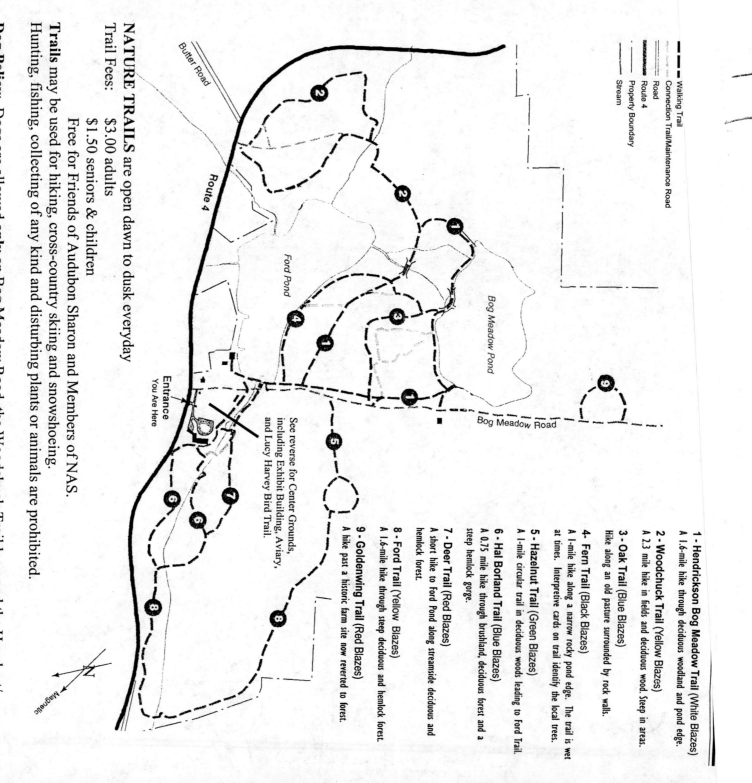

AUDUBON CENTER IN SHARON

1 - Hendrickson Bog Meadow Trail (White Blazes)
A 1.6-mile hike through deciduous woodland and pond edge.

2 - Woodchuck Trail (Yellow Blazes)
A 2.3 mile hike in fields and deciduous wood. Steep in areas.

3 - Oak Trail (Blue Blazes)
Hike along an old pasture surrounded by rock walls.

4 - Fern Trail (Black Blazes)
A 1-mile hike along a narrow rocky pond edge. The trail is wet at times. Interpretive cards on trail identify the local trees.

5 - Hazelnut Trail (Green Blazes)
A 1-mile circular trail in deciduous woods leading to Ford Trail.

6 - Hal Borland Trail (Blue Blazes)
A 0.75 mile hike through brushland, deciduous forest and a steep hemlock gorge.

7 - Deer Trail (Red Blazes)
A short hike to Ford Pond along streamside deciduous and hemlock forest.

8 - Ford Trail (Yellow Blazes)
A 1.6-mile hike through steep deciduous and hemlock forest.

9 - Goldenwing Trail (Red Blazes)
A hike past a historic farm site now reverted to forest.

Walking Trail
Connection Trail/Maintenance Road
Road
Route 4
Property Boundary
Stream

NATURE TRAILS are open dawn to dusk everyday

Trail Fees: $3.00 adults
                $1.50 seniors & children

Free for Friends of Audubon Sharon and Members of NAS.

Trails may be used for hiking, cross-country skiing and snowshoeing. Hunting, fishing, collecting of any kind and disturbing plants or animals are prohibited.

Dog Policy: Dogs are allowed **only** on Bog Meadow Road, the Woodchuck Trail loop and the Hazelnut/Ford Trail loop. Dogs must be on a leash at all times and must not defecate on trails. Please respect these rules for the safety of the wildlife and other visitors. Dogs are not allowed at the aviary.

See reverse for Center Grounds, including Exhibit Building, Aviary, and Lucy Harvey Bird Trail.

Entrance
You Are Here

Butter Road
Route 4
Ford Pond
Bog Meadow Pond
Bog Meadow Road

N Magnetic

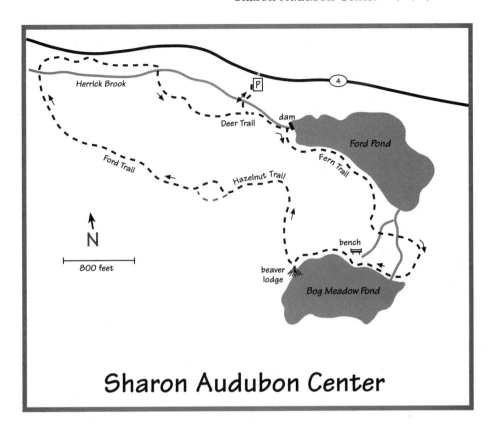

Herrick Brook

P

4

Deer Trail

dam

Ford Pond

Fern Trail

Ford Trail

Hazelnut Trail

N

800 feet

bench

beaver
lodge

Bog Meadow Pond

Sharon Audubon Center

The Trail

From the map kiosk near the parking lot, walk left to follow the sign for Ford/Hal Borland Trail and cross the wooden bridge over Herrick Brook. Ahead is the Explorer Hut. The spillway was built of native stone. Examine the brook banks for signs of nocturnal foragers such as raccoon. Come to the Deer Trail junction at the hut and turn left to follow its rectangular red blazes among hemlock, sugar maple, red oak, and yellow birch—all northern hardwood forest indicator species. The woods are very rocky; chunks of gneiss rock jut up from the forest floor. On your left, skunk cabbage and cinnamon and sensitive ferns grow in the gurgling brook's drainage under the hemlocks. Red trillium (wake-robin) and jack-in-the-pulpit line the chipped path.

Emerge from the forest at the Ice House. The spillway of Ford Pond is just ahead to the left. Turn right, pass the Ice House, and follow the Bog Meadow/Fern Trails, which fork left away from the old road track. In late spring wild raisin shrubs, a viburnum, put forth their bouquets of small white flowers. In late summer the blue-black fruits provide food for wildlife. The rock wall of the dam is on your left and Ford Pond is visible as you reach the top of the dam. There is a nice view of the pond from the bridge over the spillway. Hills just beyond form an attractive backdrop. The pond surface is covered with yellow-green filamentous algae, fertilized by the droppings of Canada geese. Water-loving birds like red-winged blackbird, warbling vireo, and tree swallow all utter their breeding songs in spring and early summer.

Return to the right and walk to the Bog Meadow Trail trailhead. As you enter the woods, turn left onto the green-blazed Fern Trail to follow closely along the pond's edge (Bog Meadow Trail continues straight). The moist, dark soil is punctuated by boulders, many of which are covered with gray-green lichens. White ash is common in the damp earth, along with the previously mentioned northern hardwood trees. Pretty royal fern joins sensitive fern in damp soil, while Christmas and evergreen wood fern form clumps amid the rocks. Hay-scented and interrupted ferns grow nearby on higher ground. Along the shore the tiny white bells of highbush blueberry decorate the shrubs in late spring. Lowbush blueberry plants are also in flower then. Cinnamon fern becomes abundant; tapping its tawny fertile fronds in this season liberates a cloud of rusty spores.

Some of the red maples along the water's edge were girdled by beavers long ago. An old bank lodge is visible on the far shoreline. One uncommonly large American chestnut tree has a wire-mesh cage around it to protect it from the rodents' sharp incisors. American robins hunt for earthworms on the muddy banks with cocked heads. The wonderfully fragrant carnation-like aroma that wafts to your nostrils in late spring emanates from the delicate pink blossoms of mountain azalea shrubs. A slope rises gradually on the right. Black birch colonizes patches of bare earth and even establishes itself on boulders. Reach the Fern/Bog Meadow Trails intersection and continue straight on the Fern Trail. Note more old beaver-cut trees along the shore. The path divides briefly to bypass one long-fallen casualty of the beaver's industry.

On a mid-June visit I watched a male yellow-bellied sapsucker drinking from rows of oblong sap wells he had drilled in a young black birch. After the sapsucker left, a ruby-throated hummingbird took its turn lapping up the sweet liquid, rich with oil of wintergreen, as it hovered on whirring wings. Sap provides a vital early-season nutrition source for hummingbirds after they first return from the south. Begin walking again and swing right, away from the pond, through red oak, red maple, and witch hazel growth. Reach a four-way intersection with the Bog Meadow Trail and turn left onto the white-blazed Hendrickson Bog Meadow Trail. Witch hazel, from which the astringent is distilled, is abundant here along with beaked hazelnut and some chestnuts.

Very soon reach a wet area bordering a stream and cross a wooden bridge. Skunk cabbage, wetland ferns, and golden ragwort, blooming yellow-orange, thrive in the dampness. A white-tailed deer bounded across the trail when we were there, white flag erect. A boulder at the end of the boardwalk/bridge has sprouted delicate maidenhair ferns. Above the boardwalk I noticed what turned out to be a wood thrush sitting low on a nest in a witch hazel about eight feet up. Moments before, I had heard one singing close by; probably its mate. The trail rises now just a bit. Wild geranium blooms in late spring along its borders. Cross another small stream on steppingstones. Gaudy Baltimore orioles and well-camouflaged red-eyed vireos sing from a fern-filled small clearing on the right. The trail swings left among oak, maple, and ash.

Soon come to a Y fork for the Woodchuck Trail on the left; continue right on the Bog Meadow Trail. Some of the red oak are quite large, while most other species are fairly young. Pass a big rock outcrop on the right. A

A wild and idyllic scene greets the walker along the shore of Bog Meadow Pond.

rocky slope rises up to the left, and then the trail bears right past highbush blueberry shrubs to Bog Meadow Pond, a far more natural scene than that at Ford Pond. Green frogs give their comical banjolike gulps and swamp sparrows sing their cheery musical trills from the lush bordering vegetation. Tussock sedges dot this marshy end. A forested ridge looms 400 feet above the pond, creating a wild and idyllic scene. To the right of the path grows one of the most luxuriant stands of skunk cabbage and cinnamon fern I have ever seen. It is reminiscent of the Carboniferous age. The path actually follows the top of an earthen dam, and soon you'll reach a concrete outflow piled high with old beaver-deposited cuttings.

Cross the outflow on a short boardwalk. Honeysuckle and arrowwood shrubs line the path. A large, hairy poison ivy vine climbs a tree to the right; some also grows along the ground. Red maple is the dominant tree here. Over the ridge I spied nine turkey vultures rocking easily on the rising air currents while the wild cries of a raven came to my ears. The trail then passes through a small but dense stand of giant reed. Leafy twigs recently cut by beaver float on the water as you reach a boardwalk where a bench makes it a perfect place to enjoy a snack. While eating lunch, I noticed red and black ants tending their aphid "cows" on an arrowwood bush immediately behind me. The ants protect the aphids from predators in turn for the aphids' "honey dew" secretions, an arrangement which seems to suit both well. In the shallows a smallmouth bass sought sustenance.

Gentle breezes carried the rapidly spinning winged seeds of red maple onto the pond surface. As children we used to call maple seeds helicopters. Each tree species has evolved ways to ensure that its seeds are borne as far from the parent tree as possible. On the opposite "shore," a red maple swamp covers an area larger than the pond itself. Continue walking down the boardwalk and come to a T intersection. At the end of the 100-foot-long left branch at the water's edge is a wide deck outfitted with benches. Return to the main boardwalk and turn left to continue. Witch hazel is still very common and red oak is now the most dominant large tree. One tree has a wood-duck box affixed to it. These are definitely drier woods; hickories and bracken ferns appear.

Pass through a gap in an old stone wall where chipmunks seem to be the prevalent life form. In late spring black cherry, black raspberry, and diminutive bluets all produce flowers along it. Paralleling the stone wall, the sun-bathed path is alive with butterflies basking and seeking nectar. A bit farther on is an old beaver-cut area now green with sedges and shrubs. Reenter shaded woods where pink-blooming wild geraniums are plentiful in June. A very wide rock wall is now close at hand. In places it is ten to twelve feet thick and waist high. What effort must have gone into its construction! Come to an intersection amid white pines where the aroma of pine pitch is evocative. The Bog Meadow Trail goes right, but before following it, turn left and walk 150 feet to the pond shore in order to examine the active bank beaver lodge. The lodge is anchored against a large, multitrunked red maple.

During my June visit the smell of beaver castorium hung thick in the air. It had a strong horse-manure-like quality. Beaver secrete the substance to mark their territories against intrusion from others not of their clan. Return to the main trail and turn left. The woods are composed mainly of young white pine, red maple, and gray birch. Walk up a slight hill and emerge at the edge of a field where pairs of bluebird nest boxes have been erected. A tree swallow poked its bicolored head out of one box as I passed by. This small, sandy meadow has scattered red cedar and gneiss rocks. The cedar (juniper, actually) indicates that it was once pastureland.

Pass through another gap in a rock wall and reenter oak woods, then immediately reach the four-way intersection with the Oak Trail. Continue straight on the white-blazed Bog Meadow Trail downhill under oak and maple with a few hickories and white pines. Below the trees are witch hazel, beaked hazel, and chestnut saplings. A singing wood thrush, a drumming yellow-bellied sapsucker, and the burry-sounding scarlet tanager added their voices to the forest. Sessile-leaved bellwort (a.k.a. wild oats) is one of the most common forbs of these oak woods. It reveals its modest, pale-yellow pendant flowers in spring. I was fortunate indeed to see and hear a big female pileated woodpecker. She sat on the horizontal branch of a nearby oak and called intermittently, with her bill closed.

Come to a split in the trail just before a large rock outcrop. Turn left onto the Hazelnut Trail here. Almost immediately cross the old woods road in a bit of a depression and continue straight, uphill. To the left stands a Native American wigwam replica. The voices of ovenbird, eastern wood pewee, and veery signaled their presence. White-blooming starflower brightens the forest floor under the oak, maple, birch, and hickory. New York fern and wild sarsaparilla are abundant. The Hazelnut Trail splits and rejoins a short distance farther along; you can go either way. The right fork is fairly wide and shaded. Gradually climb through oak woods and soon reach the intersection of the Hazelnut and Ford Trails. Turn right onto the Ford Trail to continue. A scarlet tanager sang continuously from the oaks during my mid-June walk.

The trail is narrow and bordered by lowbush blueberry in the acidic soil below the oaks. Chestnut oak seedlings are numerous in these open woods. A male white-breasted nuthatch uttered its *wer-wer-wer* song. This "upside-down" bird is a common year-round resident of oak forests. Little oak fern, which looks like a miniature edition of the big bracken, maple-leafed viburnum, and striped maple join the species mix. The last is decorated with strings of small green winged seeds at this season.

Now start downhill steeply. I found a flight feather from a barred owl below the sixty-five-foot-tall oak trees. Many of the red oak have trunks that split just above the ground. After undulating, the trail enters shady hemlock woods virtually devoid of ground cover and then descends more steeply again. The increasing volume of vehicular traffic tells you that you are nearing the highway. No Hunting signs mark the sanctuary boundary to your left.

The path swings to the left and is a bit difficult to follow here. Continue fairly steeply downhill and enter maple, ash, and birch forest. Still walking downhill, swing left at a boulder and then pass an old hemlock snag bearing deep pileated woodpecker excavations. A rock wall now appears on the left. At the bottom of the hemlock-shaded slope Herrick Brook flows left, carrying water from Ford Pond. Follow downstream along the edge of the bubbling brook to a wooden bridge over it, scanning the mud for tracks of deer and other woodland denizens. Walk through skunk cabbage; bruised leaves emit a fetid odor. Now enter a small clearing much warmer than the dank forest. The trail bears right, close to the highway. Continue through two tiny clearings and reenter woods. Oriental bittersweet draping the woodland edge is characteristic of disturbed areas like this.

Unwittingly I flushed a perfectly camouflaged American woodcock from its daytime hiding place on the forest floor. The bird sat tight, however, until I was within five feet of it. These plump, long-billed "shorebirds" extract earthworms from moist soils with their marvelous bills, which are flexible at the tip. Pass an old wooden gate on the left near the road, where Japanese barberry, another invasive exotic, is also present. The trail drops below the road, and in its soft, dark mud the cloven-hoof tracks of white-tailed deer are easily spotted. Fallen hemlocks are rather numerous. Come to a T intersection with the red-blazed Borland Trail. It is named for the late Connecticut naturalist and nature writer Hal Borland. Turn right to move farther away from the busy roadway. Pass a big uprooted hemlock immediately to your right and proceed through a moist area where blue violets bloom in late spring.

Cross Herrick Brook on a wooden bridge and pass under an overt hanging grapevine. Climb the hill shaded by hemlock trees. Among the hemlock are a few big old yellow and black birch that were here first. Climb moderately and then level off in the hemlock on the flank of the slope. The explosive, sneezy "song" of an Acadian flycatcher caught my attention here. Shaded ravines are a favorite haunt of this little Neotropical migrant. Continue uphill on the red-blazed trail through an area of large, moss-covered boulders. Black-throated green warblers and black-and-white warblers sing from the trees as the boulder-strewn slope rises to the right. Enter birch, maple, and oak woods where the trail levels off.

Ahead is the brown Explorer Hut. The sound of water flowing over the Ford Pond spillway is pleasantly audible. Water flows under the spillway as well as over it as during times of high water. Stay to the right of the hut, then turn sharply left around it and then right to recross the small wooden bridge that leads up the steps and back to the parking area.

HOW SWEET IT IS!

Sapsuckers are unique among woodpeckers in that they are adapted to exploit an abundant resource unavailable to other members of their tribe. They drill rows of small holes through the outer bark of maple, birch, and other tree species with sweet, high-calorie sap, and then repeatedly visit the sap wells to lap up the liquid as well as the insects that have been attracted to its flow.

I was fascinated to witness the comings and goings of a pair of yellow-bellied sapsuckers on a four-and-a-half-inch diameter black birch near the trail during a mid-June visit. The sap wells covered a grid eighteen inches high and encircled the trunk about nine feet above the ground. Each hole was horizontal, and some were quite large for sap wells (three-quarters of an inch by one-quarter of an inch). They were drilled all the way to the inner bark, or cambium (growth), layer. The upper, eight-inch-high portion of the grid was obviously fresh and appeared wet from the flow of sap. The lower portion was old and dark, no longer producing. Both birds fed only from the fresh, top portion of the well field.

The male sapsucker, distinguished from his mate by a red throat, made squeaky, mewing sounds as I watched, while a ruby-throated hummingbird buzzed in the immediate vicinity awaiting its opportunity to feed. On at least one occasion I saw the tiny hummingbird sampling the sweet fluid on hovering wings. After the male sapsucker left, his mate appeared and took her turn, wicking up the sweet, oily sap with her bristle-tipped tongue. Then the male returned. With my wristwatch I timed the length of their visits to the well field and the intervals between visits. The intervals between visits ranged from three and a half to almost ten minutes, with five to six and a half minutes being most common. The male did not remain long when he returned after only three and a half minutes had elapsed since his previous visit. Perhaps that wasn't sufficient time for the wells to have filled again.

Both male and female generally spent about three minutes engaged in lapping up sap at each visit. On two occasions I witnessed the male arriving with a bill already loaded with insects. These he had probably collected from one or more additional well fields in the vicinity. He proceeded to dab his already insect laden bill into the sap wells, seemingly in an effort to soak up as much of the sweet fluid as possible. Both sapsuckers flew off each time in the same direction, and I concluded that they were returning to their nest cavity to feed their ravenous young.

Getting There

From the gray granite clock tower in Sharon at the intersection of Routes 4, 41, and 343, turn onto Route 4 and drive south for 2.35 miles. Turn right off Route 4 into the Sharon Audubon Center and then bear right for less than 0.1 mile to the parking area.

—R.L.

Pine Knob

Sharon

Pine Knob is a rocky, wooded hill in the village of Sharon. A series of trails loop over its long summit ridge and through the valley below. The result is a walk that offers varied landscapes, from pastoral stream-side strolls to scenic views from rocky overlooks. It is a popular walk enjoyed by hundreds of adults and children alike every year.

The walk over Pine Knob is in Housatonic Meadows State Park and Housatonic State Forest. The Pine Knob Trail is marked with blue blazes, the Red Trail with red blazes, and the Appalachian Trail with white blazes. The Appalachian Trail in Connecticut is maintained by the Connecticut Chapter of the Appalachian Mountain Club.

Look Forward To

- brookside walk
- beautiful views
- pine and hemlock groves

The Trail

From the parking area in a mixed grove of sugar maples and Norway spruce, the trail enters a shady woodland with false Solomon's seal, jewelweed, and jack-in-the-pulpit growing beneath the leafy canopy. Jewelweed is a succu-

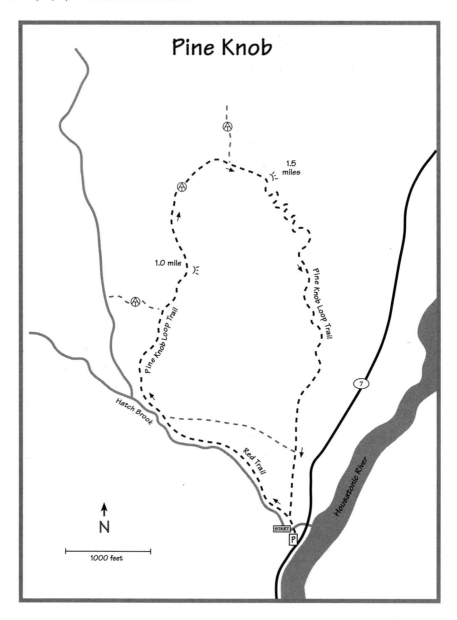

lent herb that grows in shady, moist places. The flowers are rusty orange or pale yellow and delicately hang from the plant on filament-like stems. When held underwater the undersides of the leaves seem to turn from green to silver-chrome; the reason for the common name "jewelweed." In late summer, the small, ripe seed capsules will pop open in your hand, a trait which gave the plant its other common name: touch-me-not. Jewelweed is an excellent remedy for poison ivy. If you contact poison ivy, bruise some jewelweed stems and rub it over the exposed area. As with most herbal remedies, some people swear by the stuff while others, who haven't had the best of luck using it, just swear at it.

Just after leaving the parking area the path crosses Hatch Brook on steppingstones and briefly parallels a stone wall before crossing it. Here Pine Knob Trail continues straight (north) and a red-blazed trail leaves left (northwest). Take the red-blazed trail, which quickly begins to climb along the crest of Hatch Brook ravine. The path passes through groves of hemlock sprinkled with isolated specimens of oak, ash, and maple. The brook is a noisy, cheerful companion as it trips over stones and ledges in a seemingly endless series of little waterfalls. As you walk above the stream look for the slender, ghostly white stems of Indian peace pipe popping through the leaf litter of the forest floor in late summer. There are also patches of tasty wintergreen as well as tangles of maple-leafed viburnum, mountain laurel, and witch hazel. The white flowers of mountain laurel bloom in late spring, while the spidery yellow blossoms of witch hazel appear in early fall.

The trail then levels out and comes to a beautiful section of brook where the stream bed is a bedrock shelf pocked with small potholes. Skunk cabbage, Christmas fern, princess pine, and trillium cover the ground while the sweet songs of veeries and warblers float through the trees. After passing some large boulders the path rejoins the blue-blazed Pine Knob Trail. Turn left onto Pine Knob Trail (north), which begins a moderate climb through woods of maple, oak, and hemlock, with Canada mayflower, ground cedar, and Indian cucumber beneath.

At a small, level spot the Pine Knob Loop Trail intersects the white-blazed Appalachian Trail (AT). Turn right (northwest) onto the AT, which continues up the hillside through a boulder-strewn area that is home to wild geranium, with loose clusters of nickel-sized lavender flowers in the spring. Wood thrush can also be found here hunting for insects beneath the umbrella-shaped leaves of wild sarsaparilla.

The path then begins a steep, rocky climb to the first overlook, passing beneath hickory, oak, and maple with blueberries, wild rose and stump sprouts of American chestnut lining the treadway. The rocky overlook is a nice place to rest for a bit and enjoy the broad southwest view featuring Mine Mountain and Dean Hill beyond. Turkey vultures frequently glide by, reminders that some creatures have found easier ways to reach the mountaintops.

From the overlook the trail continues to climb, then levels out on the ridge top. This is a lovely stretch of forest with hemlock, chestnut oak, and black birch sheltering lady-slippers, mountain laurel, wild azalea, and lots of chipmunks. These cute little striped rodents aren't quite as vocal as red

Rocky ledges provide sheltered views from Pine Knob Loop Trail.

squirrels, but close. When startled they let out a sharp chirp to warn other chipmunks of trespassers, then scurry for shelter.

The trail then comes to the summit of Pine Knob, sprinkled with tussocks of grass and rugged, rocky outcrops. In winter there are nice views through the leafless trees. The path then steeply descends to a forested, level area where the AT leaves left (north) and the Pine Knob Trail turns right (south-southwest). This is a lovely walk through tangled thickets of mountain laurel, which flowers in late spring; a few weeks later the sweetly fragrant blossoms of trailing arbutus appear here.

The path then makes a brief scramble to a gorgeous, rocky overlook carpeted with blueberries, huckleberries, dogbane, and sweet fern. Pitch pine, chestnut oak, and white pine cling to the steep slope. Below, the Housatonic River valley flows south, framed by the forested flanks of Mine Mountain, Dean Hill, and Coltsfoot Mountain. Phoebes, cardinals, wood thrush, and chickadees call from the trees, while hairy woodpeckers leave small, frayed excavations in nearby tree trunks. This spot is a lovely place to linger and relax before beginning the descent to the parking area.

From the overlook the trail turns left and falls steeply down the rough hillside. Near a large rock formation the grade moderates, descending through deep woods of oak and mountain laurel. The path then comes to the edge of a cliff, which it follows past a century-old red cedar to a little stream and a small, mossy waterfall. From here the terrain becomes more gentle, and the treadway crosses a series of streams and stone walls as it meanders through the cool shade of tall white pines. A section of the Pine Knob Trail then leaves right. Continue straight (southwest) past the red-blazed trail on the right and recross Hatch Brook. The parking lot is a few yards farther on.

CHIPMUNKS

Chipmunks are among the most common animals encountered in the woods. These small ground-dwelling squirrels are about eight inches long including the tail and are covered with chestnut-colored fur marked with five stripes along the back. Their preferred habitat is mature hardwood and mixed hardwood and softwood forests dotted with brushy thickets and boulders or crossed by stone walls.

Their burrows have a tidy two-inch-wide entrance hole and can be found near fallen logs, rock walls, and other sheltered places. The tunnels can be as much as thirty feet long, but there is little or no excavated soil near the burrow. As chipmunks dig their burrows they carry the excavated soil from the burrow in their cheek pouches, dumping it a few yards away.

In preparation for winter, chipmunks do not put on a layer of fat but gather seeds and nuts, storing them in caches near their burrows. The animals have very little fat and rely on the caches of food to sustain them through the colder months. In winter chipmunks do not hibernate, but they do sleep for days at a time. On mild winter days they awaken, have a snack, and go back to sleep.

About late February chipmunks breed. They aren't shy about displaying their affections, and make quite a spectacle of themselves. Males and females chase each other through the woods with reckless abandon, zipping around trees and over rocks with amazing speed. A month later the babies are born, and in April and May the little ones go off on their own.

Chipmunks are omnivores and eat everything from apples to mushrooms, grasshoppers, small frogs, and lots of different seeds and nuts. After they discover a tasty nibble they usually carry it to a favorite feeding area, such as a stump, rock, or low branch. These areas are used time after time and can be spotted by looking for the piles of shells and other litter that accumulates beneath them.

Getting There

From the junction of Routes 4 and 7 in Cornwall Bridge proceed 1.0 mile south on Route 7 to the parking area on the left.

—C.S.

6 Dudleytown

Cornwall

- Dudleytown Trail, Mohawk Trail
- 4.0 miles
- 300-foot elevation gain
- 2.0–3.0 hours
- moderate

Some people don't consider ghosts to be part of the natural world, but these folks have probably never visited Dudleytown. In the rocky, forested hills of Cornwall run miles of gray stone walls. They line the abandoned roads and surround the forgotten pastures, orchards, and cellar holes of Dudley-town, one of the most famous and infamous of Connecticut's ghost towns (see essay below).

On this walk you will explore an area once claimed and cleared by people, and now the habitat of tall forests, wildflowers, coyotes, turkeys, and chickadees. In some respects these woods are very similar to other forests in the northwest hills; you will recognize the trees, birds, and flowers. In other ways this region is like no other. Many people claim to feel something mysterious among the trilliums and starflowers, that on these hills the wind speaks through the creaking trees with a different, more malevolent voice. For generations Dudleytown has been known to instill an uneasy feeling in many of its visitors. This is, of course, simply a legend—a legend you are about to become a part of.

The walk over Dudleytown Hill and Coltsfoot Mountain passes through land owned and maintained by the Dark Entry Forest Association. Part of the walk traverses short stretches of abandoned trail which are not reliably blazed or maintained. There are no bridges at stream crossings. The Mohawk Trail is blazed with pale blue marks. Turns are noted by two stacked blazes with the top blaze offset in the direction of the turn.

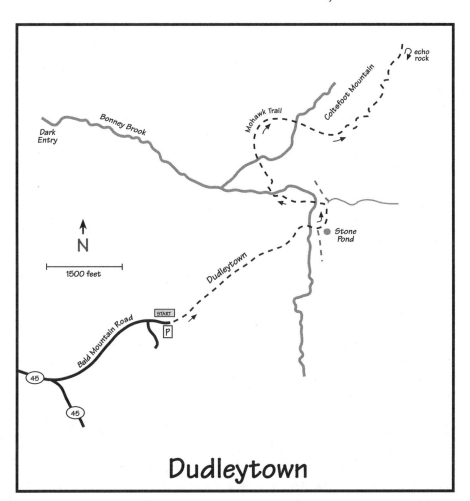

Dudleytown

Look Forward To

- exploring a ghost town
- beautiful mountain views
- wildflowers

The Trail

From the parking area the trail heads east along an abandoned road lined with saplings of striped maple and cherry. Above the thin understory a seamless canopy of red maple, white and yellow birch, and ash bathes the trail in shadow. In spring the robins like to hop along the ground looking for insects, while in the colder months mixed flocks of chickadees and titmice congregate in the evergreen branches of isolated white pines. The old road, which is unblazed but easy to follow, leads over the crest of Dudleytown Hill and into the remains of Dudleytown. The path descends easily past black birch and hemlock that seem to guard the trail. Beneath the trees the long, pliant stems of false Solomon's seal arch over the ground, while coltsfoot and Canada mayflower grow nearby.

The road then crosses a shelf of bedrock near a network of beautifully crafted, four-foot-wide stone walls. Nearby, beneath a phalanx of oak, maple, and ash that moan in the ever present wind, is the first of many cellar holes. A little farther on, the road levels out and proceeds through a broad, flat hardwood forest. Another cellar hole is passed on the left just before the trail crosses a tributary of Bonney Brook. The area you have just crossed, between the bedrock shelf and Bonney Brook, is the heart of the ghost town. If you are going to feel something unusual in Dudleytown, it most often happens here (see essay).

The trail crosses the brook by way of a stone culvert which is an excellent example of the stoneworker's art. Each block is carefully placed and has endured decades of New England's weather. In spring the tall, straight stems and wide leaves of false hellebore grow in the wet, mucky soil of the stream's narrow flood plain. The delicate fronds of polypody fern grow in niches of the waterside boulders, while burgundy-flowered trillium and patches of thorny barberry bushes brighten the drier spots.

From the brook the path leads to a small, stone-lined pond where water striders share space with the swimming larvae of mosquitoes. A brushy side trail enters right. The main trail veers left (northeast) and gently descends through the woods, a stone wall keeping you company on the left. As the trail levels out, the old Mohawk Trail enters left. From here faded blue blazes continue straight ahead as well as to the left. Leave the treadway of the abandoned road and turn left (north). The trail follows faded blue blazes over a small brook and through brushy woods of cherry and black birch. The path then enters a cool hemlock grove at the edge of a broad, rocky stream. Cross the brook and proceed about ten yards farther to the present Mohawk Trail.

Turn right (north) onto the blue-blazed Mohawk Trail. The path wanders through damp groves of hemlock and oak, with thickets of mountain laurel appearing here and there. Patches of ground-hugging partridgeberry mingle with the mottled brown-and-green leaves of trout lily, whose dainty yellow springtime flowers add a cheerful touch to the woods. After crossing a small brook the path turns uphill, passing through a break in a stone wall near an enormous old white pine. Canada mayflower blooms here in spring, as do wintergreen and bloodroot.

The trail continues to ascend the south flank of Coltsfoot Mountain, winding through woods peppered with rock outcrops and stone walls. The occasional chatter of red squirrels scolds you as you pass by, and the cloven-hoofed tracks of deer appear now and then in the soft treadway. Shortly after passing an abandoned trail the path steepens and weaves through a matrix of bedrock outcrops. The large, shattered blocks of stone resemble the ruins of long-forgotten castles. Coyotes linger here in the twilight of dawn and dusk, and flocks of turkeys often search for seeds beneath the dark hemlock boughs. In the recesses created by the jumbled boulders polypody fern grow.

As the trail gains elevation there are peekaboo views to the right (east). Pileated woodpeckers have chiseled large holes from the trunks of some of the largest trees, and in spring a small tree called serviceberry blossoms, its gray branches transformed into a delicate bouquet of white flowers.

A small brook flows through a stone sluiceway in Dudleytown.

After a moderate climb to the ridge crest, the trail reaches a bedrock pinnacle called Echo Rock. It is now largely surrounded by trees that hide most of the view, but it is still a lovely place to rest and feel the breeze blow over the mountain. For a better view follow the trail along the edge of the ridge to a sloping, open area of driftwood-colored windfalls and large slabs of bedrock. Stunted stands of oak are interspersed with windblown hemlock and birch. Thickets of staghorn sumac, whose leaves turn scarlet in fall, are separated from each other by open stretches of grasses and brambles.

As you settle into the soft grass, a beautiful view is spread out before you. To the east is the low ridge of White Rock, with Mohawk Mountain beyond. In between are the tended fields and leafy woodlands that are the signatures of Connecticut's northwest hills.

From here the Mohawk Trail continues on toward Cornwall village. To return to your starting point follow the trail back through Dudleytown—if you dare.

THE LEGEND OF DUDLEYTOWN

The Dudleys came to Connecticut from their native England before the French and Indian War. When they settled on the wild hilltop in Cornwall township that would soon bear their name, they had every hope of beginning a prosperous community. What they created was a town whose mysterious fate is as puzzling as it is haunting.

Dudleytown was home to a flock of ambitious, gifted people who rose to national as well as regional prominence. Samuel Tilden, who ran unsuccessfully for the presidency in 1876, was the grandson of a resident of Dudleytown. And the wife of Horace Greeley, who lost the presidential election of 1872 to Ulysses S. Grant, made her home in Dudleytown. Ministers, college presidents, and even an advisor to George Washington were all Dudleytown residents. But that is the good news; Dudleytown also has a much darker side.

Of the many people who lived in Dudleytown, a disquieting number of them suffered strange deaths or went unaccountably insane. If you dig around any town's history long enough, you will find the odd strange occurrence. But Dudleytown genuinely had more than its share; so many strange happenings, in fact, that the community was thought by some to be cursed. There were stories of people retiring for the evening in perfect health, only to awaken the next day totally insane. And not one or two, but many.

Even after the last resident of Dudleytown moved away in the first decades of the twentieth century, the strange events on Dudleytown Hill continued, especially near certain old foundations close to the brook. It was there that hikers once reported a dark form rising from an old cellar hole. Others recounted feeling a cold, frightening presence near them as they explored an old foundation.

There is no neat ending to this story, no tidy explanation. So when you walk the abandoned lanes of Dudleytown, be watchful as you pass beneath the creaking trees and by the old cellar holes. Dudleytown may be a ghost town with real ghosts.

Getting There

From the junction of Routes 4 and 7 in Cornwall Bridge, take Route 7 south 1.0 mile to the intersection with Route 45. Turn left onto Route 45 and proceed 0.9 mile to Bald Mountain Road. Turn left onto Bald Mountain Road and continue 0.7 mile to the end of the street. Park along the side of the street near the Dark Entry Forest Association's sign. Do not block the nearby driveways.

—C.S.

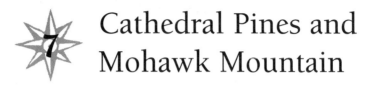

Cathedral Pines and Mohawk Mountain

Cornwall

- Mohawk Trail
- 3.7 miles
- 740-foot elevation gain
- 2.5 –3.5 hours
- moderate, with difficult sections

Change eventually comes to everything. Such is the case with Cathedral Pines and Mohawk Mountain. These beautiful places of forests and streams lay in the path of a train of tornadoes that swept through the hills in the summer of 1989. In the forests, and in the human communities around them, things have not been the same since.

This walk guides you through those changed hills, from the Nature Conservancy's Cathedral Pines to the succession landscapes of Mohawk Mountain. There are bits of forest that seem to have passed the centuries unchanged—and acres that have changed beyond anyone's worst nightmares. It is a guided tour through nature's moods, with views that are unforgettable. The walk is entirely on the Mohawk Trail, which is blazed with pale blue marks. Turns are noted by two stacked blazes, the top blaze offset in the direction of the turn.

Look Forward To

- mountain views
- ancient trees
- tornado-damaged forest
- songbirds

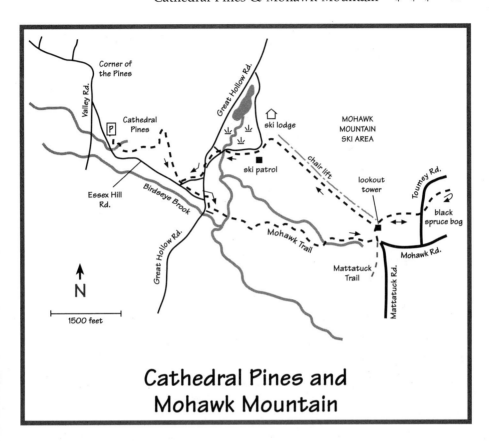

Corner of
the Pines

Valley Rd.

Great Hollow Rd.

ski lodge

MOHAWK
MOUNTAIN
SKI AREA

P

Cathedral
Pines

ski patrol

chair lift

lookout
tower

Toumey Rd.

Essex Hill
Rd.

Birdseye Brook

black
spruce bog

Great Hollow Rd.

Mohawk Trail

Mohawk Rd.

Mattatuck
Trail

Mattatuck Rd.

N

1500 feet

Cathedral Pines and Mohawk Mountain

The Trail

From the parking area follow the pale blue blazes south past a large pine windfall. This area was once the heart of Cathedral Pines. Today the trunks of the once great forest are heaped one atop the other in disarray. Beneath them grow the first wave of trees and other plants that constitute a first succession woodland. Pin cherry, with candy-scented blossoms in May, is joined by hemlock and red maple, as well as thickets of honeysuckle, raspberry, and elder. In the few unclaimed spaces goldenrod, dandelion, wild strawberry, and trillium grow.

Succession woodlands are wonderful places to look for birds, and a typical spring day here will find red-winged blackbirds, goldfinches, catbirds, chickadees, warblers, blue jays, and sometimes the honk of Canada geese or the shrill call of a red-tailed hawk.

The path heads uphill, past a small, bubbling drainage, then ascends a staircase of wooden steps set into the hillside. Soon the open landscape yields to a deep forest of towering white pine and hemlock spared the wrath of the tornadoes. They are all that remains of the cathedral pines (see essay). The evergreen canopy is high overhead, and the massive, majestic trunks inspire humility in many of the hikers who pass through.

Continue uphill into a hemlock grove where deer are frequent visitors and pileated woodpeckers carve large, rectangular holes in the trees. The path crests the top of a rise, then descends into a shallow swale before again heading up the rocky hillside past an enormous white pine on the right. Starflower, partridgeberry, and Canada mayflower grow along the ground, while chipmunks scurry for shelter in the crevices of nearby boulders.

The path then enters another section of forest damaged by the tornadoes, with blowdowns of hemlock sheltering crowds of pin cherry. Turning south, the path merges with an old woods road and gently descends through the hemlocks, keeping a stone wall in sight to the left. Eventually the hemlocks yield to a mixed hardwood forest of ash and red maple with thorny barberry beneath. Deer trails cross the path here and there, and wild turkey come through in groups of ten or more.

At the junction with Essex Hill Road, turn left (west) onto the road and follow it a short distance to a stop sign. Turn right (south) onto Great Hollow Road and proceed to the base of the hill. Here the trail turns left (east-southeast) and follows a private driveway past a residence on the right. Continue across a wooden bridge into an open field marked with ruts of an old logging road.

Follow the wide, grassy path uphill past horsetail, dandelions, apple, willows, and weeping bushes of multiflora rose. Catbirds and phoebes sing in the trees, while hawks often soar in ever widening circles overhead. As the path continues uphill it enters an area of near complete devastation, which marks the primary debris field of the tornadoes. Thick growths of saplings mingle with brambles and roses to make areas off the trail appear nearly impenetrable. It is just as well, for this area has an abundance of ticks, and you will encounter fewer of the nasty creatures on the trail.

The path climbs the slope of Mohawk Mountain through a seemingly endless area of blowdowns, saplings, and songbirds. Indian paintbrush blossoms here in summer, and the tart clusters of wild grape that hang from sapling white birch ripen in early fall. The path then leaves the sapling woods and enters a grassy field with pleasing northwest views. Quarry Hill is the small hill to the north and White Rock is the ridge to the northwest with Coltsfoot Mountain beyond.

A jumping mouse searches for food in Cathedral Pines.

The field is home to woodland jumping mice, little brown furry things with six-inch-long tails, and eastern coyotes, which nibble on the mice whenever possible. Deer, rabbits, and grouse visit now and again, and if you believe some of the local folks (and there is no reason not to), the nearby hills are home to a few mountain lions.

From the field continue uphill, briefly returning to scrubby woods before leaving the storm damage and entering a more mature hardwood forest. The path crosses a small brook where colonies of trillium and wild oats bloom in spring beneath the branches of alder, black birch, cherry, and red maple. After crossing a second stream and skirting a ski trail, the path enters a beautiful woodland savanna framed by stone walls, with large ash and maple trees above soft woodland grasses. Warblers and thrushes are here in spring and summer, which adds to the beauty of this charming spot.

The path then turns left and climbs over many stone walls as it meanders past oak, white pine, ash, and black birch to the junction of the Mohawk and Mattatuck Trails. Turn left on the Mohawk Trail (north) and proceed about twenty yards to the top of the ski lift and some beautiful views. To the left is a small stone tower which kids like to play on, but the best view is from the grassy ski trail just beneath the lift.

To the north are the Taconic Mountains, including Mount Race and Mount Everett in the Berkshires. To the northwest are the Catskills of New York. In fall, when the foliage is at its peak, this is an especially nice place to be.

From the ski lift it is a short walk along the trail to Black Spruce Bog. This fragile ecosystem is home to many plants common to more-northerly climates. A boardwalk guides you over the moss-covered boulders and roots where black spruce and leather leaf grow. After returning to the ski lift you can retrace your steps to the parking area or take a different way back.

For something completely different, follow the ski lift downhill (northwest) to the base of the hill. From the National Ski Patrol building follow the dirt road past the softball field and through the swamp where Canada geese share space with great blue herons. Beavers sometimes construct dams near here and the resulting ponds often flood the road, which may mean some wading. Blackbirds, grackles, yellow warblers, and yellowthroat are some of the birds you can see here.

Take a left (west) onto Great Hollow Road and proceed to Essex Hill Road. Turn right on East Hill Road and follow it until the Mohawk Trail enters the woods on the right. From here follow the blue blazes back to the parking area.

JULY 1989

Cathedral Pines is a blend of tall, straight-trunked white pine and hemlock ranging in age from about 100 to 300 years old. Some of the oldest trees began growing here about 1676, at the end of King Philip's War. In 1883 the forest was purchased by the Calhoun family, who protected it from logging until they donated the forty-two-acre grove to the Nature Conservancy in 1967. In 1980 a small tornado damaged some of the trees, but the majesty of the pines remained largely untouched. At the time people breathed a sigh of relief that the storm had mostly missed this priceless legacy. What no one could possibly know, however, was that Cathedral Pines would nearly disappear in less than a decade.

The morning of July 10, 1989, was a typical summer day, with warm temperatures and fair skies. In the early afternoon, however, mountainous dark clouds began building over the upper Hudson Valley of New York. As the squall line matured, a cluster of thunderstorms began to form, and the entire assemblage rolled southeast toward the Taconics and Berkshires.

As the storm front passed over the southern Berkshires, it filled the sky with heavy, swirling clouds and gusty winds, turning the late afternoon into twilight. When it entered Connecticut the swirling cloud bank had become a rotating cloud wall that barreled through the sky toward Cornwall.

At 4:30 in the afternoon two fully formed tornadoes touched down on Cemetery Hill in Cornwall, destroying acres of forest. One storm headed southeast toward the village center, while another rolled south toward Corner of the Pines. The storms lasted but a few horrific minutes. Then it was over.

The tornadoes of that July afternoon in 1989 destroyed something older than the town of Cornwall, older than the state of Connecticut, older even than the country. Cathedral Pines had been nearly completely destroyed. Only a few of the oldest trees survived.

Today the massive trunks of a fallen inheritance are slowly being covered by young hardwoods. Not only are the massive pines gone, but even their legacy is vanishing. When pine forests are damaged, they often do not heal themselves, but simply disappear. In their place grow stands of hardwoods instead of pine. And that fact of succession—that this spot may never again host such a grove of trees—that, indeed, is the deepest tragedy. For then comes the realization that the storms not only stole the present, but robbed the future. Even centuries will not bring back Cathedral Pines, a fact which makes the small surviving grove that much more precious.

Getting There

From the junction of Routes 4 and 125 in Cornwall, turn onto Pine Street (opposite where Route 125 meets Route 4). Proceed past the Cornwall Town Library to a stop sign at the intersection with Valley Road. Turn left onto Valley Road and proceed 0.2 mile. Veer left onto Essex Hill Road and proceed 0.2 mile to a small parking area on the left near a large boulder.

—C.S.

Burr Pond

Torrington

- Wolcott Trail
- 2.5 miles
- 80-foot elevation gain
- 1.5 hours
- easy

In the mid-1800s Milo Burr built a rock dam across a tributary stream of the Still River to create a permanent source of water power for America's first condensed-milk plant and for the water wheels of Burrville. His dream was to transform the little community bearing his name into an industrial town. The milk plant was owned by none other than Gail Borden. The resulting pond eventually measured 0.75 mile long but powered the milk plant for only a few years.

Today the pond and state park, north of Torrington, are part of a popular 1,800-acre recreational complex of deciduous and hemlock woodland, wetland, and pond and streams that also encompasses Paugnut State Forest and Taylor Brook Campground.

The water wheels are gone, but the scenic pond that gave them life remains. Evidence of the passage many millennia ago of a mile-thick ice sheet also remain in the form of boulders, some of them gigantic and oddly shaped. Visible reminders of the area's human history remain as well.

This walk circumscribes Burr Pond on the Wolcott Trail, usually remaining near the shoreline. The trail's name remembers Civilian Conservation Corps (CCC) Camp Wolcott, whose men constructed the park's recreation area and the current dam during the Great Depression of the 1930s.

From the southern end of Burr Pond, an optional round-trip extension of five miles the—Muir Trail—takes you past a swamp and to the wooded summit of Walnut Mountain (1,325 ft.), where a limited view is possible.

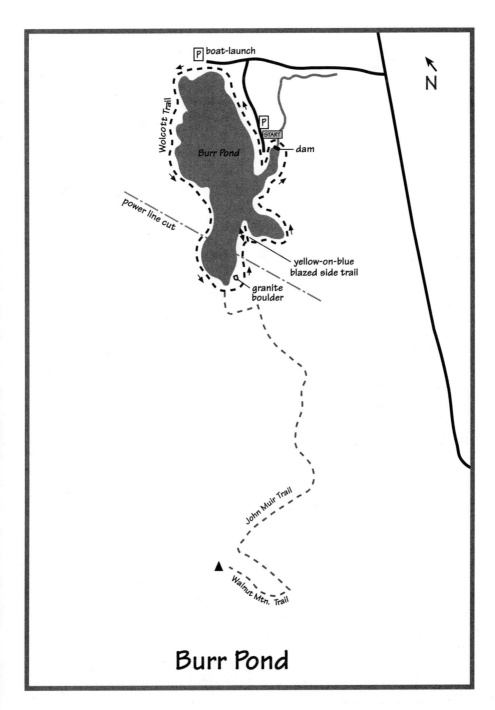

Burr Pond

Look Forward To

- scenic view of Burr Pond

- massive glacial boulders

- luxuriant laurel and azalea blooms

The Trail

From the gravel parking lot located on the east side of the campground road, cross the paved park road toward the pond and pick up the blue-blazed path behind the kiosk. The trail enters hemlock-birch (both gray and black) woodland with a mountain laurel shrub layer and then splits almost immediately. Stay right and come to the main Wolcott Trail at a T intersection. Turn right (north) and walk along the east shore of Burr Pond. Chalky gray birches with straight boles contrast artistically with the dark trunks of eastern hemlocks. Gneiss (pronounced *nice*) boulders with alternating gray and white banding protrude from the forest floor. In June the laurel shrubs, especially those receiving ample sunlight, are heavy with nickel-sized pink-and-white blossoms.

Bird song fills the air, virtually the only sound that disrupts the stillness. I picked out the voices of tufted titmouse, American goldfinch, white-breasted nuthatch, tree swallow, great crested flycatcher, and song sparrow from the chorus one day in June. On summer weekends this is a busy place, but that day the flat surface of Burr Pond served as a mirror for the tranquillity of the shore. The level trail enters shadier hemlock woods which also contain some red oaks. Some of the hemlocks are imposing at two and a half feet in diameter. On the left is a white birch with the very thin, white, peeling bark that sets it apart from the darker gray birch. A black-and-white warbler and then an ovenbird made known their presence with vibrant song.

Pass a rock outcrop located to the right as American beech, yellow birch, and white ash trees appear. Witch hazel and young gray birch grow in the understory. One big, smooth gray beech is disfigured with carved graffiti as high as an adult can reach—and higher. Unfortunately it will remain visible for decades. The trail swings left as you parallel Burr Mountain Road on the right. In early July the sweet fragrance of azaleas hangs heavily in the still air. The pond is visible through the numerous yellow birches. Ducks often loaf on the nearby boulder islet that protrudes from its surface.

Cross two small boardwalk bridges over tiny streams and enter a damp overgrown area where gray catbirds fuss at intruders. Cross another trickle leading to the pond. Elderberry, yellow loosestrife, and meadow rue bloom in early summer, while tall sedges and sensitive fern are nonflowering indicators of damp soil here. Arrive at the boat-launch parking area, which the trail crosses. Reenter the woods and pick up the trail on the far side of the lot. Black birch and white ash predominate. The showy rose-purple blossoms of purple-flowering raspberry add color to the scene in early summer. Cross a small bridge over a rocky stream. Some very large red and black oaks appear as a house up and off to the right comes into view. A resort facility follows on the right.

The forest is composed of hemlock, beech, oak, and red maple as the path swings slightly left. American beech, which, like hemlock, is very tolerant of shade, joins its evergreen partners at this northern end of Burr Pond. A six-and-a-half-inch red-eyed vireo sings its monotonous phrases loudly, but invisibly, from the forest canopy. Now cross a boardwalk over a boulder-strewn feeder stream, and then almost immediately a second shallow flow. The leathery fronds of evergreen wood fern poke up from the scant soils atop the rocks. Red trillium, or wake-robin, and Christmas fern, another evergreen fern, grow in the moist rich soil below the beech and hemlock.

Pass a large dead hemlock snag to your right amid sizable live specimens of the same species, and reach an old, 150-foot-long boardwalk through a wet area of cinnamon fern, elderberry shrubs, hemlock, and smooth winterberry. Smooth winterberry is a small tree or shrub with tiny, five-petaled, greenish white flowers that bloom in early summer. The acidic soil here is a rich, almost black, muck. Goldthread, a six-inch-tall wetland indicator with three evergreen leaflets, sports shiny, dark green, scalloped leaves. The yellow-orange runners by which it spreads give it its name, and its white star-shaped flowers appear in spring. Two vines, one poisonous, the other not, grow here as well. Virginia creeper has five leaflets and smooth stems, whereas the infamous poison ivy has three leaflets and "hairy" stems.

Another creeper hereabouts is the brown creeper, a small, inconspicuous, but common woodland bird which hitches up tree trunks in search of insects in bark crevices. The wetland itself is home to a ground-dwelling warbler, the northern waterthrush, usually first evidenced by its loud, ringing song which trails off at the end.

Now reenter higher and drier hemlock woods and pass a house-sized glacial boulder to your right. Rock tripe, a leafy lichen, and mosses cover its surface. The boulder's flat face holds a memorial brass plaque twelve feet up honoring Phil Buttrick (1886–1945), a forester and later secretary of the Connecticut Forest and Parks Association who supervised the work of building CCC Camp Wolcott.

Pass two more short bridges over feeder streams. Water striders skate over the dark waters, supported by the water's elastic surface tension, and an impish red squirrel, uneasy at any intruder's presence, scampers off. Note the old beaver cuttings within an inlet of the pond close at hand on the left. The yellow flowers of bullhead lilies protrude above the pond's surface in summer. Indian cucumber-root, which has an edible tuber the size of your little finger and rather small greenish yellow blossoms, thrives in the moist rich soil. The public beach is visible across the pond. Pass through an area of hemlocks whose lower branches are all dead, and then by a very big red oak with a gneiss boulder behind it.

American beech predominates again as the hillside rises gradually on your right. White pine becomes numerous and is then displaced by hemlock. Here I watched a red squirrel as it gathered dry beech leaves from the ground and then take them in its mouth up a nearby tree trunk, presumably for lining its nest. The forest floor is dotted with rounded gneiss boulders. Catch a glimpse of the pond to the left through an opening, while up ahead a power-line cut comes into view. Pass another big beech covered with graffiti. The ground below your feet is cushioned with a thick layer of decaying hemlock needles.

Enter the sunny north-south power-line cut. The clearing stimulates plant growth and insect diversity. Black-throated green warbler, veery, ovenbird, song sparrow, and cedar waxwing are all in full voice here in late spring and early summer. Cross a small rocky stream bed, nearly dry in summer, and reenter hemlock-beech woods. There are also a few oak, maple, and birch. The trail now begins to rise gradually, passing through a small boulder field of the now familiar gneiss rock. A red oak with five trunks stands on the left; it assumed this multiboled form after its terminal bud was destroyed long ago. Cross through another smaller boulder field and over a small dry brook bed, after which the trail rises and bears left. You can still spy the pond through the trees, although you are farther from the water now on this sloping hillside.

Come to a trail junction on the left. Going straight leads to the Muir Trail and the wooded summit of Walnut Mountain, a five-mile-out-and-back hike from this spot. Turn left to continue around Burr Pond. Descend gently along the rocky slope through oak, birch, and hemlock. The Wolcott Trail continues to be blue blazed as you enter a hemlock grove; from this vantage point a massive granite boulder rears up to your left like a mammoth, pyramidal, black arrowhead, apex skyward. It stands on end and is fully fifteen feet high. Return to the trail and continue downhill under a canopy of hemlock, red maple, and gray birch. A stunning view of Burr Pond lies ahead and below as the deep forest gives way to the light-filled power-line right of way.

Cross the open swath and reenter the forest, passing a large boulder on the right. The pond is visible downslope through the trees on the left. Princess pine, a six-inch-tall club moss that resembles a miniature evergreen tree, grows below the maple and birch, oak and hemlock. Reach a yellow-on-blue-blazed trail on the left which ends at the tip of a rocky peninsula jutting northward into the southern end of the pond. Turn left to follow this short side trail as it winds down under hemlocks, past large boulders, through laurel thickets, and up and over a bedrock outcrop to a very picturesque view of the pond.

Highbush blueberry, mountain laurel blooming abundantly from mid-June to the beginning of July, and small hemlock have found a foothold on this rocky promontory. The scene and feel is reminiscent of northern New England. The park's public beach is visible along the right shoreline. Return to the main trail and turn left, then cross a small drainage seep and bear left as the trail continues to hug the shoreline closely. Lovely black-throated blue warblers prefer to nest in mixed woodlands like this, which offer nesting sites in laurels and hobblebushes.

Follow the path through a mass of boulders that came to rest along what is now the shoreline of Burr Pond; pass a particularly sizable one to the right of the trail. The runners and dime-sized, paired leaves of partridgeberry grace the edges of the path through these mixed hemlock-deciduous woods, in which rocks abound. The slope rises to the right as you pass between large boulders. Come to the cemented rock work dam built by the CCC in the 1930s; the stream feeding the reservoir, Burr Mountain Brook, flows over the dam's spillway. Cross the brook on a small wooden footbridge built on top of a previous concrete and iron bridge foundation. The earlier bridge was obviously capable of supporting heavy vehicles.

Turn left after crossing the bridge to follow the trail back toward the parking area. Do not continue straight on the wide Starks Hill Pond Road. Reach an iron gate at the park picnic area and make a sharp right turn for a short distance uphill, following the blue blazes through hemlock back to your vehicle.

THE ICE SHEET COMETH

The area around Burr Pond and indeed the north-south-trending depression it now occupies are peppered with stones that were swept along by, and in fact became the scouring grit for, the advancing Pleistocene ice sheets that left their permanent marks and products on the New England landscape between 400,000 and 13,000 years ago.

Huge cabin-sized gneiss and granite boulders enhancing the rough terrain of the area were transported to this locality by a massive sheet of glacial ice more than a mile thick which eventually overspread the region three times during what is popularly known as the ice ages. The last of these ice ages, when mean annual temperatures were only five degrees lower on average than today's temperatures, began to reverse a mere 16,000 or so years ago.

The ice sheet formed over millennia, as summers became gradually but steadily cooler. The length of time between the end of one winter and the beginning of another is usually about seven months today; during the ice ages this hiatus of warm weather separating seasons of snowfall became ever briefer, until they had dwindled away altogether. Snow fell nearly year-round. It had barely begun to melt when a new winter season descended. In time, snow accumulated ever deeper, compacting to form ice under its own crushing weight. As the ice sheet inexorably ground its way south-ward, it flowed over the land's surface with an incredible abrading force, wiping clean whole areas of their soils, vegetation, and animal life and leaving gouges, scratches, and rock debris (glacial till) behind.

Ahead of the ice sheet tundralike conditions prevailed. Bitter winds and frigid temperatures made southern New England a very different place from what it is today. But eventually the climate began to ameliorate. Summer returned, and lengthened over the centuries until ice no longer covered the land surface year-round. As the ice sheet retreated, it left vast deposits of rock, gravel, sand, and silt behind—material brought here by the ice from farther north.

The biggest and heaviest objects were first to be dropped by the shrinking ice sheet. Some boulders the size of houses were left oddly perched on native bedrock of a different composition altogether from the relocated fragments. These glacial erratics still dot the countryside of New England today.

Smaller stones were dumped later. The actions of water and ice rounded the rocks as they ground against each other and the bedrock, as well as being tumbled in cataracts of foaming meltwater. Yankee farmers used the more manageable stones to construct the walls, or more properly fences, that are so much a part of the New England landscape today.

Outwash streams carried most of the finer materials away from the glacier's decaying mass. These deposits, some literally thousands of feet thick, are still mined today in Connecticut for their water-sorted deposits of sand and gravel.

Getting There

From the north on Route 8 take Exit 46 for Pinewoods Road. Travel 0.25 mile to Winsted Road and turn left. Drive 1.0 mile on Winsted Road to Burr Mountain Road on the right. Follow Burr Mountain Road for 0.5 mile to the state-park entrance on the left. Enter the park and drive 0.1 mile to the parking area on the left.

From the center of Torrington to the south, drive north on Route 8 to Exit 45 for Winsted Road. Turn right and follow Winsted Road for almost 3.1 miles to Burr Mountain Road on the left. Follow Burr Mountain Road for 0.5 mile to the park entrance on the left. Enter the park and drive 0.1 mile to a parking area on the left.

—R.L.

River Road

Kent

- Appalachian Trail
- 2.9 miles
- 20-foot elevation gain
- 1.0–1.5 hours
- easy

Decades ago a road hugged the west bank of the Housatonic River as it flowed south through Kent. Much of that road is today part of the Appalachian Trail (AT) and doesn't resemble a road at all. The path is well worn and easy, emulating the river which usually slides along with a relaxed, unhurried gait. A large number of those who walk the Connecticut section of the AT consider this stretch the best of all. There are stone walls and foundations, the remains of a red pine plantation, and the picturesque Housatonic River always close at hand.

The river walk is entirely on the Appalachian Trail, a 2,143-mile-long footpath from Springer Mountain in northern Georgia to Katahdin in Maine. The AT is managed by the Appalachian Trail Conference and maintained in Connecticut by the Connecticut Chapter of the Appalachian Mountain Club. The entire trail is marked with white blazes. Access trails are marked with blue blazes.

Look Forward To

- lots of water birds
- old red pine plantation
- foundations and wildflowers

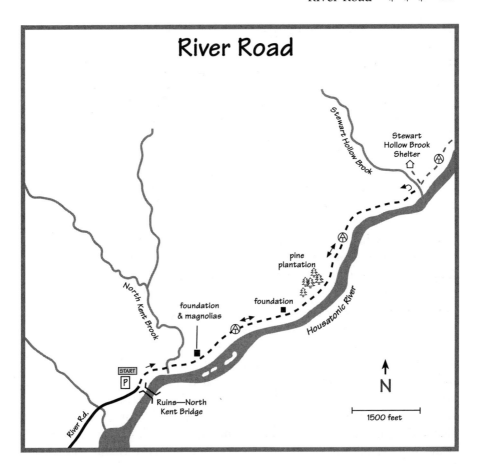

River Road

The Trail

The parking area on River Road is not just a place to leave the car, but an area with attractive wildflowers. Queen Anne's lace mingles with the yellow blossoms of false sunflower and the lavender flowers of wild bergamot. Wild bergamot, also called bee balm, is similar to the species cultivated in perennial gardens. The leaves have a minty fragrance. Bee balm is also called Oswego tea in honor of the Oswego Indian Nation of New York. In colonial times the Indians used bee balm to make a soothing, tasty tea. The Indians shared their tea with the colonists, who used it as a substitute for East Indian tea. Bee balm's whorls of lilac-colored blossoms bloom in summer to fall and are a magnet to butterflies and hummingbirds.

From the parking area pass around the gate and walk along a wide, easily followed path. The trees that grow here are representative of those that thrive in the rich bottom land soils of flood plains, including sycamore, maple, and ash. Black locust also grows here, the twisted trunks lending a spooky look to the forest. In late spring the thick, sweet scent of locust flowers fills the air.

After a short walk the path comes to an open area on the left where an old foundation hides in the weeds at the edge of the grass. The delicate magenta flowers of pink-eyed grass bloom here in summer. At the edge of the clearing is an apple tree, with soft, white-pink blossoms in May, and a magnolia, with lotus-shaped flowers in spring.

Proceed along the riverbank, crossing a shallow drainage that empties into the river. Growing among the rocks are coltsfoot, a low-growing plant with dandelion-like flowers in March; yellow flag, a water iris with bright, butter-yellow flowers in late May; black-eyed Susan; and joe-pye weed.

Just beyond the small stream the trail enters a picturesque stand of hemlock and white pine. The wide and shallow Housatonic River is a constant companion to the right, where Canada geese, mallards, wood ducks, and black ducks often feed. Another interesting water bird to look for here is the common merganser (see essay).

The evergreens slowly yield to a collection of hardwoods, including sycamore and silver maple, a species that loves the occasional flooding that occurs along rivers. To the right is an open area with a short side trail which leads to the riverbank. Cedar waxwings like to gather on the branches of the snags that line the riverbank. Hummingbirds sometimes zip along the water's edge looking for flowers, and crayfish hide in the muddy shallows. In fall goldfinches flit among the seed heads of thistle like yellow sparks against the sky.

From the clearing the Appalachian Trail continues north along the bank, the path wide and the terrain a series of easy ups and downs. In addition to the waterfowl, which are plentiful all year long, many animals come to the river. Deer come down the hillside to the left to drink, and raccoon love to scour the shoreline at night.

The path then enters a grove of sugar maple near a small stone foundation to the left before entering a massive plantation of red pine. The pines were planted in the 1930s, and decades later this grove became known as one of the most beautiful places along the Connecticut section of the Appalachian Trail. In the 1970s, however, the trees began to die from an insect-caused blight. Today all the trees in the original grove have died, and the dead pines are slowly being replaced by a first-succession habitat of sapling black birch and brambles. Even in death the stately trees have a certain majest—and usefulness. The Connecticut Chapter of the

The Housatonic River as it passes along the AT riverwalk.

Appalachian Mountain Club has harvested some of the dead trees to build shelters along the trail.

From the pine plantation the trail passes a long, narrow field to the left. The soil here is poor, sandy, and so well-drained that the plants of the field need to be drought tolerant. Two plants that meet that criterion are knapweed and wild sensitive plant. Knapweed has an open habit and wiry stems topped with small, thistlelike flowers. Wild sensitive plant is small, reaching only about six inches high, with small, bipinnately compound leaves. Wild sensitive plant conserves moisture in an ingenious way: To reduce the leaf area exposed to drying winds, the plant simply folds up its leaves in windy weather. It will do the same if you touch it repeatedly with your finger. Kids love to watch this little plant do its thing.

From the field the trail follows a stone wall into a forest of hornbeam, red oak, maple, hickory, tulip tree, and witch hazel. There are also specimens of linden, which bear sweetly scented flowers in summer; flowering dogwood, which blossoms in spring; and some very large sassafras trees. All parts of sassafras are wonderfully aromatic, with a spicy fragrance. Just scratch a twig and enjoy an aroma which, in colonial times, European nobility paid huge sums of money to enjoy.

The trail then wanders closer to the river and the land closes in a bit, with a steep hillside to the left. The river narrows and the current is faster, producing sweet sounds as it tumbles over the rocks. After crossing Stewart Brook on a log bridge, a side trail leading to Stewart Brook Shelter leaves left. The Appalachian Trail continues along the riverbank for some distance farther. To return to the parking area, simply retrace your steps.

COMMON MERGANSERS

Common mergansers are commonly seen and uncommonly beautiful water birds. The word "merganser" has been in the English language since 1555, but the birds have been paddling along the Housatonic River since long before that. The male common merganser is a flashy dresser and can be easily recognized by its emerald-green head and snow-white body accented with a black racing stripe down its back. The female is more reserved, with a gray-plumed body and a rust-colored head.

Common mergansers gather in flocks of twenty to thirty birds in the warmer months. They can be recognized even from a distance by their habit of facing upstream and chasing each other over the water. They feed on small fish and frequently dive underwater in pursuit of a meal. Common mergansers are exceptionally strong swimmers, their bright orange-red bills lined with serrations to hold onto their slippery prey.

In late winter, usually early March, the flocks break up and the birds form mating pairs. They build their downy nests in a number of places, from hollow trees to unused raptor nests or in a sheltered spot on the ground. The birds lay about ten eggs which hatch a month later, creating a flock of fuzzy little mergansers. Two months after they hatch, the baby birds are on their own.

Common mergansers like the Housatonic River because it overlaps their traditional wintering and breeding ranges, allowing hikers to view these beautiful water birds from River Road virtually all year long.

Getting There

From the junction of Routes 7 and 341 in Kent, take Route 341 west across the Housatonic River. Take the first right after the bridge (Skiff Mountain Road). Proceed 1.1 miles to a junction with River Road. Turn onto River Road and proceed 2.7 miles to the gate and parking area. Caution: River Road is quite narrow; please be careful and courteous when driving on it.

—C.S.

White Memorial Conservation Center

Litchfield

- Mattatuck Trail, Pine Island Trail, unnamed trail, Little Pond Trail
- 4.7 miles
- 40-foot elevation gain
- 3.0 hours
- easy

At 4,000 acres, the White Memorial Foundation properties constitute the single largest holding of conservation land in the state. With thirty-five miles of footpaths, the largest natural body of water in Connecticut, extensive wetlands, boating facilities, a museum, and the longest boardwalk of any preserve covered in this book, White Memorial literally has something to offer every outdoor enthusiast. The property is multiuse in nature, with horseback riding, swimming, camping, bicycling, cross-country skiing, and of course hiking all permitted in designated areas.

Alain C. White and his sister, Mary W. White, created the foundation that bears their name in 1913. Their parents, originally from Danbury, had made the family fortune in the fur trade during the 1800s when beaver-felt hats were all the rage. Their story is told in the conservation center building that houses a museum containing excellent exhibits about the natural and cultural history of the area.

This walk in the northern portion of the property leads you astride the Bantam River, along wetlands bordering Duck Pond, through Mallard Marsh, and over a 1.2-mile-long boardwalk that circumscribes Little Pond. White Memorial is my favorite location for exploring freshwater wetlands in the state because the boardwalk system enables one to get right out into it. The biologically rich set of wetland ecosystems is clearly the highlight of this place.

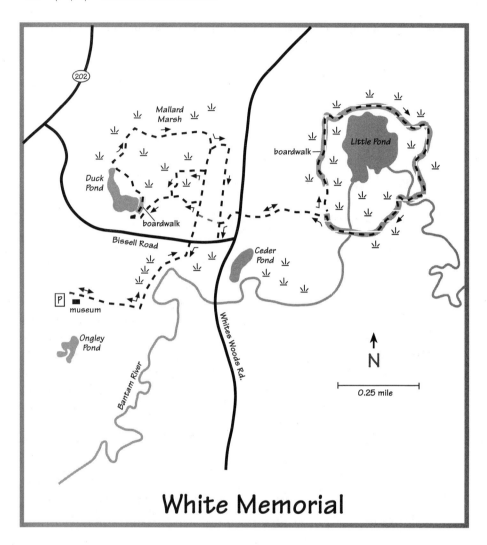

White Memorial

White Memorial is by extension an excellent area for wildlife observation. The extensive well-maintained and well-marked trail system makes a visit here a pleasurable experience for the whole family. Not surprisingly, this popular facility is visited by more than 30,000 visitors annually.

Normal museum hours are Monday through Saturday, 9:00 A.M. to 5:00 P.M.; Sunday, noon to 5:00 P.M. Winter hours may vary slightly. An excellent trail map is available for purchase at the museum shop. It is recommended that you obtain one for additional excursions on this large property. Restrooms are located in the Nature Center, and there are pit toilets at the picnic area and at several other points near the heart of the property. Pets must be on a leash at all times.

Look Forward To

- ponds and wetlands

- extensive boardwalks

- aquatic wildlife

- wonderful birding

The Trail

Begin by walking toward the museum building, passing through a roofed-over structure that contains a large map of the property. Continue on the gravel roadway located to the left of the museum, and turn left just before you reach a metal gate ahead. For a short distance follow along the meandering Bantam River, which flows south into Bantam Lake. On your left is a vegetated marsh showing signs of beaver activity. Bluegill sunfish inhabit the shallow waters, from which clumps of tussock sedge stick up like soft steppingstones. Small northern pike inhabit the pond too, feeding on the bluegills. In spring the trilling of the toad chorus can be almost deafening. Look for the white, four-petaled blossoms of cuckooflower along the shore in May and June. Pass the start of the Nature Interpretation Trail on the left, instead continuing straight on the blue-rectangle-blazed Mattatuck Trail through a shady grove of eastern hemlock and white pine.

Reach paved Bissell Road, where you'll find a map kiosk. Cross the road and continue through more shaded evergreens where olive-green and yellow pine warblers sing their sweet musical trills in spring and early summer. The white pine grow tall and straight in this woodland, and the wonderful aroma of pine resin fills the air in sunny openings. Low-growing Canada mayflower plants line the edges of the old roadway. Continue straight where the Mattatuck Trail turns left. Brown-and-white-striped northern waterthrushes nest in the wetland on the left. Come shortly to the red-triangle-blazed Pine Island Trail on the left; turn onto it. This path is open only to foot travel.

The trail bisects the wetland from where the fast cascading songs of waterthrushes emanate. Highbush blueberry is hung in spring with the tiny white bells that attract bees and other pollinators, while wild sarsaparilla is a very common herb in these woodlands. Recognize it by its three-part leaf and greenish yellow flower globes. The root was used by Native Americans to prepare a cough remedy. Mountain laurel and swamp azalea shrubs are also here. At the trail intersection, turn left and walk through wet hemlock woods. Skunk cabbage, starflower, sphagnum moss, cinnamon fern, and wild calla are wetland indicators here. Wild calla belongs to the same family as jack-in-the-pulpit.

Come to a T intersection, turn left, and walk 150 feet to another T junction, this one with the blue-blazed Mattatuck Trail. Turn right and cross a dark-flowing brook. The yellow blossoms of bullhead lilies protrude above the water in spring and summer. Arrive at Duck Pond and turn sharply right onto the Pine Island Trail. Wood duck nest boxes are visible on posts in the pond. Alain White was responsible in reintroducing this beautiful species of cavity-nesting waterfowl in 1924. Originally wood ducks used the big nest cavities chiseled out by pileated woodpeckers, and we were lucky enough to see one of the magnificent red-crested woodpeckers on a spring walk. Follow the trail along the southeastern shoreline and over a wooden boardwalk.

Signs of former beaver presence are here too. My wife, Chris, and I spotted a smaller fur bearer —muskrat—swimming in the pond on a late May visit. We also spied a snapping turtle. To the right of the boardwalk a six-inch-diameter American chestnut stands protected from the sharp incisors of beavers by a fence. This species rarely attains even this size since the chestnut blight of the early twentieth century virtually annihilated it. Stay straight where the red-blazed Pine Island Trail turns right. You are now on an unnamed and unblazed, but easy to follow, path. Cross a wooden bridge where the remnants of a former beaver dam are evident.

Turn right at the grassy T intersection and walk along a red maple swamp. Note the mass of sticks and soil that was once a beaver lodge. In spring wild geranium blooms purplish pink along the grassy path, while the blossoms of foamflower have a frothy appearance and the leaves are hairy. Note too the green jointed stems of horsetails, holdovers from the Carboniferous era some 300 million years ago. Cross a stream on a tiny wooden footbridge in the midst of an extensive cattail-red maple swamp known as Mallard Marsh. Cross a second small footbridge, enter a dimly lit hemlock-pine grove, and join a wide old woods road and turn right. Soon turn left at the first trail junction, following the red arrow for the Pine Island Trail.

Heavy snowstorms in early 1997 snapped a good many pine and hemlock here. The soft, brittle wood of white pine is especially susceptible to such damage. Black-throated green warblers are partial to pine stands,

A 1.2-mile-long boardwalk encircles Little Pond, enabling visitors to explore an expansive freshwater wetland without damaging it.

and ovenbirds are also common breeders in woods like this with relatively little ground cover. Turn right at the next old woods road where toothwort, a mustard, flowers white in spring, and walk south. The caterpillars of two uncommon native white butterflies depend upon this plant for food. Turn left when you reach the Little Pond Trail, just before Bissell Road. It is blazed with a black square on white. Amble through a young pine-oak woodland where Canada mayflower carpets the forest floor. This little lily is also known as wild lily of the valley, although its cluster of tiny white flowers are not bell shaped. Clintonia, or blue-bead lily, is also exceedingly common here.

Come to paved Whites Woods Road, cross it, and walk past the gate, following a wide old woods road through mixed woods. For those who wish to shorten this hike, there is room for a few vehicles to park off Whites Woods Road at this point. Stay straight when you arrive at a Y in the road. Japanese knotweed (a.k.a. Japanese bamboo) grows profusely at the damp intersection; this plant is aggressive and invasive. Just beyond the intersection lies a shrubby open area where Russian olive bushes have been planted. Gray catbirds meow their catlike alarm calls from the thickets. On the right a sandy clearing has been planted with tiny spruce and pine. Pass by boulders in the trail at the woodland edge, and follow the path to the margin of the wetland that encompasses Little Pond.

Reach a T intersection from which one can go in either direction to circumnavigate the pond. Turn left and immediately pass the intersection for the Pine Island Trail on the left. Continue straight on the Little Pond Trail, walk under power lines, and bear left. The water is visible past red maples to the right. Arrive at the beginning of the Ralph T. Wadhams Memorial Boardwalk, which traverses more than a mile of this extensive and scenic wetland. It wends through a shrub swamp ringing the pond, which enables you to have a rather intimate wetland experience that affords wonderful glimpses of wildlife. In autumn the foliage spectacle alone makes a walk over the mile-long-plus boardwalk worthwhile. The boardwalk is narrow (perhaps two and a half feet), however and negotiating it on a busy weekend can provide an added challenge.

Among the birds we saw and heard in late May were swamp sparrow, great crested flycatcher, Canada goose, osprey, mute swan, common yellowthroat, yellow warbler, tree swallow, red-winged blackbird, and willow flycatcher. The flycatcher is recognized by his sneezelike *fitz-bew* song. The migrating male osprey was diving for fish and the mute swans were in the process of nesting within the cattails to the left. As the female sat on the nest, she used her bill to pull dead vegetation toward her so as to fortify the nest. Mute swans are native to Eurasia, and the big, aggressive birds have become a nuisance in many parts of the eastern seaboard. Growing up out of the dark, tannin-stained water are meadowsweet, royal fern, tussock sedge, pickerelweed, and narrow-leafed arrowhead. Buttonbush forms a dense tangle of woody vegetation that produces attractive one-inch-diameter white flower heads (the buttons) in summer. In late May it is just beginning to leaf out. Farther along are also winterberry shrubs which bear masses of bright red fruits in fall.

Muskrat lodges—mounds of cattail leaves and mud—are readily apparent in the marsh. Muskrats are mostly vegetarian but will eat animal food on occasion—something beaver never do. An old discarded section of boardwalk served as a basking platform for seven painted turtles on our walk; their smooth green shells shone in the bright sunlight. Looking down from the elevated walkway we also saw a largemouth bass. In the fall it was evident that beaver were shoring up their lodge at the southeastern end of the pond with quantities of mud and sticks. I noticed scent posts along the watercourse where beaver had rubbed scent from their castorium gland onto the mud as a territorial sign to others of their own kind.

When you reach the junction with another boardwalk on the left, stay straight. Going left eventually leads to South Lake Street and the Litchfield Country Club. The dangling yellow flowers of wild currant graced the edge of the boardwalk in late May. Skirt the edge of red maple woods where there are also white pines. Interestingly, currants and gooseberries are the alternate host for the destructive white pine blister rust, a fungal disease. Pass a huge gnarled and very picturesque highbush blueberry which has more than ten main stems. Olive-drab warbling vireos nest near water; listen for their pleasant, deliberate phrasing. The boardwalk now turns left to follow the Bantam River. Lots of escaped Tartarian honeysuckle thrives at the woodland edge.

Come once again to a boardwalk, turn right, and cross the river on a wooden bridge; the golf course is visible to the left. Emerge from the woods edge to open marsh, where colorful and sweet-singing yellow warblers are very common nesters. Canada geese nest among the cattails as well. Watch for their fuzzy yellowish goslings if you visit in spring. Decades ago this species never nested south of Canada, but the establishment of refuges and feeding programs has created some populations of Canada geese that migrate only short distances or not at all. Cross the Bantam River over the Francis Howe Sutton Bridge, which has an iron central span. Tall, plumed common reed, or *Phragmites*, has invaded this end of the pond.

Reenter deciduous woodland to complete the loop around Little Pond. Turn left and follow the wide pathway back toward Whites Woods Road. Cross the road and continue on the Little Pond Trail to the woods road, where you should turn left. This leads south a short distance to paved Bissell Road. Turn right and walk 100 yards to the Mattatuck Trail on the left. Along the way pass another stretch of pavement on the left. Follow the blue-blazed dirt roadway of the Mattatuck Trail back through the hemlock-pine stand and along the Bantam River as when you began the hike. Reach the dirt road (turn right) that leads back to the museum and parking area.

HATS TO HABITAT

North America's largest rodent, the beaver, thrives once again in Connecticut and the rest of New England, but this wasn't always the case. Beaver were reintroduced to the state in 1914 after a very long absence. In colonial times these semiaquatic mammals, which sometimes exceed seventy pounds, were trapped and hunted for their luxuriant, waterproof fur until they were literally extirpated from southern New England.

Beaver were, in a very real sense, responsible for the exploration of this continent. In the seventeenth and early-eighteenth centuries, both Britain and France established vast trading empires which saw beaver pelts exchanged for all manner of trade goods. The pelts were processed and used to manufacture beaver hats, which any self-respecting gentleman of that age felt compelled to wear on his head. The demand for beaver hats thus created a great impetus for exploration and empire building among the colonial powers in North America.

Perhaps it is ironic, then, that the family of May and Alain White, the donors of this property, came to financial prominence as a direct result of its good fortune in the fur industry. For ultimately it enabled their heirs— a brother and sister who loved nature—to set aside this large piece of real estate in perpetuity for the benefit of both wildlife and people.

Today the loud slap of a beaver's tail on the water is once again a common sound in rural and even suburban New England. The animal's great resurgence has led to population increases for many other species of wildlife as well. Great blue herons, for instance, are becoming more common these days, due to the creation by beaver of wooded swamps as breeding habitat all over the region.

Wetlands are, after all, among our most productive ecosystems, and certainly among the most interesting. With the help of humans, beaver, those master builders, have contributed mightily not only to their own welfare but to the future welfare of much of New England's wildlife.

Getting There

From the intersection of Routes 202 and 63 in Litchfield drive west on Route 202 for 2.1 miles to Bissell Road on the left. Almost immediately turn right from Bissell Road onto Whitehall Road and travel down Whitehall Road for 0.5 mile to the parking area on the right.

—R.L.

Candlewood Mountain

New Milford

- Housatonic Range Trail
- 3.0 miles round-trip
- 640-foot elevation gain
- 3.0 hours
- moderate, with steep sections

Just north of Lake Candlewood and barely west of the Housatonic River lies the hard, granitic spine of Candlewood Mountain. In this area the Housatonic has done a very strange thing: It has cut directly across the billion-year-old granitic mass of the highlands rather than follow the course of lesser resistance—the relatively soft marble valley. Geologists are still puzzled by this seeming contradiction to the laws of earth science.

The name Candlewood refers to a tree we now commonly know as pitch pine. The high resin content of its soft wood causes it to burn with a bright, illuminating flame. Few pitch pine remain on the mountain named for it; instead, white pine is by far the most numerous pine here today.

This hike will take you along and over the ridge's hard granite backbone, topping two promontories in the process. Both summits are wooded and deny one distant views, although a limited view of the Housatonic Valley is possible from a location on the mountain's eastern flank known reassuringly as Kelly (or Kelly's) Slide. The trail, however, makes up for the paucity of panoramic views with an ample assortment of picturesque and challenging ledge outcrops, fragrant pine-oak woodlands, and shady hemlock groves which harbor abundant bird life.

Although an out-and-back hike, its interesting geologic features and rich fauna and flora combine to make the return walk along Kelly Slide even more noteworthy than the ascent.

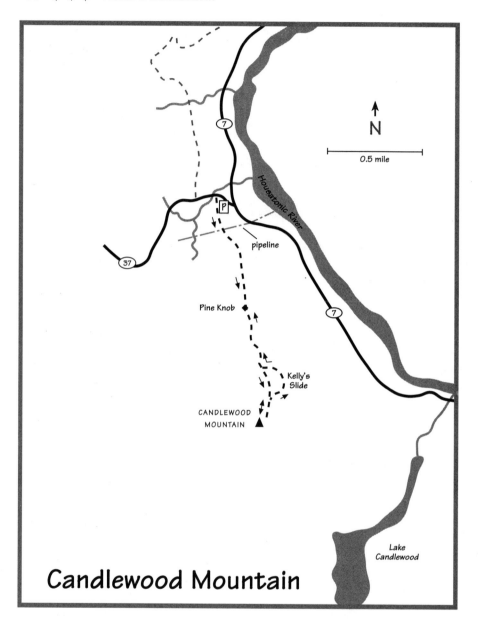

Candlewood Mountain

Look Forward To

- picturesque granite ledges and boulder fields
- fine view of the Housatonic River Valley
- fragrant pine-oak woods and cool hemlock groves rich in bird life

The Trail

Enter the woods, walking gradually uphill within a shaded, cool hemlock stand. As a precursor of much more to come, cross over bedrock and boulders of gray granite. Follow blue triangular blazes to a sign for the Housatonic Range Trail System, where you can pick up a leaflet. There is little undergrowth in the hemlock's deep shade, although red, black, and white oak do appear, as well as a few yellow birch. The first outcropping appears on the right, and to your left, just beyond the forest edge, are several houses. The trail swings right and goes up over rocks.

In summer, gaudy scarlet tanagers, solitary (now blue-headed) vireos, and black-and-white warblers sing and nest in these woodlands. The eastern hemlock increase in girth just before you pass through a boulder field and reach the linear clearing of the Iroquois Gas pipeline. In summer you'll notice the dramatic temperature difference as you step out of the shade and into the warmth of the sunny gas line cut. The odors are different too. Brilliant blue indigo buntings build their nests in trees along the edge of clearings like this, and butterflies draw nectar with their coiled, tubular tongues from the abundance of blooming flowers that thrive in sunny openings. Below to your left, well beyond the roadway, is a quarried cliff face.

As you continue walking uphill, cross gray bedrock and reenter hemlock woods, where a gray squirrel may scold your unwanted arrival. The path leads gradually upward across the surface roots of hemlock. White pine and chestnut oak are also present. Chestnut oak trunks are characterized by their rough, blocky bark. You now pass through quarried granite on the small hillside, jumbled and angular, in the shade of hemlocks. Soon a picturesque, twenty-five-foot-high rock wall, topped by pine and hemlock, rises up to the right. Make a sharp left turn here, stepping down along the outcrop. Turn right, then almost immediately left, and be sure to watch closely for blue blazes in this area. Follow along the outcrop wall on the left, then swing right in a small grove of impressively large white pine and hemlock. The path now bears right and leads you gradually up the rocky slope and over a granite ledge to the left.

The short green fronds of common polypody fern create a soft cap for the gray stone, while chestnut oak is now common. Walk up over bedrock and swing right, continuing up the slope. This section is a bit tricky; the trail becomes more challenging, although hemlock roots provide some grip for your feet. The sweet trills of olive-green and yellow pine warblers may fill the late spring and early summer air as you make your way up the steep slope. Soon you arrive at a small bedrock clearing surrounded by oak, white pine, hemlock, and black birch, all of short stature. Spongy (when moist) reindeer lichen, soft haircap moss, lowbush blueberry, pink lady-slipper orchids, mountain laurel, and even some wintergreen in shaded spots grow on the thin, acidic soil along the perimeter of the clearing. Oaks notwithstanding, the combination of exposed granite bedrock and acid-tolerant vegetation harkens to thoughts of northern New England.

The first pitch pine, certainly not a plant of northern New England, make their appearance here also. Some views, albeit screened, also are possible. Continue walking and reenter the shaded hemlock–white pine forest. Strikingly beautiful orange, black, and white Blackburnian warblers sing loudly and continually from evergreen boughs during their breeding season. Catching a glimpse of the striking males through binoculars may not be easy, however, as you make your way up this hillside shelf trail. From below to the left, the enthusiastic bubbling song of the tiny winter wren reached my ears during a late June outing. Few songs are more beautiful and sustained than this one, in my opinion.

While passing through another granite boulder field, note that the dark, damp soil beneath the hemlock is springy and peatlike. As you continue upward, reach a small sheer cliff on the right perhaps thirteen feet high. The trail bears left and then right, passing through two very large diameter evergreen trees—a hemlock on the left and a white pine to the right. Listen in summer for the songs of interior woodland nesters such as wood thrush and ovenbird, as you pause among the granite chunks of another boulder field and then continue along the rock outcrop. Small, smooth-skinned black birch hold fast amid the rock slabs. The vertical, unyielding granite surface is partially covered with rock tripe, a leafy lichen (tan above, black below) whose algal component turns green and begins producing nutrients after it absorbs moisture. The waste acids the lichens produce eventually etch even this hard rock.

The trail now turns sharply right, demanding that you scramble up the multitiered granite outcrop. You'll need both hands in some places, and exercise caution, as dead leaves underfoot can be slippery. Turn left after you reach the top. As I caught my breath there, I enjoyed listening to the ethereal music of a hermit thrush drifting down the slope. Short chestnut oak, white pine, black birch, and lowbush blueberry vegetate the slope above the outcrop. Soon come to a fork in the trail, and continue straight on the blue-blazed trail (the unblazed trail goes downhill). These rather open pine-oak woodlands remind me of Cape Cod, with the very notable exception of the rocky slopes. Soon reach the fairly level summit of Pine Knob (700 ft.). A screened view is possible to the left.

The trail now winds first moderately and then steeply downhill through dry oak woodland. Some of the oak trunks are decorated with gray-green lichens. As you descend, reach shaded and cooler forest where hemlock again thrive. Continue past rock outcrops and a jumble of boulders, then turn right. Note the one-foot diameter black birch that has forced its way up through a crevice in the granite. The level path swings left and then leads through cutover and resprouting red maple woods. Bear left again and walk down over boulders and ledges. Virginia creeper vines, whose leaves turn scarlet in fall, stretch across some slabs. Walk downhill rather steeply for a short distance and enter hemlock woods again. An overhanging ledge on the right, opposite a large black oak, could provide shelter during a downpour.

The trail swings right and leads over granite slabs. Striped maple, with attractive, tight-fitting, green-and-white bark, dot the woods; some are decorated with winged seeds. The roots of a large wind-thrown oak on the right still hold a lot of soil in their grasp. As you climb gradually through rocky oak, pine, and birch woodland and bear right, come to a trail junction. The blue-blazed trail goes left; Stay right and scramble up over

A limited but pleasant view of the Housatonic River is possible from the steep slope known as Kelly Slide.

rocks to a horseshoe-shaped granite bowl. Blooming mountain laurel shrubs ahead add to the beauty of the scene. The blossoms of Connecticut's state flower are more white than pink here on Candlewood Mountain. Continue up through rock outcrops brightened by mountain laurel. Chestnut oak is now the dominant tree, as a few sassafras trees appear. Here I inadvertently flushed my first ruffed grouse of the day, which burst from the forest floor in a heart-stopping explosion of feathers. Soon reach the lower end of the Kelly Slide side trail, which is marked with a sign. Stay right and walk past lady-slippers, Canada mayflower, lowbush blueberry, and wintergreen, all acid-tolerant plants.

Swing gradually right and walk uphill through sunny patches of dry oak-pine woodland with a fairly thick growth of huckleberry and lowbush blueberry below the oak. Huckleberry resembles blueberry, but huckleberry leaves, both top and bottom surfaces, are flecked with tiny resin dots. At a fork in the trail another sign on the left indicates the direction to Kelly Slide; this is the upper end of the Kelly Slide side trail (both are blazed blue). Pass it up for now, staying right and continuing fairly steeply uphill. Below the thirty-foot-tall oak, huckleberry and lowbush blueberry—both with green fruit in late June—grow in profusion. A few smooth, gray-trunked Juneberry (shad) trees supply red fruits to grouse and other wildlife. Here I flushed my second grouse of the day. The trail levels off on bedrock and continues through low pine-oak woods. The tiny male "cones" of white pine, empty now of their yellow pollen, may pile up on the ground below the pines in spring.

A few sunny openings come into view as the summit is neared. Scrub oak, also known as bear oak, and red cedar, both light-loving species, makes their first appearance. Eastern towhees give their distinctive *chewink* call and scratch in the leaf litter. Emerge into a level clearing on granite bedrock. Swing right through scrub oak, white pine, red cedar, and pitch pine, which has relatively short, stiff needles, some of which poke out directly from the trunk. Coyotes leave telltale scat composed of cottontail fur and bone on the rock. Arrive soon at a stone bench where you can sit and enjoy your lunch. You are now on the 991-foot-high summit of Candlewood Mountain. Unless you climb a tree there are no views, except perhaps in winter. The blue-blazed Housatonic Mountain Trail turns left just to the left of the bench and continues south down the mountain.

When ready, retrace your steps back to Kelly Slide side trail on the right. Even if you don't make the full Kelly Slide loop, which can be tough going over downed trees and boulders, walk the short distance downslope to where a fine view of the Housatonic Valley can be had. Walking this section of the trail under wet or icy conditions is not recommended, however. The trail enters oak, hemlock, and white pine woods, descending over rocks. The hillside drops away to your left, then you descend more steeply, going down the slanting ledges as one might a staircase with the path skirting the perimeter of the slide area. With granite bedrock so close to the surface on this tilted slope, deep soils could never develop. When waterlogged, the thin soil holding the root systems literally slides right off the mountainside, exposing the bedrock. In some places the shallow root systems of hemlock and other trees are evident above the clean light-gray stone.

You may want to go no farther along the hillside, instead retracing your steps to the main trail, turning right to follow it back to your car. Or you can continue following the trail as it skirts the mountainside. At the end of the horizontal ledges, follow the trail down to the right; a small downed hemlock obscures this turn. Watch your footing. Numerous young wind-thrown hemlocks along this portion of the trail may make walking difficult. On a hot summer day though, you'll appreciate the natural air conditioning emanating from the granite ledges. Pass under a big, lengthy fallen tree where a long, tapered black wing feather belonging to a turkey vulture caught my eye. Perhaps the big black carrion eaters nest among these rugged ledges.

The trail continues down over massive chunks of granite strewn along the slope, and then scrambles up the slope over a boulder field after swinging left. Continue bearing left and pass several ledge crevices large enough to shelter a bent-over person. A luxuriant growth of evergreen fern caps the ledge. More small "caves" come into view as you walk up, finally joining the main trail. Turn right and follow the main trail back to your vehicle. Be sure to stay straight (left) at the trail junction, and be careful also not to miss the sharp right where you make the short but steep descent down the ledge.

PARTRIDGE IN A SHAD TREE

Ruffed grouse are somewhat chickenlike, but far more interesting. Normally they rely upon their excellent camouflage to aid them in melting into the background. If that fails, grouse take wing with an explosive blast that leaves most potential predators, including humans, stunned. Swift fliers for short distances, grouse spend much of their time on the ground. They are also rather able climbers, clambering about on surprisingly spindly limbs and nimbly plucking ripe fruits such as Juneberry (a.k.a. shad or serviceberry) in summer and fall or buds in winter.

In spring male grouse court by selecting or returning to a favorite fall-en tree to make music. Grouse "drum" the air by very rapidly beating their cupped wings forward and upward until they are but a blur to the eye. The drumming begins slowly and then builds to a crescendo of whirring wing beats. This action creates a very deeply resonant sound reminiscent of a distant lawn-mower engine starting up and then sputtering out. Such very low frequency sounds are capable of traveling up to a quarter-mile, even in densely wooded areas. Males also drum to protect their territories from other males. In addition, males raise their crests and dark shoulder ruffs, fan their tails, and strut. It is a quite a show, certain to impress hen grouse and hiker alike.

For their part, female grouse with chicks are among the most brazen of creatures in the forest. Should your path happen to come too close to a grouse hen and her brood, you will probably suffer her wrath. This can be exemplified by several levels of intensity, but usually begins with the female making odd mewing sounds which may have you wondering what you are listening to. She may then walk boldly, wings partially extended and crouching low. In extreme cases, a female grouse will actually attack an intruder in a valiant effort to drive them away from her offspring. It is an amusing but intimidating display which usually succeeds.

In fall, grouse develop rows of fringe along the edges of their toes, providing them with a type of home-grown snowshoes. And to escape the subfreezing cold of winter nights, grouse burrow deep into the snow, relying upon its insulating properties to help keep them warm. When you're in the winter woods, look for their single-file tracks in the snow, about three inches apart.

Getting There

From the junction of Routes 202 and 67 in New Milford, follow Route 202 west for 0.5 mile across the Housatonic River to its junction with Route 7. Turn right onto Route 7 and drive northward for 2.8 miles to Route 37 on the left. Follow Route 37 for just over 0.1 mile to its junction with Candlewood Mountain Road on the left. Park on the wide shoulder to the left of the intersection of the two roads.

—R.L.

Sunny Valley Preserve

Bridgewater

- Silica Mine Trail, Lakeside Trail
- 3.4 miles
- 350-foot elevation gain
- moderate

Tucked away in the extreme southwestern corner of Litchfield County lies Sunny Valley Preserve, an 1,850-acre Nature Conservancy composite of numerous parcels. One portion, the Silica Mine Hill section, when combined with the Lakeside Trail section, produces a loop hike on well-maintained trails which melds both uplands and vista with lakeshore (actually riverside) walking—an unusual and pleasing juxtaposition.

Just north of the preserve the Housatonic River deviates from its course through the relatively soft rocks of the Marble Valley and inexplicably turns and cuts across harder gneiss and granite bedrock. After flowing through the southern Marble Valley on the eastern side of these harder rocks, the river enters the schist and gneiss bedrock of the western uplands. In this region, of which the preserve is a part, dams cause the river to back up, creating "lakes." Lake Lillinonah, very popular with boaters, is one of them. Shepaug Dam raises the river's water level about forty-five feet above the original Housatonic River channel at this point.

Rocky Hill, around which the river makes an s-shaped configuration, and other promontories rise up rather steeply along both sides of the river valley, creating a scenic landscape with fine hiking and nature study opportunities.

Look Forward To
- ledge vista
- forest with a primeval feel
- attractive fern glades
- Lake Lillinonah

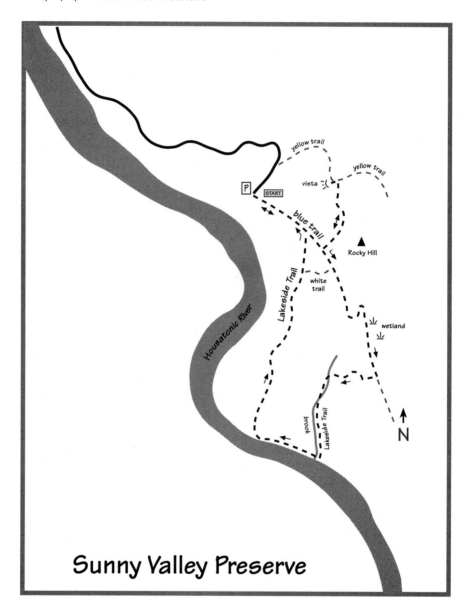

Sunny Valley Preserve

The Trail

From the map kiosk at the trailhead, follow the blue-blazed trail into the forest of black birch, sugar maple, red oak, and American beech and up a gentle slope along an outcrop on the left. Private property borders the preserve to the right. The path then levels out. In summer the forest is alive with the songs of tufted titmice, scarlet tanagers, and red-eyed vireos. Schist rocks, with a high content of the mineral mica, glisten. Large white oaks and tulip trees are visible in the forest, and below them Christmas, New York, and hay-scented ferns. There are also hemlocks and black oaks. More dark gray outcrops protrude on the left. The trail swings in that direction and climbs steadily now, crossing a tiny stream bed green with skunk cabbage. White ash and shagbark hickory join rather large black birch trees in the forest.

Climb through shady hemlocks and reach the red-blazed Lakeside Trail on the right. Continue straight on the blue-blazed trail. Shards of milky-white quartz (silica) appear underfoot. Silica, the most abundant mineral on the planet, was once mined here and used to make glass. The slope rises steeply on the left as you pass another rock outcrop, and then drops off to your right. Hermit thrushes sing their incomparable ethereal tunes from the shaded woods. Mountain laurel and witch hazel shrubs appear, and then the trail levels out under hemlocks where gray slabs of rock, uptilted at 45°, rise out of the forest floor above you to the left.

Come to the white-blazed connector trail on the left, which winds up through the outcrops to a vista point. Turn left onto it and walk up the rather steep hillside. Black-throated green warblers nest in the evergreens. Crest the hill shortly, treading on a duff-cushioned trail under hemlocks, oaks, and hickories. You are standing on the shoulder of Rocky Hill. Walk downhill briefly and curve left, then right, under hemlocks whose lower limbs are dead. Start climbing gradually again through hemlocks, black birches, and oaks with notably straight trunks. Copious amounts of glittering mica schist rocks litter the trail. Level off briefly, note the sharp drop on the left, then swing left and descend easily. Chestnut oak joins red oak on this drier, rock-littered slope.

Follow the trail right, along the hillside. Listen for the *ee-o-lay* refrain of the wood thrush here. Begin climbing at a moderate incline, then level off again. Schist slabs, set at the now familiar 45° angle, sit exposed on the right. This rock was formed about 400 million years ago and later distorted by great heat and pressure well below the earth's surface. Solomon's seal, so named because the root purportedly resembles King Solomon's royal seal, grows on the outcrop. Striped wintergreen blooms in summer along this trail, while lowbush blueberry and little oak fern indicate acidic soils. The trail undulates on this rather sheer hillside with a fairly dramatic drop-off to the left. Black oak, distinguished from red oak by its darker, more fissured bark joins white oak, red maple, mountain laurel, and sassafras. Silvery cushion moss softens the margins of the path.

Eastern wood pewees whistle their melancholy *pee-a-wee* songs from the treetops, while through the leaf litter the twin green leaves of pink lady-slipper are evident. This orchid blooms in June. It is definitely sunnier now, due to decreasing hemlocks on this drier slope. White oak, red maple, black oak, and small black birch are now common. Come to a very short side trail on the left that leads to the vista point atop the ledge (at the junction with the yellow-blazed trail). If you visit on a summer weekend, the roar of invisible motorboats far below will be in the air. Rolling forested ridges are laid out to the west, while at your feet a nine-inch-diameter pool formed in the outcrop serves as a tiny reservoir for rainwater. Close inspection may reveal mosquito larvae wriggling about. Common polypody fern grows on the outcrop.

While I was maneuvering into position for panoramic photos from the ledge, I was suddenly distracted by the loud scolding of titmice and chickadees. Following the racket led me to a black oak nearby. I searched the site of the commotion with my binoculars. Focusing upon one particularly agitated titmouse, I saw a medium-sized shiny black rat snake resting on a horizontal limb. It appeared to be looking right at me. Running for my pack and the longer lens it contained, I returned just seconds later to find the snake gone. I searched for it, but to no avail. It apparently had slid into a large knothole situated just below the limb it had been basking on. Disturbed first by a flock of agitated birds and then by a nosy human, it had decided to take its leave. After the snake's retreat, the birds' noisy jeering stopped almost as if on cue.

Black rat snakes are very adept climbers and are known to prey upon birds and their eggs and nestlings. The frantic alarm calls of the titmice had enlisted the aid of chickadees, a downy woodpecker, and even a black-throated green warbler in the campaign against this shiny black threat in the trees. I had seen instances of "mobbing" before, directed mostly at hawks, owls, and even myself on occasion, but never at a snake. It was something I had read about, but, since black rat snakes are rather uncommon in most of southern New England, I had never witnessed such a thing until now. The incident stayed with me all day and well beyond; it certainly made my day that mid-July.

Retrace your steps downhill back to the junction of the white and blue-blazed trails and turn left onto the blue trail. Walk through the shade cast by hemlocks to a small foundation made of schist immediately left of the trail. Bits of quartz are piled along the foundation's edge. Continue walking through slanting schist ledges on both sides; some form natural overhangs which can shelter small creatures. Proceed easily downhill under oaks and hemlocks to another intersection with the white-blazed trail on the right, where you should continue straight and gradually downward past more jumbled outcrops. Soon bear left.

More quartz litters the trail, and then a very massive, straight and tall tulip tree appears on the right. Its lowest limb exits the columnar trunk fifty feet above the ground! It has reached this size in a small dip between hillsides, probably because moisture tends to collect here. A little farther on, pass a small pit that has chunks of quartz lying about on top. The trail swings left after descending gently across a seep area on bog bridges. Note the wetland indicator plants—sensitive and cinnamon ferns, jewelweed, nettles, and skunk cabbage.

Regain drier ground and bear right along the base of the slope. A brilliant male scarlet tanager sang his burry, robinlike song from a hickory during a summer visit. Pass through a small fern glade, begin ascending, and then bear sharply left. Listen for the soothing trickle of water flowing over moss-covered boulders to your right. The trail swings right, up a moderately steep but short slope held in place by shallow, exposed hemlock roots. Soon you are walking on more-level ground along a tiny stream flowing down on the right under young hemlocks. Bear right and amble up through a jumble of schist boulders on the oak-and-birch-covered slope. Some slabs are capped by common polypody fern.

Cross a flowing rivulet on rocks. Upstream a few feet is a small wetland dominated by the broad leaves of skunk cabbage, sensitive fern, and sphagnum moss. The moss is yellowish green and spongy, fine habitat for green frogs. You know they are present when you hear their single or double twang, often compared to the sound made by a plucked banjo string. A group of males in chorus sounds as though they are all gulping for air. Pass an eighteen-inch-diameter, rough-barked tupelo tree growing along the flowage on the left—that's right, a tupelo (a.k.a. black gum)! This species is more common in the southeastern U.S., thriving in moist soils everywhere there. Odd to find it here on the flank of Rocky Hill. A passing bird probably dropped the seed into this fortuitously damp spot decades ago.

Follow the trail as it turns left under red maple and white and chestnut oaks. Clumps of tussock sedge and buttonbush and a film of bright green algae are visible in the "perched" wetland below on the left, while beeches grow above it. Continue through hemlock-oak woods on a level path parallel with the wet area. Tupelo seedlings are fairly numerous on the forest floor, and cinnamon ferns crowd the wetland shore.

Now bear right, away from the water and the gulping frogs. Shortly come to a Y; stay left on the narrower trail that swings left. Solitary (recently renamed blue-headed) vireos sing their measured phrases of dialogue

Lakeside Trail leads to the wooded shores of Lake Lillinonah, a wide section of the Housatonic River.

from the trees above. Where openings in the forest canopy allow sunlight to penetrate, lacy ferns thrive in yellowish green gardens. Enter shaded and rocky hemlock woods. The hemlocks are joined by black and chestnut oaks, and the slope drops away to a small hemlock ravine on the left filled with attractive hay-scented ferns.

Proceed downhill gradually, then more steeply. Black birch saplings sprout from what was once bare soil in a sunny, rocky opening in the forest. Look back over your left shoulder for a pleasant view of the ledge outcrops. Although the trees are not particularly large, the forest has a primeval feel here. Perhaps it's the lacy green garden of ferns from which straight trunks of hemlocks rise up like Greek columns. Reach another very attractive, sun-dappled clearing crowded with ferns. During a mid-July visit the uncontrollably bubbly and joyous song of a tiny winter wren added to the magical atmosphere.

Reach the red-blazed Lakeside Trail at a T junction and turn right onto it. Continue through more lacy hay-scented ferns to a rotting hemlock adorned with bracket fungus. A tiger swallowtail butterfly glided through the sunlight and a fiery-throated male Blackburnian warbler sang from high in a hemlock tree as I passed through. Reenter the cool of the hemlocks and climb gradually on the somewhat rocky trail. A few prickly Japanese barberry bushes indicate soil disturbance. Walk through a shallow "ravine" between ledges and then level out under black birches and hemlocks adjacent to ledges on the left.

Pass through another hay-scented fern gap (hay-scented fern is often common on rocky ground) and reach an unblazed side trail on the left. Keep straight on the red-blazed trail and walk down through mixed woods and occasional fern glades which also contain the New York and Christmas species. The woodland is composed of beech, white ash, shagbark hickory, black birch, and hemlocks. Red-eyed vireos and hermit thrushes fill the forest with song in spring and early summer after returning from the tropics to breed. Continue steadily downhill past outcrops, then level off and bear left. Note that quite a few young wind-thrown hemlocks have been downed here. Hemlocks have very shallow root systems and are therefore prone to such a fate.

The trail turns left, and immediately left again. The small flood plain of a brook on the right is covered with a monoculture of skunk cabbage, named for the fetid odor of its crushed leaves. The huge "celery stalk" stem and large leaves of cow parsnip grow tall here as well. Continue walking along the small stream in the tiny ravine as you listen to its quiet flow. Remnants of a rock wall are visible beyond the brook. Pass a rather large, straight beech tree standing left of the path. Most of the woodland is young hemlock—very shade tolerant, like beech—as well as oak, birch, ash, and maple.

The ravine deepens slightly. Many young hemlocks are snapped off seventeen feet or so above the ground. There are also some large sugar maples in the woods and fair-sized tulip trees near the stream. The flowing water is closer and more audible now. Proceed steadily downhill on a path softened by a thick layer of hemlock needles, and pass a twin beech on the right which has one trunk broken off low. This is an attractive hemlock ravine. Continue downhill moderately steeply, and soon glimpse the waters of Lake Lillinonah through the trees ahead. Walk through the remnants of a stone wall just above where the brook enters the "lake" (actually the Housatonic River).

Reach a T junction near the water's edge and turn right to remain on the red-blazed trail. Cross the brook, pass through the same stone wall again, and begin a gradual ascent through tulip tree, black birch, maple, and hemlock woods. Listen for scolding red squirrels as you walk through a stone wall where a big tulip tree marks a corner. Walk through a muddy seep area where canopied jack-in-the-pulpits grow. White and red oaks and moisture-loving tulip trees form the canopy. Waves created by passing motorboats wash the shoreline. The occasional ring-billed gull may put down on a boulder near shore for a rest. I found a very attractive clump of white Indian pipes growing up against the side of a gray granite outcrop— an eye-catching contrast of color and texture.

Resume walking gradually uphill as the trail bends right. Pass a massive American beech, fully three and a half feet in diameter growing along a stone wall behind a boulder. The life span of this species may reach 400 years. This is the largest specimen I have seen anywhere in a long time. A long-dead farmer may have left this beech standing when he cleared his fields because it provided shade and sweet nuts for his livestock.

Walk uphill away from the river through a boulder field, and then through a woodland where little grows below the shade cast by hemlocks, oaks, beeches, and tulip trees. Dip slightly, then swing left and begin a very gradual climb. Pass between outcrops. A patch of elderberries grows in the sunlight, surrounded by elephant-gray granitic gneiss rocks.

The trail makes a sharp right and ascends briefly amid boulders and ledge into a slight dip between outcrops where hemlocks, tulip trees (yellow poplar to some), and ashes grow. Bear left, climb again, and then level out, following along the shoulder of the slope. Black-throated green warblers make their compact, well-built nest cups on the boughs of hemlocks in these woods. Through my binoculars I spotted two on a warm summer afternoon.

Begin climbing again. Schist rocks, with very visible mica crystals, appear just before you reach level ground and bear left under hemlocks and white and red oaks. The slope drops off to the left. Gray squirrels bound along on the forest floor. Look for the little excavations that indicate the rodents have been retrieving acorns.

Reach the junction with the white-blazed connector trail on the right. Continue straight on the red-blazed trail slightly downhill through hemlock, oak, and birch woods. Walk parallel to a stone wall on the left, beyond which the hillside falls away more steeply. Keep walking downhill; above the trail on the right are rock outcrops. Reach the intersection with the blue-blazed trail. Turn left and retrace your steps back down to your vehicle.

MOB MENTALITY

An old saying has it that there is safety in numbers. Small birds certainly find truth in this axiom when confronted by a potential predator. The presence of the black rat snake in the oak tree was quickly telegraphed to other nearby avian residents by the first tufted titmouse to discover the snake. And although the snake couldn't hear the screams of the excited birds, it certainly saw them jumping about, just out of reach. And that is the key: The birds doing the mobbing are generally smaller and faster than the predator being mobbed. But rat snakes, when sufficiently warm, possess the ability to move with great speed. Reason enough for the birds to remain just out of harm's reach.

When chickadees mob screech owls, or crows dive upon red-tailed hawks, or crows themselves are set upon by any number of smaller species, the mobber has always chosen a larger and slower target. Something akin to fast fighter planes flying circles around a cumbersome bomber. Usually this kind of harassment succeeds in driving away the potential predator. Perhaps this is because without the element of surprise working in its behalf, the predator's chance of procuring an easy meal is greatly reduced.

In reality there is still some conjecture among bird behaviorists about the true role or roles that mobbing may play. But whatever its advantages, birds continue to rely upon it as an apparently effective predator-deterrent device.

Birders often use to their advantage the knowledge that small birds will mob a potential predator. By whistling an imitation of the screech owl's call (even a poor approximation will often do), the birder can usually attract a number of birds, often of a variety of species, to his or her location. The agitated birds flit about, attempting to locate the source of the quavering owl call, but to no avail. It is a popular ruse which sometimes works amazingly well, and at other times doesn't work at all. It can be overdone, however, especially when birds are nesting, and because it could expose them to a real predator, this tactic should be used sparingly and only in the proper situations.

Getting There

From the junction of Routes 202 and 67 in New Milford, take Route 67 south for 3.1 miles to where Route 133 merges on the right. Follow Route 133 south for 0.8 mile and turn right onto Hat Shop Hill Road. Drive down Hat Shop Hill Road for 0.6 mile to a triangle. Jog right, then immediately left around the triangle and drive straight on Hemlock Road for 1.8 miles to the gravel parking area on the left at the end of the road. The small lot has room for four to five vehicles.

—R.L.

Devil's Den Preserve

Weston

- Laurel Trail, Godfrey Trail, Sap Brook Trail, Hiltebeitel Trail, Deer Knoll Trail, Pent Trail
- 3.3-mile loop
- 230-foot elevation gain
- 3.0 hours
- moderate

This, the largest contiguous nature preserve in southwestern Connecticut, is owned and managed by The Nature Conservancy (TNC). Its 1,746 acres boast a very well marked twenty-one-mile trail system. The full name of the property is actually Lucius Pond Ordway–Devil's Den Preserve, which honors the father of the donor of the property, Weston resident Katherine Ordway. Ms. Ordway began purchasing portions of the property for TNC in 1966, and by 1969 1,400 acres had been protected. Locals refer to it simply as "the Den."

The land's human history is a very long one, as it is the site of ancient Native American encampments. Godfrey Pond, built as a millpond in the 1700s, now provides refuge for a multitude of aquatic and semiaquatic plants and creatures. Much of the preserve's forested acreage was cut over for use in charcoal making, an important industry here until the early part of the twentieth century. A replica of a charcoal mound stands along Laurel Trail.

In such a densely settled part of the state as this, the preserve represents very important forested habitat for wildlife as well as a place of solitude for humanity. The preserve's rugged terrain, crossed as it is by so many bony ridges, makes the Devil's Den a delightful place for a day's exploration. But how did it come to be known as the Devil's Den? The unfortunate appellation stems from the discovery of what was thought to be the imprint of the Devil's own cloven hoof in one of the rocks on the property.

The preserve is open sunrise to sunset; all visitors must register at the kiosk, which has trail maps, interpretive booklets, and displays. A small

Devil's Den Preserve

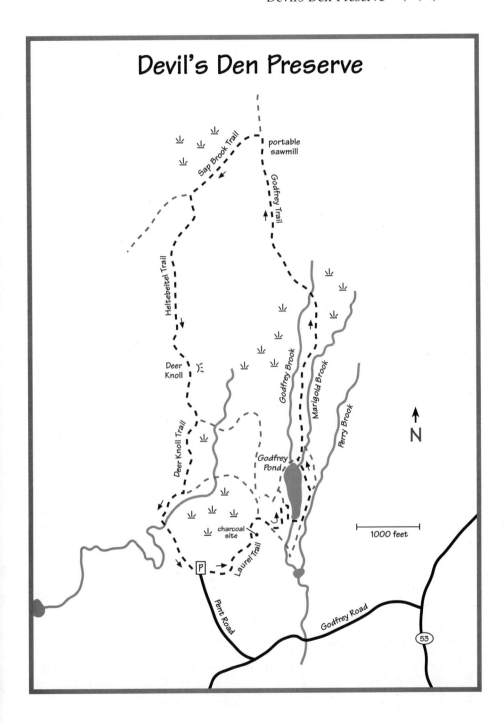

donation is requested. There are no restrooms available. Cross-country skiing is permitted on red-blazed trails. Pets, horses, bicycles, and picnicking
are not permitted.

Look Forward To

- Godfrey Pond

- rocky ridges

- scenic overlook

- expansive woodlands

The Trail

From the gravel parking area follow the red-and-white blazed Laurel Trail
past the wooden gate in the direction of Godfrey Pond. White oak are very
numerous and chestnut oak, black birch, and red maple are common too,
with a thick understory of mountain laurel and some witch hazel. The trail,
which is wide and chipped, leads you uphill, then bears left. Red oak
becomes dominant; among these acorn-bearing trees blue jays and tufted
titmice are year-round residents. In late summer, dog-day cicadas fill the
warm air with their mechanical buzzing. Walk downhill now amid gneiss
boulders. Lowbush blueberry and pinesap, a plant which lacks chlorophyll
and draws its nourishment from oak and pine roots, pokes out of the leaf
litter. It resembles Indian pipes, another saprophyte.

The trail swings left as American beech trees, many scarred by graffiti, appear. In damp soil tulip trees, cinnamon fern, and sweet pepperbush,
which produces dense spikes of pretty white flowers in summer, thrive.
Scarlet tanager, red-bellied woodpecker, American robin, and Baltimore
oriole are among the summer residents of these woods. Many of the red
oak are very straight and tall, indicating that they grew up in a forest rather
than an open field. The trail bears right and reaches a stone wall on that
side. Sassafras, with its variously lobed leaves, joins witch hazel in the
understory of these dry oak woods. Start downhill, bear left, and pass
gneiss boulders just prior to reaching the replica of an 1800s charcoal
burner's site. Logs have been piled into a wigwam form. At one time there
were forty active sites within the preserve.

A short distance past the charcoal site, bear right and pass a big gneiss
boulder on the right. Striped wintergreen, with bold dark-green-and-white
leaves, grows along the trail. Pass through a stone wall and arrive at a T junction at marker #22. A rock outcrop and the Cub Scout Trail are on your left.

Turn right, however, and go gradually downhill toward Godfrey Pond. The trail is now blazed red, white, and yellow. Ironwood saplings make an appearance, as do maple-leafed viburnum and greenbrier. Shortly come to a Y fork at marker #23; turn left here. This trail is blazed yellow and white. Pass through a boulder field and walk downslope through black birch and some hickory. Gray squirrels thrive amid the nut bounty. Ferns, mostly lacy hay-scented, as well as a patch of evergreen Christmas fern, enliven the slope.

Stone walls on the right intersect at a very rocky brook, which you cross on a small wooden bridge. Keep alert for green frogs, characterized by parallel pleats down their backs, on the damp rocks. Fountain mosses give the rocks a furry appearance. To your left a stone wall sits atop a rock ledge, while at the end of the bridge, at marker #24, is a T junction on the same side. Bear left onto the yellow-and-white-blazed trail and parallel the brook bed. Note the appearance of yellow birch, an attractive member of the northern hardwood forest community. Mountain laurel borders the path. At marker #26 bear right and walk slightly uphill to a view of Godfrey Pond. A wooden bench is situated at the end of a level old stone-and-concrete dam which has a sluiceway in the center.

You'll enjoy the nice view of the pond, with its root-beer-colored, tannin-stained water, from this vantage point. More sweet pepperbush blooms along the shore in summer and a vigorous poison ivy vine climbs up a tree by the dam. A few buttonbush display their pompomlike white flower heads. While we sat enjoying the scene during an early August visit, a large snapping turtle cautiously poked the tip of its head out of the water near shore, its reptilian eyes fixed on us. It seemed to be playing hide-and-seek. Bluegills, potential meals for the turtle, swam heedlessly nearby. Other pond inhabitants include green frogs, gray tree frogs, and patrolling dragonflies.

The trail now turns right and leads to a trail intersection at marker #25. Turn left and cross the pond outlet. In late summer and fall check the pond shallows for globular, gelatinous masses known as bryozoan colonies. The minute colonial animals are embedded in the surface of the sphere and wave tentacles to direct diatoms and other single-celled plants into their mouths. Below the dam, rusting machinery is all that remains of the former mill apparatus. On the far side at marker #33 is another T intersection. Turn left and follow the red-and-white-blazed trail through rocky oak, beech, birch, and laurel woods as it parallels Godfrey Pond.

Come to marker #34 at a Y. Follow the chipped left fork, which is Godfrey Trail, downhill gradually through white, black, and red oaks; laurel; and witch hazel. The yellow-blazed path is lined by soft cushions of silver mound moss. Cross a mostly flat rocky area just above the pond, where buttonbush and lilies grow, and enter a shaded forest. The slope to your right and the bed of Marigold Brook are punctuated by many large granite boulders. Swing left to cross the brook on a wooden bridge and continue along the pond shore. Some of the rocks display large crystals of dark mica, glassy quartz, and pink feldspar, the three constituents of granite.

Another path soon merges from the right at marker #30. Turn right onto the now yellow-and-white-blazed Godfrey Trail and walk gradually uphill away from the pond in the midst of some fairly large beech trees. Then descend easily to approach the edge of the brook, where sugar maple, yellow birch, tulip tree, and straight-boled black birch are common. Swing left and reach a T junction at marker #36. Turn left to continue on the Godfrey Trail, which is blazed red and white in this section. To distinguish between the New York and hay-scented ferns growing here, note that New York fern is tapered at both ends. Walk by boulders and continue on this old woods road. Pass a sizable twin red oak on the left, its two pillarlike trunks diverging near its base. This forest patriarch bears no branches for forty feet up its twin trunks. A bit farther on, a twin tulip tree rises on the left and a large old beech near that.

Swing right, pass through low rock outcrops, and then bear left almost immediately. In a rock on the right is a miniature natural pool six inches in diameter. It serves as a source of drinking water for some forest dwellers. Where sunlight penetrates the canopy, stands of hay-scented fern shade the forest floor. The trail bears left and crosses Godfrey Brook via a wide wooden bridge. Moisture-loving cardinal flower blooms along the brook in summer with a red so intense it seems to glow in the subdued forest light. Spicebush and sweet pepperbush also thrive in the moist soil, as do skunk cabbage and rue anemone. Fluorescent-orange toadstools growing among the emerald-green mosses of the rocks may also catch your eye.

The brook veers off to the right as you continue to follow the old woods road straight ahead through oak-beech woodland. Tulip tree, yellow birch, and shagbark and pignut hickories are also common. Reach a low-lying spot with red maple and cinnamon and New York ferns as the trail curves right. Red maple are extremely tolerant of varying moisture levels, growing in both dry and saturated soils. Walk upslope gradually, bearing left through a boulder field. Eastern chipmunks use the boulders as observation posts and escape from enemies by dashing under their cover. We noticed one peering at us intently from the summit of one rock, pausing from its hickory-nut meal.

Tumbled remnants of rock walls lie on the right as you climb gradually, then descend gently and curve left. Pass gneiss boulders where light-gray, flaky-barked white oak are numerous, and then level out as you pass through hay-scented and New York ferns. Many ironwood trees grow in the understory of these open, easy-to-walk-through woods; their slender, muscular trunks are unmistakable. The path undulates gently, then rises and swings right.

Numerous boulders dot the forest floor—the reason why this land was never suitable for crops. Cross through a damp area on corduroy and then over a tiny brook bed which is dry in summer. Incredibly absorbent sphagnum moss covers some stones to the left. Pink knotweed grows in the moist soil at your feet and blooms in summer. Look for delicate and beautiful maidenhair fern along both sides of the trail.

Note the magnificent two- and three-trunked tulip trees—the tallest species of our eastern forests—and the big red oak on the right. Through the trees to your right you'll glimpse the rusting hulk of portable sawmill machinery that operated here during the late 1800s and early 1900s. The steam boiler and large flywheel are most obvious. Red and white oaks, American chestnut, and tulip tree (a.k.a. tulip poplar) were harvested. The sawmill shut down for good in 1922. The trail proceeds gradually left and up past stone walls and ledge outcrops. Soon come to the Sap Brook Trail

More than 75 years after this portable sawmill processed its last hardwood logs, the rusting machinery is still visible from Godfrey Trail.

intersection at marker #39. Turn left onto this relatively narrow, yellow-and-white-blazed trail and walk past an outcrop on the right; then curve right and into young oak, maple, and birch woods with mountain laurel, huckleberry, and sweet pepperbush beneath.

Big chestnut oak with deeply furrowed brown bark stand near the undulating path. Ovenbirds—heavily streaked, ground-nesting warblers—inhabit these woodlands in spring and summer, preferring to spend the "off-season" in the Tropics. Gain ground gradually and swing left through rocky woods of oak, birch, and laurel. Yellow birches are quite common, along with black birch. Both have oil of wintergreen in their sap. Huckleberry, which can be confused with blueberry, also does well in rocky, acidic woodlands like these. Huckleberry leaves, unlike those of blueberry, are peppered with minute yellowish resin dots on both surfaces.

The trail bears left and descends gently to a T intersection at marker #38. Turn left onto the Hiltebeitel Trail and cross a tiny flowage on rock as the path bears left. On your left is a low-lying, seasonally wet area with sweet pepperbush, mountain laurel, highbush blueberry, and sphagnum moss. Step over a living fallen beech which has transformed three side branches into surrogate vertical trunks, testimony to the prolific sprouting ability of this species. Bear left and continue through rocky oak, birch, and maple woods with many old fallen trunks on a sinuous but level trail. In general the forest seems young, with many slender stems. Huckleberry is especially abundant. Its blue-black fruits are sweet in late summer. Cross over a flat bedrock outcrop amid mountain laurel, witch hazel, and chestnut oak, and pass the rusted remains of a cast-iron stove on the right. Here we came across a long column of red and black ants carrying ant larvae in their pincers. Perhaps this was a victorious raiding party returning with the spoils of war.

At a rock outcrop on the left, the yellow-blazed (indicating it's for hiking only) trail swings in the other direction. Cross the bedrock floor of a small, sunny opening where only stunted oak and a few other species such as shadbush and mountain laurel eke out an existence. In the warm sunlight of the clearing, huckleberry shrubs produce plenty of delicious fruit. Chestnut oak, which does well on dry sites, remains the dominant large tree. Its sweet acorns mature in one year. Silver mound moss is common on the sandy soil as you weave through oak and laurel. Cross another small bedrock clearing and then pass an outcrop covered with rock tripe lichens. Follow the path gradually up over the outcrop, which is decorated with the gray-green doilies of other lichens. Walking along the top of the low outcrop brings you to a T intersection. The trail to the right is blocked; turn left.

Cross over a seasonally damp area on a single split log. The trail continues to be blazed with yellow only as it bears right, then left, and gradually climbs past a rock ledge on both sides. Descend fairly steeply for a short distance and swing right. These outcrops appear contorted, as if the rock melted and later resolidified. And that is exactly what happened deep within the earth under great pressure and heat. With the aid of a log ladder—steps cut into a log lying at a low angle—climb to the top of the outcrop and gain the vista point on Deer Knoll. The open granite prominence, studded with a few pitch pine, affords a pleasant view to the east of low, rolling, tree-clad ridges.

While we munched on a snack during our early-August outing, we watched industrious ants as they hauled away crumbs at our feet. The rock isn't totally naked. Haircap moss and reindeer lichen have colonized it. Lichens produce acids as a byproduct of their metabolism, and that ignites the slow process of turning rock into rock flour and finally soil. In pockets where soil has collected, small oaks, including scrub oak, have gained a foothold.

Continue on the trail and notice the rock turned on end. It contains prominently visible quartz veins. Quartz is the major reason why granite is so erosion resistant. Proceed down the rocks and off the outcrop, entering oak woods and bearing left down the rocky path through laurel. A few small oak fern, miniature versions of bracken fern, are present here. The trail swings this way and that and reaches a T junction at marker #20. Turn right onto the Deer Knoll Trail, which appears to be an old rocky woods road, and walk over exposed beech roots. American beech has characteristically shallow roots. Some of the trees show signs of old pileated woodpecker excavations where the crow-sized birds sought out carpenter ant colonies.

The path bears left over rolling topography and continues to an intersection with the Harrison Trail at an acute angle on the left. Stay straight on the Deer Knoll Trail. Sweet pepperbush and red maple thrive in the damp soil here. Descend gently and bear left on the rocky trail. Both New York and then hay-scented ferns are common just before you reach another T at marker #5. Turn left and cross a seasonal stream. You are now heading in the direction of the parking area. Pass marker #4 on the left where a small trail intersects. This too leads back to the parking area, but by a more circuitous route. A short distance farther, at marker #3, is the junction of the McDougal T. West Trail. Continue straight on the Pent Trail, which is marked with red-and-white blazes.

Rock outcrops come into view on the left. The yellow concrete marker indicates the boundary of watershed land. Reach a marsh overlook on the right which affords only a narrow view. An observation area has been created just off the trail. Aquatic vegetation such as buttonbush, lilies, and bur reed are visible from here. Gaudy black-and-yellow tiger swallowtails sip nectar on the spherical flowers of buttonbush in summer. A rock wall continues along the right side of the roadway and leads you back to the opposite end of the parking area from which you began your walk.

WOODLAND TO CHARCOAL

In the eighteenth and early nineteenth centuries, before the widespread use of coal, iron furnaces were fueled with locally produced charcoal. To make the huge quantities of charcoal required to keep the iron furnaces functioning, vast tracts of woodland were cleared. In addition to fuel to fire the furnaces, charcoal was also an important component used in the production of a wide variety of other products, including filters, drawing ink, gunpowder, medicines, and paint.

Charcoal making was a labor-intensive process carried out by men known as colliers. After cutting up to thirty cords (one cord is eight feet by four feet by four feet) of wood (often American chestnut) to the proper length and seasoning it for a year to eliminate moisture, the collier used the logs to construct a mound in the form of a wigwam. Trees were cleared around the vicinity of the collier's hut in successively larger circles. The mound was then covered with ferns and sod to keep it from igniting completely. Air flow was controlled through vents in the bottom of the mound.

The collier spent about one month tending the slowly burning mound, and lived in a hut of his construction nearby. Rock fireplaces are the only remainders today of such huts at Devil's Den. You can still find the rock-pile remains of a fireplace and bits of charcoal at the charcoal site along Laurel Trail. This is just one of forty such sites identified on the Devil's Den property.

Charcoal production, along with land clearing for agriculture, created a landscape that would be virtually unrecognizable to anyone living today. Whereas Connecticut today is fully 70 percent wooded, during the middle of the 19th century, 70 percent of the state was devoid of trees!

Getting There

From the Merritt Parkway (Route 15), take Exit 42 and travel north on Route 57 for 5.0 miles. Turn right (east) onto Godfrey Road and drive for 0.5 mile to Pent Road on the left. Turn left onto Pent Road and follow it for 0.35 mile to its terminus at the preserve's parking area.

—R.L.

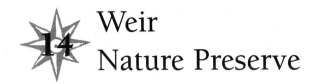

Weir
Nature Preserve

Wilton

- Yellow, White, and Blue Trails
- 1.1-mile loop
- 1.0 hour
- 50-foot elevation gain
- easy

This small Nature Conservancy property of 110 acres in southwestern Connecticut is one of my favorite places for exploring nature and enjoying the outdoors. My first visit, which happened to coincide with remarkably beautiful autumnal weather during the height of the foliage season, turned out to be a truly delightful ramble through unexpectedly lovely woodlands and old pastures. This is a place where you'll want to linger.

Perhaps it was the day—crisp, a bright blue sky and intense sunlight illuminating the colorful leaves—that caused me to feel a real sense of peace and serenity here one does not often find. Given that the preserve is located adjacent to one of the most densely settled regions of the state, this feeling of contentment as I walked the well-marked trails was even more of a surprise. There is also a palpable sense of human history as well, perhaps as a result of the Weir Farm site next door.

The bucolic Weir Farm National Historic Site, the former home of J. Alden Weir, a notable American impressionistic painter, borders the Weir Preserve on the northeast. Enjoying this lovely National Park Service property was an added bonus for me. The historic site is open from 8:30 A.M.–5:00 P.M., Wednesday through Sunday. Weir Preserve is not far from Devil's Den Preserve in Weston, another property owned and managed by The Nature Conservancy. Dogs and bicycles are not allowed in Weir Preserve.

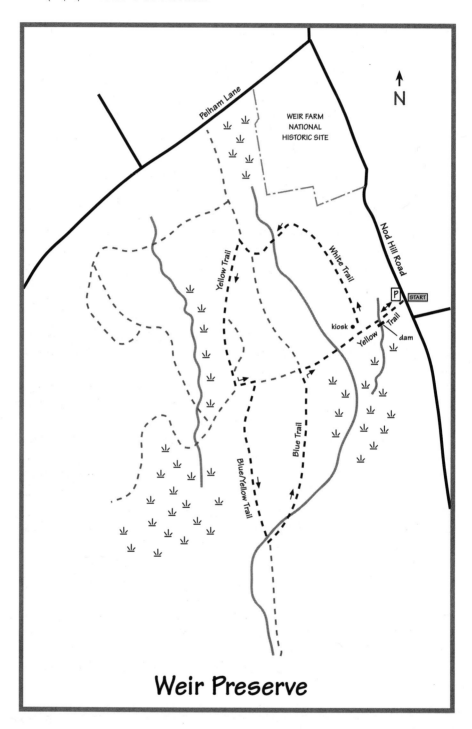

Weir Preserve

Look Forward To

- picturesque laurel thickets

- sturdy stone walls

- granite boulders and ledge outcrops

- pleasing meadows

The Trail

Enter the preserve on a wide former woods road bordered on both sides by stone walls. The predominant tree is sugar maple; there are also white ash, black birch, and Christmas fern, which remain green year-round. Descend gradually to an intermittent stream where spicebush shrubs are abundant. Well-named shagbark hickory, contrasting smooth-barked ironwood, and witch hazel, which bucks the tide by blooming in fall, are here as well. Winterberry, the holly that loses its leaves in autumn, produces bright red berry clusters eaten by birds. To your left lies a seasonal wetland created by a thirty-five-foot-long field-stone dam across an intermittent brook. Moisture-loving sensitive and royal ferns thrive here. The old roadway, blazed yellow, follows the length of the dam.

Walk up easily as you reach granite outcrops on both sides. Evergreen wood fern grows on the rocks. Red and white oaks appear just before you reach a trail intersection on the right. A kiosk complete with large trail map is located just beyond an opening in a stone wall. Turn right onto the white-blazed trail, toward the kiosk. American chestnut grow to sapling height here before the chestnut blight kills them. Black birch, from whose sap oil of wintergreen was once distilled, are common in these woods. A few American beech, red maple, big-tooth aspen, and red cedar (juniper) are also present. The cedar average four inches in diameter but took root here when this still was pastureland.

Pass through a gap in a stone wall constructed of gneiss rocks. The gap is outfitted with a barway made of cedar posts and cleverly embedded horseshoes used to hold the cedar rails. This substantial wall stands chest high and is four feet wide at ground level. On the other side is a small meadow of little bluestem grass, with a few small red cedar where crickets chirp. Blue and white asters add splashes of color in fall. Gray squirrels bound along the stone walls carrying hickory nuts and acorns to their winter larders. During the warm days of summer they live in leaf nests high in the hickory. On the right stand gray granite outcrops, just before you pass through another stone-wall gap with posts into another small field. On the right stands a stalwart oak which has overgrown a vertical slab of granite in intriguing fashion. In profile, the tree seems to be eating the rock.

Come to a Y fork almost immediately and turn left on a narrow path which soon enters woodland to continue on the Weir Preserve trail system (proceeding straight will lead you to the Weir Farm National Historic Site, which is worth a visit). The trail continues to be white blazed. Pass through another stone wall fitted with cedar posts and horseshoe bar holders to enter a red oak and black birch forest with an understory of striped maple, a small northern hardwood forest tree with green-and-white bark, and sassafras. Walk into a dip and cross a brook that flows seasonally through a culvert made of field stones. Strikingly plumaged and vocal red-bellied woodpeckers are common inhabitants of these oak woods, their striped black-and-white backs being unique in eastern woodlands.

Sweet pepperbush, witch hazel, and striped maple thrive in the moist soil below red maple. Curve left and climb slightly. The first mountain laurel shrubs become evident, and rock walls stand ahead and on the left. Pass through the wall and turn right, ignoring the path going left. Thickets of laurel now appear along the yellow-and-white-blazed trail. A yellow-blazed trail which is somewhat difficult to see turns off to the left almost immediately. Follow it through dense mountain laurel which tower nine feet tall. Leaves from the trees above—white, red, and chestnut oaks and red maple—display their brilliant foliage in fall; the red maple when backlit are flaming scarlet.

Walk at a gentle grade downhill on the yellow-blazed path and bear left at a rounded pink granite outcrop on the right. Some of the chestnut oak trees are fairly large; their leaves are quite broad, with wavy margins. Turn left again and walk through a heavy laurel growth and under a canopy of oak and red maple. Continue gradually downslope, then more steeply through laurel and by granite bedrock outcrops and boulders. Where the trail levels out, reach a large, handsome American beech with a two-foot-diameter trunk (diameters are always measured at breast height); its smooth, light-gray bark is characteristic. In fall the bright-yellow sunlit leaves of sassafras are a nice contrast to the gray beech trunk that serves as a backdrop.

Continue straight, past the beech, then bear left at the T intersection where another fine beech specimen awaits you. Neither, thankfully, has been defaced by vandals or disease as yet. I was fortunate to find a spotted salamander under a heavily rotted log here. After capturing its image on film I returned it to its hideaway. Spotted salamanders, identified by their bright-yellow polka dots, are one of the species that can breed only in woodland vernal pools. Follow the yellow trail left; note that the direction-of-travel arrows, however, are white. The trail is crisscrossed by the surface root network of a stand of beech trees, some of which are quite sizable. The stems of mountain laurel shrubs are gnarled in a picturesque fashion.

To the right is a slighter lower, damper area of sweet pepperbush, winterberry, and red maple. A few tulip trees and the first yellow birch grow here too. Among the largest trees are white and red oaks, while red maple, witch hazel, chestnut, and laurel make up the understory and shrub-sapling layer. The sometimes shrill cries of the ubiquitous blue jays are a common sound in these woods. Blue jays cache food such as acorns for winter use. Nervous, sometimes briefly hovering, ruby-crowned kinglets seek tiny insects, spiders, and eggs as they pass through during their twice yearly migrations. Gray squirrels bark and whine in response to the presence of an intruder while safely surveying the scene from the high limb of a tulip tree.

Yellow birch, a member of the northern hardwood forest community, now becomes common, and black birches increase as you come to a T intersection. The fall foliage spectacle can be very colorful: witch hazel, both birches, tulip tree, and aspen all turn varying shades of yellow; red maple transforms from green into red and orange; and oaks take on a coppery hue. The yellow-blazed trail goes both straight and left; continue straight, slightly up and onto a low, rocky knoll covered with laurel and birches. Moss forms a soft cushion beneath one mountain laurel. Common year-round avian residents in these woods include the tufted titmouse and white-breasted nuthatch. At a point where another path comes in from the left, a small and harmless eastern garter snake, coiled and sunning itself on the path, caught my eye in spite of the fact that it lay completely still. To my delight, it allowed me to approach—fittingly enough on my belly—to within inches for a photograph.

Continue straight ahead along a gradual slope through laurel, oak, birch, maple, and tulip tree woodland. Come to a Y fork, blazed yellow in both directions. Follow the white arrow left and walk easily uphill through more laurel. Pass two beech not spared from disfiguring carved graffiti and reach another Y intersection at two American beech trees. Turn right onto the blue-and-yellow-blazed trail and follow it through the twisted trunks of tall mountain laurel. Continue past a granite boulder split lengthwise and through sweet pepperbush, which blooms white in summer. The trail continues past more boulders and outcrops as laurel remains dense. Walk up and over an outcropping—a granite island in a sea of laurel—which offers a good view of the laurel thicket to the right.

Harmless garter snakes, which hunt a wide variety of small prey, can sometimes be approached quite closely.

Come upon an oddly shaped black birch which, after being bent over, rerooted and formed a photogenic arch—a monument to its flexibility and tenacity. This species' scientific name, *lenta,* in fact refers to its pliable twigs. Chestnut oak, black birch, and maple are the major trees, while witch hazel and beech dominate the understory. Cross a bedrock outcrop, make your way through more laurel, and walk across additional low ledges as the slope drops away to the right. You are now gazing out at about the midway level of the big trees' trunks on the right.

Now proceed gradually down. The trail turns left, but take the short spur of twenty-five feet to the top of the ledge for a view of the woods first. On the left is a wet area with tall cinnamon fern. For a nice view, follow the path to the left over the outcrop where it joins the blue-and-yellow-blazed trail again on the left.

The main trail turns sharply left and continues over rocks and through laurel to a slanted T intersection. Both directions are blazed blue. Continue straight (east) here; the path curves left. Walk through more of Connecticut's state flower, mountain laurel, which blooms in late June and early July. The trail jogs through oak, maple, birch, and sassafras woodland

and traverses another low outcropping along the side of a minor slope. Houses are visible to the right. Walk over more granite as you curve right and descend from the ledge, where large white oak and tulip trees reach up from this damper "lowland." The trail turns left ahead where a short stone wall section greets you. Ferns and shrubs fill the wet area on the right with greenery.

The path now climbs again to the summit of a modest ledge. On the right is a four-trunked red oak. From here during my mid-October visit I gazed up to witness a migrating sharp-shinned hawk and its larger relative, Cooper's hawk, spiraling overhead. A bit farther along at the base of a ledge stands a huge double-trunked red oak on the right. Here the slope drops down to a red maple swamp 100 yards away to the right. More walking over low outcrops, then turn right. A stone wall is visible on the left. Fast against the trail on the left is a boulder made of granite, one of the hardest rocks on earth. After descending from the outcrop, swing left and pass through the stone wall where black (sweet) birch is very common, then come to a T intersection immediately after a rock wall.

Turn right to follow the yellow-blazed trail back in the direction of the trailhead and your vehicle. A stone wall borders the trail on the right, and spicebush shrubs are beyond that, as well as on the opposing side. Spicebush contains very aromatic oils, and early land surveyors once regarded it as an indicator of fertile agricultural soils. In mid-October I spotted two hermit thrushes here, one of which was swallowing the high-fat-content spicebush berries in preparation for its long flight south. Pass through a stone wall; such structures now border both sides of this old woods road. On the right stands a fine tulip tree. Finally return to the junction of the white and yellow trails; note the now familiar kiosk to your left. Continue straight to reach your vehicle parked along Nod Hill Road.

FROM EDEN TO YOUR GARDEN

Snakes, quite frankly, have gotten a bad rap for millennia. Ever since evil was epitomized in the serpent that tempted Adam and Eve in the Garden of Eden, these scaled creatures have been the object of disdain by most of humanity. The fact that snakes are legless no doubt plays a major role in conjuring up the feeling of revulsion some feel toward them.

Although there are indeed poisonous snakes that pose some danger to people, in this part of the Northeast, poisonous serpents are rare indeed, and even those that are poisonous are highly overrated as far as their danger to humans is concerned. But our fear, or at least our distrust, goes deeper. Perhaps it hearkens all the way back to a primeval time on the African veldt, the cradle of humanity, where a misstep by our early ancestors might certainly have been their last.

Putting the irrational aside, snakes are truly interesting and attractive creatures when seen from a vantage point devoid of prejudice. Fourteen species of snakes are indigenous to Connecticut. Two, the northern red-belly snake and timber rattlesnake, are now found at very few sites. Seven species are irregularly distributed, and the remaining five are commonly found statewide. No doubt the most common of all is our eastern garter snake, named after the fashionable garters that once held up men's socks. Although highly variable of pattern, our garter snakes generally possess three dull-yellow longitudinal stripes, one of which runs down the center of the back. The background color is usually tan with darker blotches.

Garter snakes, which range farther north and have a wider range than any other snake, are born alive and are often found near water. In spring and fall they spend much of their time sunning themselves in order to maintain the correct body temperature. Garter snakes eat earthworms, insects, frogs, salamanders, birds, and small mammals. They have an amazing ability to locate earthworms by the scent trail the worms leave. Sometimes it is the attention-getting alarm cries of captured frogs which leads a person to one of these snakes. The larger females give birth in late summer, about five months after mating. In winter they den together in protected locations such as mammal burrows or rock outcrops, where these snakes appear to be able to withstand some freezing without consequent harm.

Getting There

From the traffic light located in Wilton center at the intersection of Routes 33 and 7, turn onto Route 33. Travel north on Route 33 (Ridgefield Road) for 2.0 miles to Nod Hill Road on the right. Turn right onto Nod Hill Road and follow it for 3.1 miles to the entrance for Weir Preserve on the left. Parking is parallel to a stone wall on the left side of the road, with space for perhaps three vehicles.

—R.L.

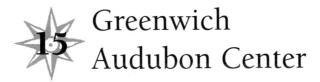

Greenwich
Audubon Center

Greenwich

- Discovery Trail, Clovis Trail, Old Pasture Trail, Riverbottom Road, Hemlock Trail, Maple Swamp Loop, Beech Hill Trail, Dogwood Trail, Lake Trail
- 3.0-mile loop
- 180-foot elevation gain
- 2.5–3.0 hours
- easy

This 500-acre preserve is situated on a rocky spine less than one mile south of the New York border and in a thickly settled suburban part of Connecticut. Owned and managed by the National Audubon Society since 1942, this property, so close to the New York City metropolitan area, is a tremendously valuable oasis for both wildlife and people.

Within its boundaries the center boasts a fair assemblage of wildlife habitat types, including meadows, deciduous woodlands, wetlands and small ponds, the Byram River, rock outcrops and cliffs, and an old millpond called Mead Lake.

The center's trail system is well marked and maintained, and there are educational exhibits about the natural history of the region inside the interpretive center. Bird feeders outside the building's windows entice many of the woodland species out where you may obtain good views of them.

The center charges an admission fee for nonmembers. The grounds and the interpretive building close at 5:00 P.M. Dogs, bicycles, and picnicking are not permitted.

Look Forward To

- massive hardwood trees—especially tulip trees
- numerous rock outcrops

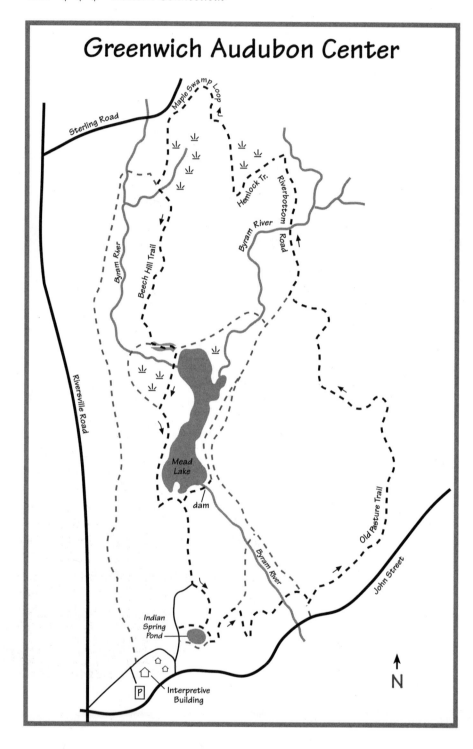

The Trail

After paying your admission fee at the interpretive building, follow the asphalt path downhill to the trailhead on the left. Some fine birding can be had right in this area. Turn right onto the Discovery Trail, then walk left and cross a small wooden bridge along spring-fed Indian Spring Pond. In summer the small pond, which bullfrogs and the smaller green frogs call home, is covered with a layer of tiny floating plants known as duckweed. Follow the sign to the Discovery Trail to the left. Take the second trail junction for Discovery–Byram River–Mead Lake–Old Pasture Trails. This leads you past a small masonry structure which protects the spring flowing out from under it.

Pass two huge tulip trees on the right, one of which is more than four feet in diameter. Tulip tree (also known as tulip poplar or yellow poplar) is the tallest species of the eastern deciduous forest, sometimes reaching heights of more than 100 feet. It is also one of the most massive in terms of girth. Native Americans constructed dugout canoes from these hulks. Stand next to this pair of forest giants and gaze up into their crowns to appreciate their size. Their beautiful yellow-green, tuliplike flowers belie the fact that these trees are related to the magnolias, not the poplars. The large flowers appear in late spring. One sapling tulip tree on the property had a leaf that measured fourteen inches across. Sapling trees in general grow outsized leaves which help them manufacture sufficient food—so important in their competition to get established among their parent trees. These woods are characterized mostly by American beech, sugar maple, black birch, and red oak, however. Some of these species are very large also.

A small stream flows by on the right from the spring on its way to the Byram River, while schist rock outcrops and boulders are already making an appearance. Pass through an old rock wall, a reminder that this was once a pasture long ago. The outcrops are covered with emerald-green mosses, and a large beech tree grows atop one. To the left of the path a sizable hop hornbeam (usually a small tree) stands with the aid of a buttress root reminiscent of tropical forest giants. A semicircle amphitheater is created by rock ledge on the left.

Come to a trail junction and follow the Clovis–Old Pasture Trails to the right. Schist rocks in the path sparkle with gleaming crystals of the mineral mica. Christmas and spinulose wood ferns, the lacy one, are indicators of rich soil. A rock wall borders the path on the left, while a hillside drops away beyond it. Some of the taller trees here are honey locusts, which are members of the nitrogen-fixing legume family. Recognize them by their deeply furrowed bark and compound leaves of many small leaflets.

Sugar maple seedlings form a Lilliputian forest below their parent trees. The trail turns sharply left now onto a downhill switchback, past a mowed grassy area with fruit trees on the right. More large tulip trees appear, one of which is triple trunked. Tufted titmice and black-capped chickadees flit about, sometimes hanging upside down in the canopy, searching for insect tidbits.

The trail swings right and crosses the brook on a section of boardwalk. In the fine silt along the brook look for tracks of raccoon, eastern chipmunk, American crow, and other creatures. Garlic mustard, a plant with pungent foliage, grows here in profusion. Enter a small sunlit clearing colonized by thorny raspberry and rose and hanging grapevines, then reenter shaded forest. Skunk cabbage grows along the brook. Cross a stone wall, descend a small hill, turn left, and then turn right to cross a wooden bridge over a flowing stream. This is the East Branch of the Byram River. False hellebore, which has pleated leaves, sensitive fern, and jewelweed (a.k.a. touch-me-not) grow in the damp soil. The first small eastern hemlock appear, and water striders skate about on the stream's surface tension looking for insect prey. Look closely into the river and you may see crayfish on the rocky bottom and small fish as well. In summer striking black damselflies flutter along the stream. The males possess electric-blue abdomens and jet-black wings.

Regain higher ground and cross a stone wall at a T intersection; this is Riverbottom Road. Turn right onto Old Pasture Trail. Granitic gneiss boulders and outcrops are numerous. Cross a tiny intermittent stream bed on a bog bridge; paved John Street is visible straight ahead. The path turns left to follow near the preserve boundary through young, open maple woods. The veery, a small thrush colored a uniform light cinnamon above with very faint spotting on the breast, breeds in these woods. Its descending flutelike song is one of the most beautiful and enchanting sounds of the forest. Oriental bittersweet vines—some three inches thick—creep up the trees. This nonnative pest "strangles" its host by constricting the flow of nutrients in corkscrew fashion.

The trail swings right and passes an open field on the right where a nest box has been placed to provide a breeding site for bluebirds. Stone walls are everywhere in evidence—at one time Connecticut had 25,000 miles of them! These fences served an important function in colonial times in keeping cattle, sheep, and other livestock out of crop fields. Native Virginia creeper, or woodbine, spreads its branches on the ground along the woodland edge. Among the large trees here is black birch, which requires bare earth for its seedlings to become established. Its other name—sweet birch—owes its origin to the tree's high oil-of-wintergreen content. Enter a forest of beech and red oak, with bracken fern in sun-dappled glades, and pass a big glacial erratic on the right. Maple-leafed viburnum forms part of the shrub layer. Also present is Japanese barberry, a small prickly shrub; it is a sign of past soil disturbance.

A gray, rocky clifflike outcrop of gneiss stands on the right, below which scampering eastern chipmunks gather fallen acorns from the many white oaks. Bluish green evergreen wood fern stands on the outcrops and New York fern covers the forest floor. To your left lies a vernal pool where frogs and certain species of salamanders go for annual courtship and breeding. In summer the wiggling of tiny black tadpoles is obvious in the shallow water. Pass more outcrops on the right, one of which bears an uncanny resemblance to the arched back of a whale. Walk through another stone wall and curve left. Large black birch are common here, as well as tulip tree, red and white oaks, white ash, shagbark hickory, and—in the understory—American beech. Blue jay, eastern wood pewee, scarlet tanager, and northern cardinal are common breeding birds in this rocky woodland.

Walk by large multitrunked red oak on the right. Associated with the oak are tight-skinned and furrowed pignut hickory trees bearing five leaflets per leaf, while seedling sassafras trees have sprouted on the forest floor. The path bears left and passes through a stone-wall "boundary" into an open area with one nest box. Sassafras seedlings, sporting a reddish hue, are colonizing this field. Now pass under the limb of a flowering dogwood, which has exquisite four-petaled white blossoms in May. Yellow cinquefoil and blue-eyed grass bloom in early summer along the path. Walk through woodland briefly and then enter a second small field, also outfitted with a nest box. A dwindling few red cedars are reminders that this was all pasture at one time. Bracken fern grows profusely in the sandy soil. Watch for butterflies such as the little wood satyr in the opening.

Reenter woods briefly, passing through an old rock wall, and then glimpse a new field on the left as you approach a Y trail junction. Stay left and follow the Old Pasture Trail to Riverbottom Road through a small field dotted yellow with the spikes of goldenrod in late summer. Bittersweet shows signs of invading this field, which also contains yarrow and black-eyed Susan, a well-known and attractive wildflower native to our midwestern states. Reenter red maple, beech, and oaks woods and walk slightly downhill. Highbush blueberry, black birch, tulip tree, and maple-leafed viburnum are also present. Spicebush is very common; its name originates from the tangy citrus odor of its sap. The red fruits provide migrant thrushes and other birds with fat-rich fuel in late summer.

Pass through a small stone wall, swing left, and continue downhill. In late June the yellow-orange petals of tulip tree flowers litter the path. On the right is another huge specimen of the species, characteristically very straight with crosshatched bark much like that of an ash. Come to a T intersection. Turn right onto Riverbottom Road in the direction of Hemlock Trail and walk through an open woodland of red maple, beech, red and white oaks, and tulip tree. The trees display tall, straight trunks. On the forest floor Christmas and New York ferns add splashes of green. Christmas fern is so named because each leaflet is shaped like a tiny Christmas stocking. Unlike New York fern, it is also evergreen. Pass through another stone wall and swing left, coming close to a very smooth, light-gray beech on the right.

Reach a wooden bridge and cross the East Branch of the Byram River on a bridge which utilizes recycled plastic decking. Skunk cabbage plants poke up out of the flood plain. These fascinating plants actually generate their own internal heat, allowing them to melt through the snow cover of late winter. The impressive trunks of tulip trees stand like massive pillars in the woods. A rock outcrop emerges on the left as the stream parallels the path on the opposing side. Follow the trail gradually uphill and at the top reach a dead end. From here the Hemlock Trail turns left and follows along the side of a hill through an attractive woodland of oak and beech. Many of the beech are less than three inches in diameter and probably represent sprout growth from the roots of the larger trees.

Hemlock trees reappear as the trail bears right and then leads downhill into a bowl. An imposing ledge outcrop rises steeply on the left to a height of forty feet. A little farther pass a wetland with skunk cabbage on the right. Raucous great crested flycatchers nest in the canopy, while ovenbirds build their domed-over nests on the ground. Listen for the ovenbird's ringing *teacher-teacher-teacher* refrain in spring and summer. Walk past a huge beech tree on the right; it has a major branch broken off down low. Pass through yet another stone wall. While this was once pasture, it now contains many specimen-size beeches. Beechnuts are eagerly consumed by many birds and mammals.

Bear left and come to a T intersection; turn right (north) onto the Maple Swamp Loop. Then swing left, and left again; just below you to the right is gravel Sterling Road. Wood thrushes, which have bright rust-colored heads and are boldly spotted with brown on bright white underparts, summer in these oak and beech woods and winter in the Tropics. After passing through another stone wall you are walking now on the spine of a low ridge, with the land falling away on both sides. After a couple of curves a big rock outcrop appears on your left. Turn right and come to an intersection with Dogwood Lane Trail on the right and Beech Hill Trail on the left. Go left and follow Beech Hill Trail south.

Although spring peepers are not often seen, we were lucky enough to find one of these tiny tree frogs, with an X-like mark on its back, crawling up the wet, slanted surface of a nearby ledge after a shower. The friction discs at the tips of its toes enabled it to climb adeptly. In spring when the males of this, our smallest frog species, congregate in breeding choruses, their high-pitched calls resound like ringing sleigh bells. Beech Trail leads to a junction with Dogwood Lane, at which point you turn left to follow Dogwood Lane, a short distance to its intersection with Lake Trail. Turn left at Lake Trail as well. Soon reach a boardwalk which leads across a wooded swamp near the edge of Mead Lake on your left.

The lake surface is largely covered with the floating leaves of fragrant waterlilies. Also known as sweet-scented waterlily, the three- to five-inch-wide showy flowers, which bloom in summer, are usually white but sometimes pinkish. Clumps of tussock sedges and alder shrubs also thrive in the shallows. Reach a T intersection and turn left to continue on Lake Trail in the direction of the parking area. Partially obscured views of Mead Lake on the left are possible from this trail. There is an isolated patch of low, creep-

Eastern cottontail rabbits emerge from sheltering shrubbery near Indian Spring to nibble on clover.

ing partridgeberry in the woods here; the flowers are tiny, twin white trumpets which bloom in late spring and early summer. The small, rounded leaves are paired and evergreen.

At the southern end of Mead Lake the path turns sharply left and meets the Discovery Trail. Before turning right onto the Discovery Trail to follow it back toward the interpretive building, you may want to turn right and walk out to the concrete top of the stone dam that created the millpond known as Mead Lake. This dam is more than 100 years old and has sprouted several leaks over the years which are in urgent need of repair. After inspecting the dam, return to the trail intersection and turn left. Walk uphill and then down again. When the trail forks you can go either way, as they both lead back in the direction of Indian Spring Pond. Watch for eastern cottontail rabbits emerging from sheltering shrubbery to nibble clover in the lawn near the pond. Along the way listen for the sweet liquid warble of a rose-breasted grosbeak. This black, white, and red bird is one of the most colorful of our summer residents. The left fork will lead to another T junction at the pond, from which you should turn right and then left at the next intersection to retrace your steps back to the interpretive building and your vehicle.

TULIPS IN THE SKY

As you walk the trails of the Greenwich Audubon Center, you can't help but be impressed by the sheer size and massive columnar form of the magnificent tulip trees, which are quite abundant in these woodlands. At the same time you may feel small and insignificant in their presence.

Tulip trees are fast-growing giants that reach their greatest dimensions in the cove forests of southern Appalachia. They are very shade intolerant but grow so quickly as to outstrip the growth of their competitors. They mature in 200 to 250 years. For sheer size alone, yellow poplars, as they are sometimes known, have virtually no rivals in our eastern forests. In the moist, rich, deep soils of the Appalachian forests, they sometimes attain heights of 150 feet and more. Some noteworthy specimens of *Liriodendron tulipifera* have grown to be 8 or 10 feet in diameter, no wonder, then, that the state of Tennessee selected this species as its state tree.

The flowers, which are pollinated by bees, are cup shaped, two inches across, and gorgeous, the petals being creamy greenish white with orange bases. In southern Connecticut they bloom in late May and early June. The trees produce many winged seeds, but most of these are infertile.

Large crops of fertile seeds are produced at irregular intervals. Even the large leaves of these relatives of the magnolia are tulip shaped.

The wood of these important timber trees is quite soft and easily worked to fabricate a variety of products. It is used to make plywood, crates, boxes, and other mundane items which are seemingly out of whack with its noble proportions. It is also used to make high-grade paper. Native Americans, and after them white settlers, used the long, straight trunks of tulip trees to fashion dugout canoes. Apparently it was such a canoe—fully sixty feet in length—that transported Daniel Boone and his family and all their belongings westward to start a new life in the wilderness in 1799.

Getting There

From the Merritt Parkway (Route 15) exit at interchange 28 and travel north on Round Hill Road for approximately 1.5 miles to John Street on the left. Turn left onto John Street and drive approximately 1.5 miles to its intersection with Riversville Road. Turn right and immediately right again into the drive that leads to the parking lot of the Greenwich Audubon Center.

—R.L.

Central Connecticut

 **16** People's Forest

Barkhamsted

- Jessie Girard Trail, South Girard Trail, Charles Pack Trail, Agnes Bowen Trail
- 4.5 miles
- 650-foot elevation gain
- 3.5–4.5 hours
- difficult

History is all around us all the time—the natural history of plants and animals, and the human history of nearly forgotten times. This walk through People's Forest combines both into a montage of mountain views, meadows, gravestones, wildflowers, abandoned settlements, bird song, and boulders. It is not an easy walk, with some challenging climbs and long strolls, but it is wonderfully rewarding. Remember the bug spray during the summer.

This walk follows many trails through portions of People's Forest in Barkhamsted. The trails are blazed in a variety of colors and styles, with signs at some intersections. Be careful when the footpaths intersect paved roadways, as the trails are less well marked there.

Look Forward To

- manitou stones
- incredible mountain views
- glacial boulders
- beaver meadow

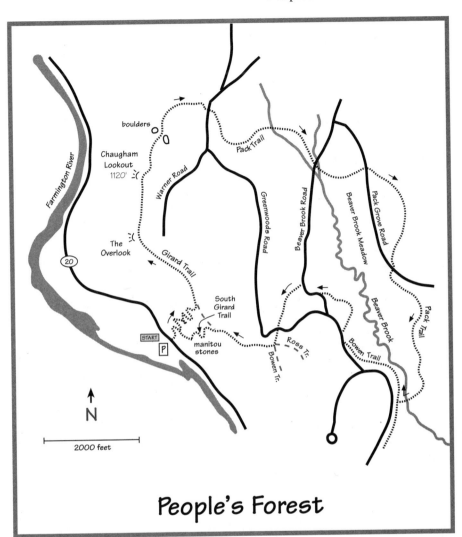

boulders

Chaugham
Lookout
1120'

Farmington River

Warner Road

Pack Trail

The
Overlook

(20)

Girard Trail

South
Girard
Trail

manitou
stones

START

P

Greenwoods Road

Beaver Brook Road

Beaver Brook Meadow

Pack Grove Road

Pack Trail

Beaver Brook

Ross Tr.

Bowen Trail

Bowen Tr.

N

2000 feet

People's Forest

The Trail

The Jessie Girard Trail begins at the sign across the road from the parking area. From the edge of the woods where clumps of daylilies blossom in July, the trail enters a forest of white pine, hemlock, and maple. A few yards from the road the trail forks left (north) and right (east). Turn left and begin a very steep climb up a bouldered ridge. This section of trail looks more like parts of the White Mountains of New Hampshire than it does Connecticut, which means it is beautiful but tough. As you hike through jumbles of boulders and groves of oak, maple, and ash, look for some of the wildflowers that grow in the sheltered crevices. False Solomon's seal is here, as are trillium, which displays its burgundy blooms in spring.

After a short but difficult climb, the path comes to a junction. Bear left (north) through patches of laurel, chestnut oak, and maple. The glossy green leaves of wintergreen appear here and there along the trail, as does Indian cucumber. The grade is much more level here, and becomes even more so at the crest of the ridge. An unmarked trail leaves left to an unnamed ledge with a limited view, while the main trail continues straight ahead. Continue through a hardwood forest of oak and hickory, accented with outcrops of ragged bedrock. Warner Road, a blue-blazed path, enters from the right. After a short, steep climb the path comes to a large, rounded ledge, called the lookout, with spectacular views down the Farmington River valley. The lookout is nestled among red and chestnut oak, red maple, white pine, and shrubby bear oak. Turkey vultures and hawks glide up and down the valley while the song of thrushes, juncos, and warblers floats through the trees. On warm summer days you can see people cooling off in the waters of the old quarry below and in the river to the south.

From the first lookout the trail enters a beautiful, shady hemlock forest. Canada mayflower, with tiny spikes of lily-of-the-valley-scented flowers in spring, share the forest floor with starflower and the tidy fronds of polypody fern. The cool hemlocks lead to the most spectacular viewpoint on the ridge: Chaugham lookout (see essay). The view opens west down a steep cliff to the Farmington River below. To the north is the village of Riverton, with the Berkshire hills beyond. Hemlock and white pine provide sheltered resting places all year long, and the mountain laurel that clings to the hillside adds a special loveliness when it blooms in late spring.

From the lookout the trail continues through more hemlocks, passing through the narrow cleft between two immense glacial boulders. These truck-sized stones were transported to this spot by the glaciers that covered this area some 20,000 years ago. From the boulders it is a pleasant walk, through tall white pine above yellow birch and beech, to the terminus of the Girard Trail at Greenwoods Road. Turn right (south) onto the road and walk a few yards to Big Spring picnic area on the right. Here you can get a refreshing, very cold drink of water using the old red-handled water pump. Just south of the picnic area turn left (east) onto the Charles Pack Trail, a path that takes you into the heart of People's Forest.

This area of lowland forest is wet in spring and gets a little buggy at times in the warmer months. Familiar Indian cucumber and mountain laurel are joined by hobblebush, an open, thinly branched shrub with flat panicles of showy white flowers in spring. Partridgeberry, a creeping ground cover with lots of small, glossy green leaves, also grows here, as does blue-bead lily, with small, yellow springtime flowers and bright blue fruits in late summer.

After crossing a brook on a log bridge the trail comes to Beaver Brook Road. Turn left and cross the bridge over Beaver Brook. Immediately after the brook turn right into the Beaver Brook Recreation Area (sign). The path continues south, crossing the brook on steppingstones beneath a stand of hemlock before climbing to a junction with Pack Grove Road. Cross the road and continue climbing, skirting a ledgy outcrop where the sharp calls of yellow-bellied sapsuckers can be heard in summer. The trail passes a huge, 150-year-old beech tree before heading downhill through a forest of beech, maple, and hemlock to meet Pack Grove Road once again.

Cross the road and continue downhill through hemlock and pine, passing a large boulder where trillium flowers in spring. Soon the remains of an old farmhouse appear on the left, its foundation composed of huge blocks of quarried stone. Tall ash trees loom overhead and shade trillium, doll's-eyes, false Solomon's seal, and meadow rue. Near what once was the dooryard, daylilies still grow, a living legacy of flower gardens long abandoned.

From the foundation the trail passes through a wet area and crosses Beaver Brook just before reaching the Agnes Bowen Trail (sign). Turn right (north) onto the Agnes Bowen Trail, which wanders along the edge of Beaver Swamp. A short unmarked path leads to a small open area near the beaver dam, where the wildlife of the swamp can be observed.

Mountain laurel in bud near Chaugham lookout.

Life in the swamp is much different than in the nearby forest, encouraging a host of different plants and animals. Elderberry mingles with swamp azalea, which bears small white, very fragrant blossoms in late spring. Summersweet forms thickets along the shore and bears spikes of small white flowers in summer. There is giant reed, a grasslike plant with mahogany-colored floral plumes in summer; yellow flag, a water iris with golden blossoms; arrowleaf and bullhead waterlilies. Many species of ducks negotiate the waterway, and scores of songbirds, from red-winged blackbirds to wrens and warblers, either visit or live here. The booming croak of bullfrogs adds a peaceful tone to late summer afternoons, and common water snakes and painted turtles sun themselves on rocks and driftwood all summer long. This is as spectacular a place as Chaugham lookout, but in a completely different way. Each time you come here, it is possible to see something new—a delightful prospect indeed.

Return to the trail, which follows the shoreline past clusters of blue-bead lily and goldthread, to Greenwoods Road. Turn right onto the road and follow it about 100 yards to where the trail turns right into the woods. After a short walk the path intersects Beaver Brook Road. Turn right and follow the road about 200 yards. The path then turns left, leaving the road and immediately climbing a short wooded stretch to intersect Greenwoods Road again. Turn right and follow the road about 50 feet. The trail turns left, reenters the woods, and quickly comes to the junction with the Ross Trail. Follow the blue-blazed Ross Trail as it climbs past boulders and rocky outcrops. The path skirts a stony buttress to the right with impressive cliffs, and then descends along the hillside to the terminus of the Ross Trail and the junction of the Girard Trail and South Girard Trail. Be cautious here, as the junction is easily overlooked. The Girard Trail continues right, while the South Girard Trail, blazed yellow, leaves left downslope. Follow the South Girard Trail down a steep, rough hillside. The path uses many switchbacks to ease the descent, but it is still tough on the knees. When the trail levels out it passes through an ancient graveyard whose interment sites are marked with manitou stones instead of tombstones. This area is called Barkhamsted Light, a fascinating, though little known, historic site (see essay).

From the graveyard it is a short walk along the trail to the parking area.

MANITOU STONES

For thousands of years the Farmington River has flowed through the mountainous gap between American Legion Forest to the west and People's Forest to the east. In the 1700s a narrow road was constructed along the bank of the river. Called the Farmington River turnpike, it ultimately connected Hartford and Albany. Along the route were small, widely scattered English villages and a few Indian settlements.

After a dispute with her father, a woman from Wethersfield named Molly Barber ventured along the road to the Indian settlement in the People's Forest gap. There she married Chaugham, a Native American, and the two lived in a cabin near the roadside.

The story goes that stagecoach drivers used the cabin as a landmark along their journey, and over time the soft glow of lamplight from the windows gave the cabin, and hence the rest of the village, the name Barkhamsted Light. Today the Farmington River turnpike is gone, replaced by the winding highway called Route 20. Stagecoaches have disappeared, as has the settlement called Barkhamsted Light. What hasn't vanished with the passing of time, however, is the settlement's small graveyard on the hillside.

If you visit the cemetery you will notice that each grave has a headstone and a smaller footstone. The stones are uninscribed, and each headstone has been notched at the corners so the marker resembles a rough image of a person's head and shoulders. These unique markers are called manitou stones and were used by some Native Americans to mark the graves of their dead in the decades before the Revolution.

According to tradition, *manitou* is loosely defined as the spirit, or force, that governs the natural world. Manitou stones were symbols of this power and also served as a conduit to it. The Indians used manitou stones in a number of different spiritual ceremonies. Some Christian Indians took the European tradition of placing headstones at the graves of their dead, and blended it with their tradition of the manitou stone. The result was a rough, effigy-style headstone that served the purpose of a European gravestone as well as a Native American manitou stone.

The tradition did not last very long, however, and in the years after Independence manitou stones disappeared from use. Today they may still be found in a few very old cemeteries, and on the hillside near the Farmington River at the place still known as Barkhamsted Light.

Getting There

From junction of Routes 44 and 318, turn onto Route 318. Cross the Farmington River and turn left onto East River Road. Continue on East River Road 2.5 miles to a parking area on the left (west) side of the road. Across the road from the parking area is a sign for the Jessie Girard Trail.

—C.S.

Indian Council Caves

Barkhamsted

- Tunxis Trail
- 3.8 miles
- 450-foot elevation gain
- 2.0–3.0 hours
- moderate

There is magic in a cave. Sometimes spooky magic, but magic just the same. This walk travels to the matrix of boulder hideaways called Indian Council Caves. Yet the caves are only one facet of this lovely walk. Along the way are abandoned homesteads and richly scented pine forests, acres of ferns, enchanted forests, and ridge-crest views. Without playing favorites too much, I think this walk takes you along some of the loveliest sections of Connecticut's Blue Trail system. The caves are a wonderful bonus.

The walk to Indian Council Caves is along the Tunxis Trail and passes through a portion of Tunxis State Forest. The trail is marked with light-blue blazes. Turns are designated by two stacked blazes, the topmost blaze offset in the direction of the turn.

Look Forward To

- boulder caves
- old foundations
- ridge-top views
- beautiful forests

The Trail

From the parking lot proceed north across Route 219 and enter woods of tulip tree, red oak, maple, hemlock, and ash with clumps of mountain lau-

116

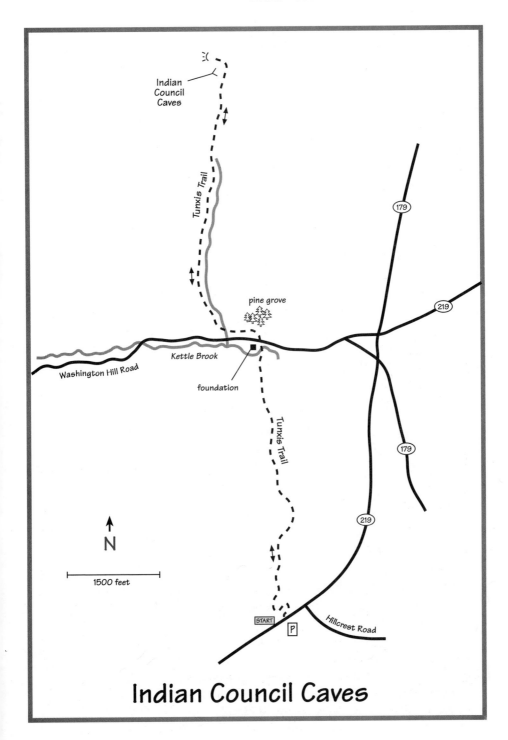

Indian Council Caves

rel, and witch hazel beneath. Tulip tree's common name comes from its interesting tuliplike flowers of green and orange, which appear in the topmost branches of the trees in late spring. The blossoms are so well concealed that most people know them only by the occasional colorful petal that descends from the canopy and lands on the footpath.

Beneath the ceiling of leaves lies an intricate matrix of cinnamon and Christmas fern, Canada mayflower, goldthread, and twisted stalk that have colonized the spaces between the boulders.

From the road the path jogs west a short way, then swings into a small wetland before climbing into a dry woodland. The path crosses an old woods road and enters a thick stand of sapling maple and black birch. While this area may seem attractive, with its overcrowded groves of slender trees, these saplings provide evidence that the area was logged in the recent past. From this disturbed woodland the trail crosses a stone wall and passes near a large white oak whose boughs reach out toward the trail. It then enters a climax forest of hickory, beech, oak, and maple with scattered thickets of mountain laurel and witch hazel.

The path continues north, climbing easily through picturesque woodlands where pileated woodpeckers live and wood thrushes sing in the summer. Chipmunks are here, their sharp squeaks designed to remind you that you are only visiting the places where they live.

As the trail gains elevation the soil begins to become more rocky, passing over ledges of metamorphic rock called gneiss. Chestnut oak begins to appear and red-tailed hawks are frequent passersby. Many hawks, most notably the broad-wing, migrate over these hills each autumn. The red-tails, however, are true Yankees, staying throughout the year. These large hawks are easily identified by their rusty red tails. They are often seen sitting atop a tall dead snag in winter, or soaring high overhead in ever widening circles in summer.

The path then crests a ridge and enters a beautiful woodland of rock ledges, wind-stunted oaks, blueberries, laurel, and pink lady-slipper. Coyote love to come here, especially in the evening hours, to prowl the game trails in search of dinner. These woods are some of the nicest you will find anywhere in the state. Walk slowly and listen for the laughter of ravens as they glide overhead.

Passing over the top of a rocky, moss-covered outcrop, the path descends around the ledge by way of a hairpin turn. The treadway swings right (east) near a small wet area and proceeds along the base of the rock. Soon the path again turns north (left), swings northeast briefly, then continues north through thick stands of laurel.

A short distance farther on, the path turns southeast, descending along the edge of a wooded ledge before swinging east where abundant ferns, starflower, and goldthread line the footway.

The trail levels out and merges with an abandoned woods road now covered with mountain laurel and ferns. The walk through here is relaxing and pleasant, the hemlock, oak, and birch offering welcome shade on hot summer days.

The path then crosses a small brook near a large boulder and enters an area of white pine, spruce, and hemlock. Near a clearing the trail crosses Washington Hill Road. Just to the left, near a large sugar maple, are the remains of an old homestead. The house is long gone, but many of the plants once cultivated in the garden remain. The glossy green leaves of vinca grow near the remains of the old foundation, and patches of ribbon grass grow in the sandy soil. You can recognize ribbon grass by the long white stripes that streak the leaves. Native goldenrods and milkweed grow here too. The yellow plumes of goldenrod attract bees in late summer, and the fragrant floral clusters of milkweed are a favorite of butterflies.

The trail crosses the road and enters a beautiful plantation of pine. The evergreen canopy far overhead provides welcome shade in the summer, and on warm days this area is filled with a sweet, piney perfume. The path descends through the pines and again intersects with Washington Hill Road just above a brook. Turn right (north) and walk along the road about 100 feet to a junction. Here one fork leaves left (west) while another continues straight ahead (north). Continue straight ahead (north). A few feet past the junction follow the footpath left (northwest) as it leaves the road.

The trail now makes an easy climb through increasingly attractive woods. Ground cedar, princess pine, and many types of ferns cover the ground beneath tall pines, cherry, and maple. To the right is a marsh where cattails, sedges, and the sculpted skeletons of dead trees can be found. Hawks frequently soar over the swamp, sometimes skimming just over the tops of cattails and other times making wide circles high overhead.

Just past the marsh the trail passes through a sea of ferns where deer often browse and songbirds sing from the trees. Soon the path merges with an old woods road at an exposed patch of bedrock. Continue north along the road, which soon narrows and fades back into a footpath as it passes through a grove of hemlock and laurel. After traversing a wet area, the trail makes a moderate climb to a rocky spot where the delicate blossoms of pale corydalis can be seen in summer.

After descending to, and crossing a small brook, the path scrambles up a rocky cobble near a grove of dead red pine trees. Black and white war-

One of the Indian Council Caves.

blers flit among the thick tangles of laurel as the path crosses a fire road that runs east to west. Continue north through a seemingly endless thicket of laurel in a woodland of red and chestnut oak.

At the top of a rise the path levels out and swings right, over a series of rocky hummocks. After a pleasant walk the trail turns east over metamorphic rock ledges studded with small crystals of ruby-red garnet. A limited view opens from the ledge, while below, hidden by the forest, lie the bouldered shelters called Indian Council Caves.

Blueberry grows in the shallow soil, and a small, gray-barked tree called shadblow, or serviceberry, blossoms here in spring beneath the oaks.

From the ledges the trail swings south and makes a steep descent past enormous cliffs and boulders to the caves. The area is a jumble of house-sized stones resting against the steep cliff face. Centuries ago Native Americans came to this place at the base of the cliff to hold councils. These events were not casual things held just anywhere, but important, ceremonial gatherings convened at places with spiritual power. There are many stony hideaaways among the rocks. Some are large enough to explore, while others have become home to porcupines, raccoons, mice, and bats. Take some time and let curiosity guide your steps. There is much magic here if you are observant, and fortunate, enough to find it.

To return to the parking area, retrace your steps.

CAVES AND TREES

Caves have stimulated the imaginations of people since ancient times. In Roman mythology caves were the homes of nymphs. In Greece the mystic oracles at Delphi were delivered from a cave, and the temples of Zeus and Dionysus were originally rocky caverns. In Germany the caves of the Harz Mountains are the fabled home of woodland fairies, while somewhere in a cave near Granada, Spain, the great Boabdil sleeps, patiently waiting to be awakened by a wandering mortal so he can restore the Moors to glory.

In New England, Native Americans saw caves as spiritual places: literal entryways into the earth and metaphorical unions between the earth and sky. They were places of power as well as protection.

Interestingly both caves and ancient trees were used as council sites, places where leaders of tribal groups would gather. The trees were usually century-old white oaks, though sometimes other trees, such as American elms, were used.

Trees and caves represented similar things to the Indians. Both provided shelter from the ravages of nature. Both old trees and caves were symbols of timeless antiquity and stability. The roots of trees and shafts of caves penetrated deep into the earth, while the canopies of the trees, and the cliff or mountain that held the cave both extended into the sky. These places, whether cave or tree, formed a physical and spiritual union between the earth and sky, joining the power of both and concentrating it in a single spot.

Indian Council Caves was and is such a place. The power is still there and can be as enriching to the spirit as the beautiful views from the cliffs above them are a treat to the eyes.

Getting There

From the junction of Routes 219 and 318 near the Barkhamsted Reservoir dam, proceed east on Route 219 1.7 miles to a small parking area on the right, about 100 feet west of the intersection of Route 219 and Hillcrest Road.

—C.S.

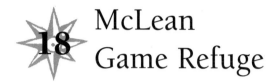

McLean
Game Refuge

Granby

- Barn Door Hills Summit Hike
- 3.5 miles
- 400-foot elevation gain
- 2.0 hours
- easy, with moderate section

At 3,700 acres, the McLean Game Refuge is one of the largest parcels of conservation land, state or privately owned, in Connecticut. Its many miles of well-maintained trails lead through extensive hardwood forests, along fast-flowing streams, past lush wetlands, and to the summit of a hill created by lava flows.

This impressive property, established for passive recreation in 1932, was declared a National Natural Landmark in 1983. The refuge is the lasting legacy of longtime state senator George P. McLean (1857–1932). A quote from the senator that gives insight into his motivation for conserving this land for the enjoyment of the public appears alongside the map of the refuge situated at the parking area off Routes 202/10. He wrote: "A place where some of the things that God made may be seen by those who love them as I loved them and who may find in them the peace of mind and body that I have found."

The property is administered by the Trustees of the McLean Fund located in Simsbury.

Look Forward To

- beautiful summit vista
- verdant spring wildflower display
- diverse bird life
- clear, cold streams

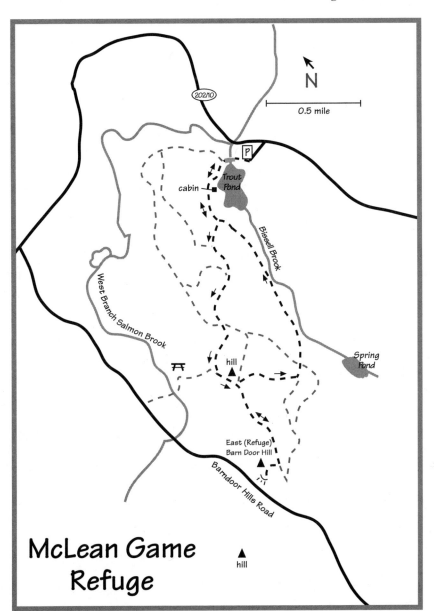

202/10

N

0.5 mile

Trout
Pond

cabin

Bissell Brook

West Branch Salmon Brook

Spring
Pond

hill

East (Refuge)
Barn Door Hill

Barndoor Hills Road

McLean Game
Refuge

hill

The Trail

A short paved road leads from the highway through open wildflower meadows where bluebirds nest to an unpaved parking area adjacent to the trailhead. A map board illustrates the refuge's extensive holdings and trail system, and lists its regulations.

Walk past the wooden gate and enter a cool, shaded hardwood forest of red maple, red and black oaks, eastern hemlock, and black birch. A steep slope rises to your left, where brilliant scarlet tanagers nest high in the canopy, while on your right broad skunk cabbage leaves and fern fronds thrive in the waterlogged soil. Follow the broad roadway as it crosses Bissell Brook on a wide wooden plank bridge. The trail curves left and arrives at a trailhead on the right where a sign gives trail distances and blaze colors. The tall and eye-catching fertile fronds of cinnamon fern grace the brook banks to your left in spring.

Continue straight along the stream on the wide dirt path to the Trout Pond, as well as to the concrete dam that created it, on the left. A fence guards the shoreline, while Canada geese and their goslings approach visitors in hopes of securing an easy meal. Restrain yourself and remember to "keep the wild in wildlife." Watch for painted turtles on logs basking in the sun. The trail climbs a low, sandy rise and passes the senator's log cabin, which overlooks the pond on the left. A pit toilet is located to the right of the path.

The trail now bears left and enters attractive pine, oak, and maple woods with some hemlock. Inconspicuous brown creepers hitch up the tree trunks using their forceps-like beaks deftly to pick insects and spiders from bark crevices. As you walk over this old woods road watch for chunks of rusty-brown basalt, the first sign that lava once flowed and solidified below the surface of this land. At a Y junction, take the right fork.

Pink lady-slipper orchids bloom in June amid the accumulated needles of red and white pine. Another species that thrives in the sandy, acid soil of this pine-oak woodland is lowbush blueberries. The trail ascends gradually and curves left. Here the roadway has been cut over time several feet down into the sandy soil. Young white pine and hemlock line the path, and soft haircap moss forms a cushion atop the sterile soil. One of the loveliest spring wildflowers of these glacial soils is bird's-foot violet. Its delicate purplish violet blossoms and finely divided leaves make it easily recognizable.

Seemingly always active are black-capped chickadees, which hang acrobatically from the ends of limbs in search of insects, spiders, and their eggs while continually whistling their territorial *fee-bee* songs. As you follow the old road to the left and slightly uphill, listen in late spring and early summer for the exquisite woodwind song of the wood thrush, one of the refuge's many birds that spend their winters in the Tropics.

Soon after reaching the junction of the blue-blazed trial (from Stony Hill) on the right, the trail curves left again. The rock outcrops are basalt, obvious by their dark brown, hexagonal fractures. Increasing eastern hem-lock growth results in deepening shade and very little undergrowth in this section. Storms had toppled or snapped many shallow-rooted hemlocks just prior to my late-May visit. Proceed downhill, curving right, and then walk uphill, level off, and curve left. Soon reach a four-way intersection with a basalt slope on your left. This is one of the basaltic promontories known collectively as the Barn Door Hills. Turning right will take you to the picnic grove adjacent to the West Branch of Salmon Brook, where tow-ering, mottle-trunked sycamores line the banks.

Turn diagonally left instead, toward the summit of East (Refuge) Barn Door Hill, where a fine view awaits you. This too is a wide old woods road leading past a twenty-foot-high basalt outcrop on your left. Walk uphill through hemlock, black birch, and red oak woods, curve left, and arrive at a trail junction on the left. In spring, round green oak apple galls about the diameter of a quarter may litter the ground. These growths are caused by a tiny wasp that inserts an egg into the stem of an oak leaf; the plant reacts by producing the growth, thereby creating a protective home for the devel-oping larva. Continue straight uphill on this blue-blazed trail toward the summit. Worm-eating warblers (named for the caterpillars they consume) build their nests in the leaf litter on the dry, oak-covered slopes. Listen for their sweet trills in spring and summer.

Tiny white flower spikes and shiny green heart-shaped leaves of abundant Canada mayflower dot the forest floor in May. The path levels off, climbs again, and soon reaches a narrow, blue-blazed path on the right that leads steeply up the hickory and oak slope past yellow-blooming star grass to the summit of East (Refuge) Barn Door Hill. This path is short, and soon you level off and walk left to arrive on the basaltic summit ledges, 580 feet above sea level. Small-statured hemlock, birch, and oak grow in these scanty soils.

Here you are perched directly above a farmstead where cows graze in pastures separating this lava hill from another of the Barn Door Hills just to the southwest. The view of the other hill's cliff face, talus, and the sur-rounding rolling green countryside is excellent. This is a wonderful spot to bask in the sun and enjoy a snack before returning to the main trail. Follow the path back down the slope to the main trail and turn left, retracing your steps to the trail junction on the right. Turn right and walk on this wide old road, first on level ground, then gradually downhill. Light gaps created in the canopy by wind-thrown and damaged trees have allowed a host of white pine seedlings to thrive here.

The trail curves left and joins with another wide pathway. Turn left and arrive almost immediately at another split in the trail. The blue-blazed trail turns right, but you should bear left, walking slightly downhill. The margins of the path are carpeted with Canada mayflower. These pine woods are also home to the lovely black-throated green warbler, one of some twenty species of small, active, and mostly colorful insectivorous birds that breed regularly in Connecticut woodlands and then undertake incredible annual migrations to and from Mexico and Central America.

Reach a major T intersection and turn left to return to the cabin at Trout Pond, near where you began the hike (turning right takes you to Spring Pond). The wide trail, which parallels Bissell Brook, is quite level as you walk under pine, oak, and birch trees. At this point the stream is screened by vegetation. Oak, hickory, and maple begin to predominate in the woodland as you continue. Here the songs and calls of red-eyed vireos, eastern wood pewees, and gray tree frogs fill the air. The tree frog has adhe-

The deeply-cut leaves of lovely bird's foot violet give the species its common name.

sive discs on its toe tips which enable it to climb and cling to branches high above the forest floor. Its grayish lichen-colored skin makes it all but impossible to find. This one-inch frog is quite vocal, however, and once you learn to distinguish its birdlike trill, you'll find that it is surprisingly numerous.

The showiest trees in the May woods are flowering dogwood. The big, white, four-petaled blossoms of this small understory tree are unmistakable. The old road now parallels the brook more closely. Sizable hemlock line the near brook banks, whereas red maple and skunk cabbage plants grow profusely in its rich flood plain. You may see a tiny blue-gray gnatcatcher as it flits about in the trees along the brook, its long tail acting as a counterbalance.

Soon come to the Y intersection near the Trout Pond. Continue straight through the pine-dominated forest. During the warm months the nasal voices of resident Canada geese will tell you that you've reached the pond, before you ever see it. The island in the pond hosts an abandoned bank beaver lodge, and old signs of the beaver's former presence still can be seen on tree trunks in the vicinity. Continue on the wide roadway back to the parking area. Notice bits of rusted barbed-wire fencing, left over from when this was pastureland, which you may have overlooked when you first entered the shaded forest.

FIRE AND ICE

The landscape so familiar to us today is actually just one snapshot in the vast library of photo albums known as geologic time. But graphic clues to the past lie all around us. The Barn Door Hills came into being some 190 million years ago, when what we now know as Connecticut and indeed North America were very different places. Connecticut had a tropical climate back then, with lush vegetation and dinosaurs constituting the dominant life forms.

As you walk the refuge trails, and especially as you make your way up the slope of the East (Refuge) Barn Door Hill, notice the dark, heavy stone that litters the woodland floor or juts out from it to create abrupt outcroppings. This basaltic traprock, as it is often called by geologists, is an igneous rock born of fire deep within the earth. As the molten material found its way to the surface through fissures and by way of volcanic flows, it solidified. In some cases, the molten rock did not reach the surface and cooled underground instead. As it cooled and shrank, it cracked into the vertical, often six-sided columns so characteristic of the dense, heavy rock we see today.

The molten rock flowed to, or in some cases almost to, the surface through cracks in the earth's crust that formed as a result of the splitting apart of the supercontinent Pangea. One major result of all this was the creation of the Atlantic Ocean.

On the local scene, the half a dozen or so Barn Door Hills which jut up from the valley today are part of a generally north-south trending series of small traprock ridges that originally cooled below the earth's surface. Subsequent erosion of softer overlying rock layers have made these hills and others like them along the western edge of Connecticut's Central Valley visible. The ridges usually, but not always, have a steep slope on one side and a more gradual slope on the opposing side. The steep, unvegetated slopes are prone to weathering through the cleaving actions of freezing and thawing. This creates a jumble of broken basalt at the cliff bases known as *talus* (Greek for "toe") slopes. Thus it is ice which in time reduces the erosion-resistant rock, born of fire, to rubble.

The earth is constantly recycling itself. Eventually the ridges will probably be covered in deep sediments again, no doubt to be overspread by lava flows and glaciers once again in their turn, ad infinitum.

Getting There

From the junction of Routes 202/10, 20, and 189 in Granby, travel south for 1.0 mile on Routes 202/10 to a paved road on the right. There is currently no sign directing visitors to the refuge along the highway. Turn right onto the refuge entry road, past a yellow metal gate (which is locked at 8 P.M.), and follow the road a short distance to its gated terminus at the parking area. A map of the trails and refuge regulations are posted here. Bicycles are not allowed, and dogs must be leashed.

—R.L.

Sessions Woods Wildlife Management Area

Burlington

- Beaver Pond Trail, Tree Identification Trail, several short side trails
- 3.0 miles
- 200-foot elevation gain
- 3.0 hours
- easy, with a few moderate sections

Sessions Woods Wildlife Management Area proved to be an unexpected but very pleasant surprise. This 455-acre property, acquired by the state from the United Methodist Church in 1981, has a great deal to recommend it. The acreage is actively managed as a public demonstration area for wildlife and resource management techniques. There are numerous working examples of these techniques as well as interpretive panels and other means of instruction. The education center also conducts programs for the public, schools, and organized groups.

Foot access to the property is primarily by means of a wide, graveled path known as Beaver Pond Trail. It and the many boardwalks and demonstration sites are wheelchair accessible. Although the managed aspect of the property might discourage those who are seeking a wilder, more natural outdoor experience, part of the loop walk described here includes a half-mile-long, more traditional woodland path known as the Tree Identification Trail.

The view from the lookout tower alone is enough to recommend Sessions Woods. The inclusion of a waterfall, a thirty-eight-acre beaver pond, and acres of delightful woodland combine to make an excursion here truly enjoyable. It is also a very suitable one for children.

The trail network is also available for cross-country skiing. Bow hunting for deer and waterfowl hunting (for disabled persons only) is permitted in season; a daily permit is required. Pit toilets are located at both

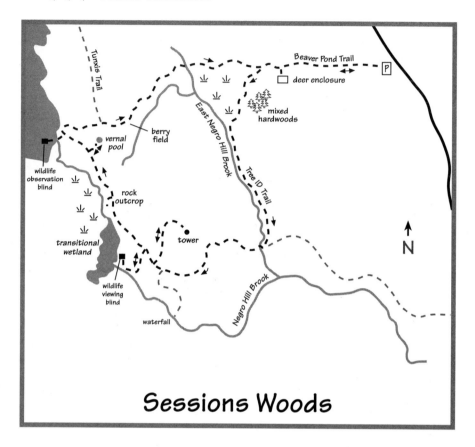

Sessions Woods

points where the Beaver Pond Trail and the Tunxis Trail meet, including the trailhead. The property is open from sunrise to sunset. Dogs must be leashed, and motorized vehicles are not allowed.

Look Forward To

- wildlife viewing
- great vista from tower
- waterfall
- beaver pond and wetlands

The Trail

The trailhead is located immediately north (right) of the parking area. Look for the wide, graveled roadway; a sign marks the beginning. Visitors are asked to register. Follow the roadway by an iron gate, passing inter-

pretive signs about the property's vegetation. Enter a woodland of pre-
dominately red maple, some quite large, as well as young black birch.
Cross a culvert where spicebush shrubs grow in the damp earth. In late
summer the shrubs produce bright red berries which are high in fat—just
the energy source southbound birds are looking for. Spinulose wood fern
clumps dot the forest floor.

Begin walking upslope, and at the crest of the rise note coppice growth
of red maple on the right. Red maple is a prolific stump sprouter, and the
thick new growth here is indicative of recent cutting. Soon reach a logged
area. Note the blue blazes that demarcate the Tunxis Trail. This major footpath follows the Beaver Pond Trail for less than a mile before turning north.
A sign informs visitors that firewood is for sale from this selectively cut
stand. Lowbush blueberry thrives in the sunshine. Schist rocks show the
sparkling presence of mica. Gneiss, a banded rock, is also present. Walk
gradually downhill through a forest of white, red, and black oak and reach
a fenced deer exclosure about 150 feet left of the path. A slanted, solar-pow-
ered electric fence keeps the hoofed mammals out so wildlife biologists can
study the effects of deer browsing on forest regeneration.

Gray birch, a pioneering species, become more numerous. Young
white pine, witch hazel, red maple, lowbush blueberry, and huckleberry
define the woody vegetation below the taller trees. Reach a small clearing on
the right where Japanese barberry has been planted as a wildlife food source.
This shrub actually has become an invasive and harmful species in many
areas now. Diseased red pines were removed here in 1985. Come to the
beginning of the Tree Identification Trail on the left. A leaflet identifying the
trees, which are marked only with numbers, may be available at either end
of the trail. No bicycles are allowed on this natural-surface woodland path.
Follow it downhill through black, gray, and yellow birch woods. Canada
mayflower, princess pine, striped wintergreen, and hay-scented fern add
color to the forest floor. Soft haircap moss borders the path.

Level out amid common white oak. Indian cucumber-root, which
produces blue-black fruits in late summer, is named for its edible tuber.
Some azaleas appear, as do American chestnut sprouts. The latter almost
always die back when they reach a height of twenty to twenty-five feet.
Killed by the blight, they'll resprout again. The slope drops off gradually to
the right as you curve left. Young yellow birch, the most beautiful of our
hardwoods, in my opinion, are now more numerous. Tiny tree frogs known
as spring peepers make their high, piping calls from the trees. Big, coarse
bracken fern, mountain laurel, and huckleberry abound as ground cedar (a
club moss) displays its spore-producing candelabra. Reach a small stream

on the right. In a good mast year, acorns litter the path. They represent a very important wildlife food source.

Pass through a stand of New York fern—the small one—and chest-high cinnamon fern to the right. Hay-scented fern is the lacy species on the left. Here the yellow birch become larger. This tree is one of the main components of the northern hardwood forest and, along with black birch, contains fragrant oil of wintergreen. Large stumps on the slope are evidence of selective cutting quite a few years ago. Come to bog bridges in a wet area leading up to East Negro Hill Brook. Sphagnum moss and New York and cinnamon ferns thrive in the moist soil. I found a dusky salamander under a log here on a late-September visit. This is a common stream salamander which, because it has no lungs, takes in oxygen through its moist skin. Cross the brook on logs.

To your right is a twenty-foot-high rock ledge with a boulder field below. Rock tripe, a lichen that turns green after rains, forms a flaky covering on the granitic gneiss. Mica crystals, some one inch across, make up one of the boulder field's rock components. Continue walking through the little valley of birch and maple, with a slope rising up to the right. One of the yellow birches is two feet in diameter. There is also a stand of young and middle-aged hemlock, mostly on the right side of the stream, indicative of a cooler environment in the ravine. Mosses and lichens thrive on the moist outcrops and boulders. The brook here flows with a soothing trickle. Some white ash trees, fond of damp soils, raise their crosshatched trunks high into the canopy.

The path follows the waterway closely downstream. Where sunlight reaches the ground, patches of hay-scented fern create light-green blotches of color. Yellow as well as black birch are numerous, and woodland aster blooms white in the late-summer woods. The summer quarters of a gray squirrel, a mass of leaves known as a leaf nest, will be forsaken for the warmth of a tree cavity in fall. Cross the brook after it makes a turn to the right. More spicebushes with red berries have established themselves here. Red berries in general are designed to be attractive to birds, since birds have excellent color vision, whereas fruits meant to be dispersed by mammals are generally dark blue and sweet. Mammals cannot see color, but they have a taste for sweets.

Some of the white ash are quite large and one has three trunks. The wood of this tree is strong and durable, and is favored for baseball bats. Pass a large white pine and then through a sunny, fern-lined opening. An interpretive sign explains the virtues of a "3-log digger dam," which created the small pool brook trout utilize. Many water striders skate across the surface film, while five- to-six inch-long fish flee at the approach of a hiker. The trail is now wider and finely graveled again as you reach the junction with the main Beaver Pond Trail. Turn right and walk uphill, then cross the brook shortly. If you look closely you may see three-inch-long brook trout in the pool on the right end of the culvert. The culvert has been buried into the soil to enable a natural stream bed to form within it.

Continue up the roadway, which bears right under birch and oak, from which tufted titmice noisily scold. Mountain laurel, Connecticut's state flower, graces the steep slope to your left. To the right below you is a seep area that remains nearly snow-free in winter, and a larger relative of the laurel—great rhododendron—can be seen. Although much more common in the Appalachians to the south, and planted widely as an ornamental, this shrub is native to the state.

Rock sedimentation basins along the road prevent runoff silt from reaching the wetland. On a late-September walk I heard the guttural croaks of a raven as it flew high overhead. With the maturation of the southern New England forest, these birds, which weigh four times as much as the similar crow, are once again being seen—and heard. Sweet fern, a fragrant fern look-alike, grows in the sandy soil to the right of the road, which climbs and curves left. Small clearings have been created along the roadway to create edge habitat. Some plants have been fitted with wire or plastic mesh cages to prevent deer from nibbling them. While edge habitat encourages new growth sought by many species of wildlife, like deer, too much "edge" can be detrimental for some interior woodland-nesting birds, such as wood thrushes.

The road now levels out and curves in the other direction. Pass an informal woods path on the right. The forest canopy is composed of white, chestnut, and red oaks, red maple, and black birch, with some doomed American chestnut saplings. Come to a side trail on the left for the waterfall marked with a bench and a sign as well as a large red pine with platy, pinkish bark. Follow the 200-yard trail into an attractive small ravine to the waterfall, which has a seasonal flow due to upstream beaver dams. Descend gradually, then more steeply, over wooden steps at the end to the flow. Negro Hill Brook flows through a jumble of large gneiss boulders, making a pleasing rumbling sound in the process. Pools are stained root-beer brown by tannins in the leaf litter, and it is noticeably cooler in this small ravine. Watch your footing, as these rocks may be very slick.

Return to the main trail and turn left. The road passes through a shrubby clearing where eastern towhees whistle their drink-your-tea refrain. Almost immediately reach a short side trail on the right which

Biologically rich beaver ponds and their associated wetlands are a primary feature of Sessions W.M.A.

leads to an observation tower at 756 feet above sea level. Pass a very large twin-trunked black birch on the way to the tower. A bench rests at the base of the 25-foot-high metal tower. From the tower, just above treetop level, you'll be treated to a wonderful 180° panoramic view toward the state's Central Valley, from Avon to Meriden. The Hanging Hills of Meriden and West Peak are visible to the right. This formation is part of the Metacomet Ridge, whose 190-million-year-old basalt rocks are actually the youngest in Connecticut. Primarily you'll see what appears to be an almost unbroken green expanse of forest—a gorgeous sight.

Return to the main trail and turn right. In September I watched black-throated green warblers deftly plucking slender green caterpillars from the pine needles. Sheep laurel, a two-foot-high relative of mountain laurel said to be poisonous to sheep, grows near the trail junction. Come almost immediately to another side trail on the left which leads to a wildlife viewing blind. Turn left and walk on a wide chipped path through a 1985 clearcut of diseased red pines, now regenerating mostly to oak and birch. Then enter a relatively shady oak forest. From the wooden blind pickerel-weed, bulrushes, and tree stumps can be seen. Early and late in the day you may also be lucky enough to spy muskrats and other wildlife.

Return again to the main trail and turn left. On a warm, sunny day the evocative aroma given off by pine needles along the sandy shoulder may waft to your nostrils. Reenter woodland that holds some low ledge outcrops. Reach a sizable boulder sloping up gradually from the road on the left; dark and light swirls in the gneiss rock make it appear almost as a bundt cake would. From its back, a better view of an old beaver flowage is possible. An osprey perched in a dead snag, clutching a fish meal in its long talons, flew off at my approach during an early-fall visit.

The swamp maples turn a brilliant scarlet in late summer along the flowage. A nesting box for wood ducks has been attached to one tree. Evidence of recent beaver activity can be found in the form of a tiny dam constructed by the rodents on the right. Walk left a short distance along the path lined with wintergreen shrubs bearing bright red fruits in fall to see a larger beaver dam. Mountain laurel shrubs put on a dazzling pink-and-white June display in this sunlit clearing.

Return to the main trail and turn left. Pass over a small culvert and enter oak woodland with some red maple and lots of mountain laurel. Come to a graveled and signed side path on the right which leads to a wooden observation platform overlooking a thirty-foot-long vernal pool. In late summer the pool most certainly will be dry, for that is the nature of vernal pools. Velvety green moss encircles the depression, as do Juneberry and winterberry shrubs. Spotted salamanders make their way to this pool to breed in early spring, and the tadpoles must complete their development before the heat of summer dries this nursery.

Return to the main roadway and turn right. Sheep laurel shrubs become common, and then you'll pass a water-control structure. On the opposite side is another side trail, which leads over boardwalks and bridges to excellent views of a red maple swamp. Azaleas, winterberry, and royal fern line the path, while bur-reed, pickerelweed, and fragrant waterlilies vegetate the standing water. A nesting platform for ospreys erected atop a dead snag has not been utilized. The vast majority of the population of this elegant fish hawk still nest coastally.

Follow the path over more boardwalk to a wildlife blind above the water which offers a nice, expansive view of the thirty-eight-acre, lily-covered pond. Breezes sometimes flip up the lily's leaves, revealing the reddish undersides of the floating fragrant lily pads. A whole community of tiny organisms thrives on the leaves' gelatinous undersides. An old, low beaver lodge, now abandoned, sits rather forlornly out in the water. Beavers were reintroduced into Connecticut in 1914 and are now thriving. More big wood duck nest boxes, the sites of nesting activities in spring, are visible on the many water-killed trees. Red-shouldered hawks nest in the live trees surrounding the pond. Retrace your steps through mountain laurel to the main trail and turn left.

Reach another overlook of the swamp at a split-rail fence where the roadway takes a major bend to the right. Pass a number of very large white pine. The New Britain Water Company owns the land just to the left. Multiflora rose, once planted for wildlife food and cover, grows in a small clearing on the right. Its harmful invasive nature has since been demonstrated in much of the country. A dying grove of red pine stands on the left but is being left to provide food and cover for birds. The natural forest is composed of oaks—white, red, and chestnut—with huckleberry shrubs below, as well as some white pine. Come to the junction of the Tunxis Trail on the left, which leads to East Chippens Hill Road and eventually to its Mile of Ledges section (see the following chapter). A pit toilet is located opposite the intersection. Remain on the wide graveled roadway.

The road crosses a stream where a water-loving tupelo tree's foliage turns vivid shades of red and orange in autumn. Another short graveled path on the right soon comes into view. It leads to a "shrub release area," or berry field, where the removal of large trees has enabled the shrub layer to obtain more sunlight and moisture. Huckleberry grows along the edges, while pioneering gray birch is colonizing the clearing. Gray birch's leaves have long, pointed drip tips. Continue on the main road through water-company property as it goes downhill past a bench on the right. Whorled loosestrife, which produces yellow flowers, grows profusely along the road shoulders.

Continue walking through oak-maple woodland where the land rises to your left. Cross a small drainage, where even in late summer spicebush, cinnamon fern, and small amounts of sphagnum moss testify to wetter times. On the left, planted cranberry viburnum (a.k.a. highbush cranberry) is surrounded by wire-mesh screening to keep deer at bay. The roadway gains ground gradually, passes through abundant cinnamon fern, and then climbs more steeply. Reach the start of the Tree Identification Trail on the right to close the loop. Continue straight on the Beaver Pond Trail back to your vehicle on the right.

WET AND WILD

To some, wetlands are the epitome of wasted and "unreclaimed" land, ugly places good only for hatching mosquitoes. In reality, wetlands are dwindling resources that afford countless benefits to both humans and wildlife.

Wetlands are natural flood-control structures which absorb the abundant snow melt and rainwater of early spring, thereby preventing flooding or minimizing it greatly downstream. Wetlands are also ground-water recharge basins that slow the flow of streams and permit the water's percolation deep into the ground. They also function as natural filtration plants where contaminants can be transformed into less harmful or even benign compounds.

Wetlands—swamps, marshes, wet meadows, and ponds—are also extremely productive wildlife habitat. From the most minute single-celled organisms to the four-foot-tall great blue heron with its seven-foot wingspan, wetlands provide food, cover, and homes to countless species. Beaver, muskrat, river otter, and mink all depend directly on their continued existence. Whether vegetarian, as in the case of the beaver, or strictly carnivorous, as in the case of the river otter and mink, these creatures are inextricably linked with the welfare of their wetlands communities.

Waterfowl—ducks and geese—of course are also closely associated with wetlands. Wood ducks and hooded mergansers nest in tree cavities and in the wooden boxes constructed for them by concerned humans. Migrating ospreys plunge into the water for fish, while great blue herons, green herons, and other wading birds nest and feed in wetlands. Great blue herons build their untidy stick nesting platforms high in the crotches of flooded timber in secluded areas. Kingfishers nest in bank burrows and hunt for fish in the clear waters. Frogs, turtles, and red-spotted newts also thrive in beaver ponds and other wetlands, feeding upon the abundant aquatic insect life they harbor. These creatures in turn often become food for larger animals.

The list goes on and on, but wetlands don't. Each year we are losing wetlands to the relentless tide of development, although wetlands-protection laws have stemmed the destruction to some extent. Pollution and acidification are also real threats. At last we have begun to appreciate the importance of what once were thought of as wastelands. By acting to save and restore wetlands, we can aid not only wildlife, but ourselves as well.

Getting There

Take Route 6 to its intersection with Route 69 in Bristol. Turn onto Route 69 north and follow it for approximately 3.0 miles. Turn left onto the entrance road for Sessions Woods Wildlife Management Area. Parking is located 0.15 mile up on the right.

—R.L.

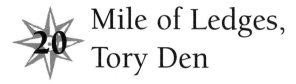

20 Mile of Ledges, Tory Den

Burlington

- Tunxis Trail, Greer Road, Yellow Dot Trail
- 4.25 miles
- 300-foot elevation gain
- 4.0 hours
- moderate, with difficult rocky sections

One of the most rugged and interesting sections of the state's blue-blazed hiking trail system is located in Hartford County very near its border with Litchfield County. Indeed, this walk straddles the boundary between the two. The Tunxis Trail and associated side trails traverse some of the most rugged terrain available to Connecticut hikers. Given that the trail network is very well maintained, accessibility is excellent.

By connecting the Tunxis Trail and the Yellow Dot Trail by way of Greer Road, it is possible to create nearly a full loop walk of moderate length which samples some of the most interesting ledge and "cave" formations along the Tunxis Trail system. The Revolutionary War–era hide-out known as Tory Den is just one of the fascinating natural features along the route.

Look Forward To

- picturesque rock ledges
- a few tight squeezes
- historic Tory Den

The Trail

The Tunxis Trail begins on the east side of East Plymouth Road at a wooden gate. Because the area is part of the Bristol public water supply, it is posted against trespassing. Hikers, however, are welcome. Start by following the

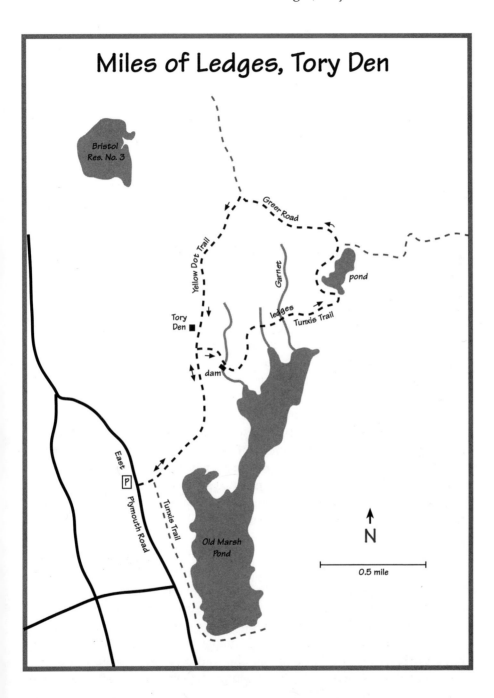

Miles of Ledges, Tory Den

level gravel tote road past a pine plantation on the right. Poison ivy grows lush here. An arm of 1.3-mile-long Old Marsh Pond is soon visible on the right. Eastern towhee and gray catbird skulk in the thickets as the blue-blazed trail rises gradually and curves left. Planted European larch stand near the water. Sugar maple, white ash, and red oak border the road, which crosses a culvert. Numerous grapevines drape the trees and touch-me-not is common along the damp roadsides. When the seeds mature into small pods, the slightest touch will cause the pod to split explosively, hurling the seeds a surprising distance.

After crossing another culvert the roadway becomes narrower. Black birch joins maple and oak, as well as spicebush. Six-inch-long olive-green-and-white red-eyed vireos are common nesting birds in these woodlands. Females weave lovely cup nests containing thin strips of birch bark at the ends of forked branches. Begin walking easily downhill along a slope to your left. Amid oak trunks festooned with climbing poison ivy vines, false Solomon's seal bears its frothy white flowers at the end of its stem. Pass a big twin red oak on the left. In the low damp spots, meadow rue and smartweed bloom in summer. Cross a flowing stream where spicebush and especially skunk cabbage are common plants. You might find a green frog here also. The shrub swamp on the right contains red, or swamp, maple.

At a point where the tote road forks, stay left. Cross another culvert where a few hemlocks have found suitable conditions and begin a gentle climb. Stay left as the road forks again almost immediately and takes you through cutover red oak and hickory woods. Rock outcrops appear on the right—the first of many to come. A few yellow birch, with fine peeling metallic bark, make an appearance, and witch hazel and maple-leafed viburnum show up in the shrub-sapling layer. After more outcrops, the old logging road swings right. American chestnut sprouts appear, as do beaked hazelnut and, on the forest floor, the flattened leaves of ground cedar club moss. Mica crystals in the rock at your feet glisten.

Hay-scented, or boulder, fern grows in the sunlit openings and low-bush blueberry and a few mountain laurel appear as the old road through this logged area levels off. Slash piles are still visible. The road bears left to avoid a seasonally damp spot marked by sedges, which have triangular stems, and smartweed. Ledges rise up on the left. Evergreen wood fern, a rock specialist, caps the outcrops. Red maple are vigorously resprouting in this selectively logged woodland, as the trail narrows through a stand of hay-scented fern. Red-eyed vireos, which are Neotropical migrants, are numerous here as well. Pass a large red oak and then walk through a gap in a stone wall. Notice the minerals quartz and mica in the boulders and outcrops to your right. A few white pine are present and below them, in the acidic soil, Canada mayflower.

Reach a trail intersection at the three-quarter-mile mark. Turn right to continue on the blue-blazed Tunxis Trail. These oak woods have not been logged as recently. Joining the oak are red maple, black birch, mountain laurel, American chestnut, and lowbush blueberry. A small plant, fairly common in dry soils and bearing light-yellow trumpetlike flowers in summer, is cow-wheat. At the edge of a logged area on the right, the trail bears left down into a dip and then up and over a ledge outcrop which forms a shallow bowl. The parallel-banded outcrop is gneiss, a metamorphic rock altered under intense heat and pressure deep within the earth some 400 million years ago. Come to another shallow depression between ledges with laurel, witch hazel, sassafras, lowbush blueberry, and some chestnut oak.

While walking gradually up the next outcrop, note the layer-cake bedding of the dark-gray rock upon which rock tripe lichen and common polypody fern have gained a foothold. Bear right and go up rather steeply over the ledge outcrop. You are now standing on top of the ledges, with a sheer drop-off to the left. Light-gray and green lichens cover much of the darker-hued stone, and white cushion moss forms soft pillows on the rock. The oak woods are attractive and wood thrushes sing their lovely *ee-o-lay* breeding songs from its depths. Cross more exposed rock slabs and descend. The right-angle cleavage planes of the outcrop have created rather convenient steps in some spots.

Turn left and go down more steeply now over a jumble of flat boulders. Level out below the ledge and bear left. Walk over rocks along the left edge of another ledge outcrop, and then turn right to climb up over the rocks of this ledge. Pass boulders capped with polypody ferns. This is the top of another outcrop, with a sheer drop on the left. Come to an eight-to-nine-foot-deep cleft in the ledge, swing right, and then immediately swing left to descend through it. Turn left after emerging, continuing rather steeply downslope. The rock has fractured into right-angle blocks which appear vaguely to be of human origin. A few smooth-skinned, gray-trunked shad trees appear. They bloom in April during the period when shad fish used to ascend rivers to spawn. Hermit thrushes sing their ethereal songs, which evoke a wilderness feeling in one traveling this rugged terrain.

Walk along the vertical cliff face covered with mosses, ferns, and lichens. Note the quartz bands. Cross a jumble of rock slabs and blocks where horizontally bedded ledges rise up on the right, then descend to a wet area with fringed loosestrife, whose yellow, down-facing flowers bloom in summer. Cross a stream via an old stone dam from whose center stones have been removed. Both ends are intact, however, and indicate its former height. The damp area behind the dam is fertile ground for fringed loose-strife. Check the soft mud for tracks of raccoons and other mammals. Climb up the far end of the dam abutment and marvel at how the dam's builders transported these heavy blocks and maneuvered them into place.

Eastern towhees, large, boldly patterned members of the sparrow family, scratch vigorously in the leaf litter with both feet simultaneously and give a raspy *chewink* call note from the safety of the shrubbery. Males are velvet black above with rusty-brown flanks and white breasts, while females are warm brown above. Both possess fiery red irises. The trail swings left as you climb up and over a lower outcrop. Walk between and over outcrops to a small clearing created by bedrock; huckleberry, shad, mountain laurel, oak, black birch, and red maple grow here. Wintergreen produces bell-shaped blossoms below the laurel in summer. Turn right and walk into a slight dip and then up and over ledge bedrock. Black-and-white warblers hitch along tree limbs seeking insects, looking like striped nuthatches. Continue up over more ledge, where white, red, and chestnut oak are dominant.

Turn right along a fifteen-foot-high bedrock wall and then immedi-ately left to make your way up through a shallow cleft; a rock on the right juts out toward hikers. Crest the lichen-covered ledge, with a drop-off to the right. Crawl up over the ledge and curve left. You can rest here but beware the sheer cliff to your right! We shared this perch with a white-tailed dragonfly, wasps, and ants as we ate lunch here during a summer visit. You may wish to sample the ripe huckleberries if you're here in sea-son. Walk downhill through low-stature oak, shad, and black birch, where white-breasted nuthatches are common year-round residents. Their nasal *ank-ank* calls are unmistakable.

Bear right and descend at a sharp angle through a crevice. Black birch is adept at colonizing narrow clefts, as it does here. Look back behind you for an impressive view of the ledge cliff on the left. Walk down into a small hollow between ridges and pass through a small canyon about 100 feet in length. Bear right and cross more boulders. The rocky trail parallels a small outcrop on the left, curves left, and passes through another cleft, this one level. Within the cleft, which appears to be a fault, the air feels definitely cooler. Climb up out of this cleft, known as Bear's Den, on the right by employing the natural steps in the 6-foot-high rock wall. Walk over the top of the 5-foot-wide "wall" and then turn right. Descend gradually. Part of Old Marsh Pond is visible in the distance to your right.

The forest floor is covered with wild sarsaparilla, maple-leafed viburnum, Virginia creeper, and sessile-leaved bellwort under sugar maple and oak. Cross an intermittent stream through a boulder field and proceed uphill easily past patches of New York fern. Bear around the left end of an outcrop and up to the right where a tulip tree stands tall and alone to the left. Cross the bedrock at a rather declivitous angle and swing left along more ledges. Lowbush blueberry and Canada mayflower are indicators of acid soil here. Bear right and proceed up and over a low ledge where chestnut, red oak, hickory, shad, red maple, and lowbush blueberry dominate the woodland. Descend over rocks, turn right, and then turn sharply left to level out. Patches of Christmas fern and princess pine club moss decorate the forest floor.

Listen for the soothing sounds of running water ahead. Walk down and bear right to loudly flowing, rock-lined Garnet Brook. The sound emanates from a miniature waterfall eighteen inches high. Even small irregularities such as this help to aerate the water. Cross the brook, which feeds the pond, on big flat stones. Green frogs often sit on stream-side rocks waiting for insects. Bear right, cross a stone wall in an area of small hemlock, climb a small slope over a low outcrop, and then level out again. Here grow a few big, coarse, bracken ferns. Walk along the minor slope and pass another rock wall to your right. You are still in oak-maple woods with a few beech, hemlock, white pine, hickory, and black birch. Young black birch possess very smooth, nearly black trunks.

The Tunxis Trail undulates a bit, then passes a low outcrop and boulders on the left. Ghostly white Indian pipes, also known as corpse plant, push up through the decaying leaves and striped wintergreen, with its variegated leaves and waxy flowers, blooms in summer. Reach a trail intersection on the right just before a rock wall. Stay straight and pass the wall on the right and the junction of another trail almost immediately on the left. The blue-blazed trail turns left just before reaching a pond. While viewing the pond from a short side trail, we were delighted to see a crow-sized adult green heron perched on a snag in the water. Disturbed, it flew to shore with its crest erect. It may well have been seeking young green frogs, which leap and squeal at an intruder's approach.

Lilies of both species float on the surface, and at the far end, near Greer Road, sits the big, high mound of a beaver lodge. Return to the main trail and turn right. Climb up over a low rock outcropping which sparkles with mica. Pass a human-made mound of stone on the right, turn right, and ascend another ledge fairly steeply. The pond is visible through the trees below. You may also glimpse the Canada geese that nest here. They are partial to beaver ponds, often building their nests directly on the lodges. Descend from the low outcrop and bear right to walk under a low canopy of grape and witch hazel, the source of the astringent of the same name. Delicate maidenhair, interrupted, and Christmas ferns thrive in the damp soil, as do moisture-loving basswood, ash, and spicebush. From this vantage point there is an open view of the pond.

Now the path rises easily and moves briefly away from the pond. Blue-headed (formerly solitary) vireo, eastern towhee, and chipmunk all started scolding us as we walked through their domain on a late-July hike. The path then returns to the pond and follows along its shore. Belted king-fishers use snags to scan for fish in the clear water, and male bullfrogs bellow from their territories. The imposing beaver lodge is now visible on the right, and to the right of it are two others. Beaver have removed the trees on the far shore, and the increased sunshine reaching the dense mountain laurel there makes possible considerable blossoming of the state flower in June and early July.

Pass through a stone wall gap by small outcrops and descend to paved Greer Road; leave the Tunxis Trail and turn left onto the road. Follow it for about one-half mile and turn left onto the Yellow Dot Trail (blazed with a yellow dot over blue) just before the pavement ends. Cross a seasonally wet stream bed and climb the rather inclined hillside into oak and maple woods where red-eyed vireos are among the most common breeding birds. Vireos and warblers consume vast quantities of forest-canopy insects in spring and summer. Cross the boulder-covered slope, where mica and quartz crystals are prominent, and come to a T intersection. Turn left toward Tory Den, three-quarters of a mile south.

Proceed through laurel and under maple and oak, where olive-drab eastern wood pewees sally forth for flying insects. Red efts are quite common even here, a fair distance from the beaver ponds where they will later live out their aquatic adult lives as red-spotted newts. Come to a ledge cliff on the right, its surface partially obscured by leafy rock tripe lichen, which metamorphose from brown to green after drinking in rain. A laurel thicket caps the top of the outcrop. Blueberry, huckleberry, mosses, chestnut, and oak are also common. Both hermit and wood thrushes nest up here, hermits on the ground and wood thrushes usually about ten feet up. The trail undulates gradually and gray birch becomes more common, while chestnut oak is quite abundant along with the laurel and a few white pine.

Walk up over bedrock where a small two-trunked gray birch is anchored, then level out and bear left through a young forest of oak, birch, and maple. Walk downslope to a dip between ledges, swing left, and continue the gradual descent. Next, bear right and climb fairly steeply, level off, and then climb low ledge. Witch hazel is the other prominent shrub in these woods. Beautiful black-throated blue warblers are partial to mountain laurel thickets and often build their well-concealed nests low to the ground in these shrubs. After leveling out again the path traverses a big bedrock boulder and trends downhill. Bear left, descending with increasing steepness, and cross a small seasonal brook. Pass through a low damp spot adorned with tall, attractive cinnamon ferns; to the right stand ledge outcrops. Here we heard the song of a Canada warbler, a beautiful five-inch-long summer resident that breeds near wetland edges and damp woodland depressions.

Pass a noteworthy red oak on the left which has seven trunks. Walk over a quartz boulder partially covered with silvery-green cushion moss; to the right is the damp bowl. The tongue-shaped leaves of pink lady-slipper crop up occasionally in these woods. Cross a ledge with a short climb, go down the other side, and bear left at the blocked connector trail on the right. A high ledge cliff is visible on the right as you level out, and tulip trees grow in the depression below it. As the ledge continues, you'll see that slabs have broken off from the rock overhangs. The cliff is now twenty-five feet high. Another damp area on the right has cinnamon fern, wild iris, and sedges growing in it. Bear right, cross a low ledge outcrop, and swing left almost immediately. Brilliant scarlet tanagers, looking out of place in our northern forests, make the long flight each May from northern South America to return here.

Level off along the slope, bear right, and ascend a low outcrop. Continue walking to another ledge cliff ahead and bear left to arrive at the historic Tory Den on the right. The cavity, thirty-five to forty feet long, is formed by a stone slab resting against another rock, while a huge boulder forms a backdrop.

Continue south past the overhanging cliff on the right and then gently downhill; soon reach the intersection of the Tunxis Trail on the left. Continue straight for three-quarters of a mile back to your vehicle, keeping an eye open for wild turkeys, especially in the logged areas.

TUNXIS TALES

If only the rocks could speak—oh, what tales they would tell! And so it is at Tory Den. Long after cataclysmic forces deformed the rock itself and much later exposed it at the earth's surface; long after earthquakes, tremors, and ice sheets jostled the slabs into their current positions, local inhabitants created a human history which is still being told today.

During the American Revolution, British loyalists—Tories—from the nearby Chippen Hill community used the den as a safe haven, taking refuge there when the patriots came a-calling. The den was owned during those days more than two centuries ago by one Stephen Graves. He was whipped by patriots for being a Tory, but his brother-in-law, Moses Dunbar, suffered a far worse fate for his lack of support for the fledgling nation. Dunbar was the only Connecticut resident, it seems, who was hanged for treason during the Revolutionary War.

During the late 1800s Tory Den was also inhabited by a recluse known as the Leatherman, who acquired that colorful moniker as a result of his habit of being attired entirely in animal skins.

Getting There

From the junction of Routes 6 (Terryville Avenue) and 72 in Terryville, west of Bristol, travel north on Route 72 for 1.7 miles to Preston Road on the right. Turn right onto Preston Road and drive east for 0.1 mile to its junction with East Plymouth Road. Turn left onto East Plymouth Road and travel 0.5 mile north to a wooden gate on the right. Park off the pavement, and be sure not to block the gate. Parking is not allowed here from sunset to sunrise.

Talcott Mountain

Avon and Simsbury

- Tower Trail, Metacomet Trail
- 3.1 miles
- 500-foot elevation gain
- 2.0–2.5 hours
- moderate

Talcott Mountain is one of the most popular places to walk and enjoy nature in central Connecticut. Here, at the end of the Tower Trail and perched on the edge of the mountain, is one of the most unusual buildings in the state, the Heublein Tower. From its weatherproof viewing deck the horizon seems endless and spectacular. Yet the tower is only one aspect of the walk up Talcott Mountain. The Native American leader Metacomet was allegedly there hundreds of years ago, and the cave named for him is still there. The Metacomet Trail wanders through the forest, providing a quiet, secluded walk through tall trees and over rocky ridges. This walk takes you where everyone goes, and where few go, all in a couple of hours' time.

The Tower Trail and its feeder paths are unblazed but very easy to follow. The Metacomet Trail is marked with pale blue blazes. Turns are indicated by two stacked blazes offset in the direction of the turn.

Look Forward To

- King Philip's cave
- Heublein Tower
- fantastic views

The Trail

On weekends and at other peak times, the walk up Tower Trail is more akin to an outing on a Manhattan sidewalk than a nature walk. To avoid the

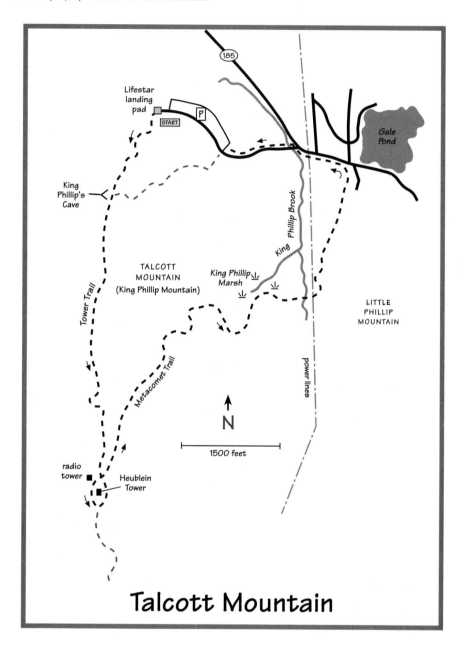

Talcott Mountain

crowds, at least part of the way, walk from the parking area up the paved road to the Lifestar helicopter landing pad, where a feeder path to Tower Trail begins. From the landing pad the trail enters the woods and proceeds south amidst specimens of yellow birch, oak, maple, and hickory. Mountain laurel and clumps of witch hazel are the understory plants, along with tufts of Christmas fern.

The path is wide and easy to follow as it begins gently to traverse the rocky hillside. The grade steepens as the woods change to waves of evergreen hemlocks alternating with oak, maple, birch, and other hardwoods. An unmarked path leads right, down the increasingly steep slope to an enclave of rock called King Philip's cave.

As the trail steepens it breaks out of the woods into a scrubby area of red cedar, staghorn sumac, red oak, and hop hornbeam. In spring round-lobed hepatica blooms near the edge of the ridge, its pale pink, blue, or white flowers providing a delicate touch to the stony landscape. A few black-eyed Susans and pink-eyed grass flower in late summer, a month or so after the wild roses that also grow here have gone by. The plants of this area are representative of the type of plant community that thrives along all the basalt ridges throughout Connecticut. The plants and trees are a hardy group, accustomed to hot, dry summers, and windswept, freezing winters.

The path continues along the edge of the ridge, with the Farmington River valley sweeping away to the west. After a short stroll a level area is reached where hang gliders launch their nimble craft into the sky. On summer days turkey vultures often soar past the launch area, providing a feathered contrast to man-made wings. You can tell turkey vultures from hawks, even from far away, by the way they glide through the air. Turkey vultures rock back and forth as they soar, while hawks do not.

From the launch area follow the wide woods road south, away from the ridge, past a large chestnut oak. Striped maple, a small understory tree with green-and-white-striped bark, grows beneath the spreading boughs of beech, oak, hop hornbeam, and shagbark hickory. After passing a low escarpment on the left where rock climbers practice their sport, the trail joins the blue-blazed Metacomet Trail as it approaches the tower.

Follow the signs to the entrance of the six-story-tall Heublein Tower, perched in whitewashed splendor atop the highest point of Talcott Mountain. The tower was constructed by Gilbert Heublein in 1914 as a summer house. The 165-foot-high structure sits atop the already impressive 875-foot-high mountain. The tower's enclosed viewing area offers perhaps the finest views in the entire state, with a 360° sweep that encompasses most of Connecticut as well as bits of three other states.

During foliage season the viewing area can be standing room only, and the natural world is sometimes chased far away by brass bands or other equally loud events conducted on the patio outside. There are days, how-

Chestnut oak on the Metacomet Trail.

ever, when bird song is still the predominant sound, and it is during these times that the uniqueness of the tower is most powerful. Designed to emulate the architectural style of Bavaria, the tower has been recognized as a National Historic Place since 1983.

From the tower retrace your steps to the junction of the wide woods road called the Tower Trail, and the Metacomet Trail. Take the Metacomet Trail north, which almost immediately enters very attractive woods of white and red oak, hemlock, beech, and a few stump sprouts of American chestnut. Polypody fern hides in rocky recesses beneath the hemlocks, while chickadees and black-and-white juncos flit among the branches. The footway wanders through the forest, soon coming to a rounded ridge where colonies of evergreen bearberry grow in the rocky soil.

The walk along the ridge is particularly enchanting, with beautiful views framed by a landscape of stone, tangles of mountain laurel, and stunted evergreen hemlocks. After leaving the ridge the path descends briefly, then passes a second ridge with winter views to the north and wintergreen underfoot. From the rocky outcrop, continue through a thick cover of mountain laurel that is stunning when it is in full bloom in late spring.

The trail then turns right (east), descending through tall oaks and maples into a moist lowland valley that separates the basalt ridges of Talcott Mountain (also called King Philip Mountain) and those of the smaller Little Philip Mountain. This sheltered area is home to maple-leafed viburnum, mountain laurel, and wild azalea, which thrive beneath the tall trees. To the left is a small wetland called King Philip Marsh, which serves as the headwaters of the brook that also bears his name. After negotiating a series of turns, the footway levels out at the base of the mountain, crosses a feeder stream of King Philip Brook, and turns right (south). Pass through the brushy scrub beneath high power lines to a dirt road. Follow the road briefly, and turn left into hemlock woods.

The path roughly parallels the power lines, staying in the woods and continuing north until it crosses Route 185 in a wet area of hardwoods and hemlock. Turn left and walk along Route 185 the short distance to the parking area for Talcott Mountain State Park.

VULTURES

From early March to late fall one of the largest birds in New England soars off the cliffs of Talcott Mountain. Turkey vultures are similar in size to eagles, standing thirty inches tall with a wingspan reaching six feet. During the day they soar the thermals, or updrafts, caused by the sun's heating the earth, gaining altitude by circling in upward spirals. Their sense of smell is astoundingly acute and helps them find their unappetizing meals of carrion.

Turkey vultures do not like to waste energy and are the best gliders of any Connecticut bird. Aside from takeoffs and landings, they seldom beat their wings, preferring to soar like the hang gliders who also ride the cliffside thermals. At night turkey vultures often gather in roosts, sometimes on the rocks of cliffs and other times in the limbs of dead trees. These roosts can give the woods a distinctly haunted feel, but a feeling is all it is. The birds have a supporting role in the dark side of our imagination through no fault of their own.

To identify turkey vultures in flight, watch how they fly. Turkey vultures rock side to side as they glide and rarely flap their wings. As they pass overhead they can be identified by their small, red heads and the silvery color of the back portion of the wings.

Thirty years ago turkey vultures were a rare sight in Connecticut, but they have increased their range and numbers substantially since then and now have the largest range of any North American vulture. From spring to fall turkey vultures can be seen across the entire United States, excluding the northernmost regions of New York, Vermont, and New Hampshire and most of Maine. In winter the birds migrate to the southeastern and southwestern states.

Getting There

From Route 44 in the center of Avon, turn onto Routes 10/202. Proceed about 2.9 miles to the junction with Route 185. Turn right onto Route 185 and travel 1.6 miles to the entrance to a parking area on the right. Proceed up the hill and park off the road. Parking is not permitted at the top of the hill, where a pad for the Lifestar helicopter is located.

—C.S.

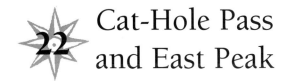

Cat-Hole Pass and East Peak

Meriden

- Metacomet Trail
- 4.2 miles
- 700-foot elevation gain
- 3.0–3.5 hours
- moderate, with difficult sections

The Hanging Hills are one of Connecticut's most easily recognized landmarks. Looming over the city of Meriden, these four traprock ridges and their accompanying rust-colored vertical cliffs seem like a massive, protective fortress. As if to reinforce this medieval image, a lone stone tower, built in the style of castle turrets, rests on the promontory known as East Peak. This walk takes you to the tower, known as Castle Craig, via a route that traverses Cat-Hole Pass, where bobcat and copperheads still live, and the cliffs high above the beautiful lake known as Meremere Reservoir.

The walk to East Peak is on the Metacomet Trail, which is marked with pale blue blazes. Turns are noted by two stacked blazes, with the topmost offset in the direction of the turn.

Look Forward To

- views from Castle Craig
- cliffside walk
- snakes?
- Cat-Hole Pass

The Trail

From the pull-off on Route 71 walk north 0.2 mile to where the Metacomet Trail crosses the highway, just south of the Berlin town line. This area is

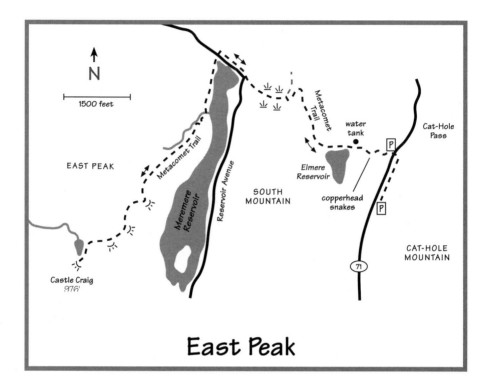

East Peak

known as Cat-Hole Pass, the bouldered debris fields on either side of the road having provided shelter to bobcats for centuries. This area is certainly not wilderness, but I was fortunate enough to see a bobcat here in the 1970s, and they are probably still here.

From the road the trail heads southwest into woods of black birch, maple, oak, and beech. The terrain is rough, with traprock boulders everywhere. A few yards from the road is a sign that reads Warning Snake Area. If bobcats weren't enough of a thrill, Cat-Hole Pass is also famous for its population of copperheads (see essay). Most people who hike this section of trail consider the sign a joke. It isn't. It is there to protect the snakes from people who whack everything that slithers with a stick. Stay on the treadway, and most of the time all you will encounter in Cat-Hole Pass are Christmas fern, witch hazel, and a few songbirds.

After an easy, short climb the path comes to a open area dominated by a large water-holding tank and the earthen dam of Elmere Reservoir. Continue across the dam at the north end of the reservoir. This is a beautiful pond with a wooded shore studded with boulders. In autumn the colorful foliage reflects in the water, intensifying the color of the leaves. At the far end of the dam, an unmarked trail leaves left (south) and the Metacomet Trail continues straight ahead (west).

Follow the blue blazes along the stony bed of a usually dry wash through woods of red maple, oak, hemlock, hop hornbeam, and flowering dogwood above witch hazel, benzoin bush, arrowwood, and wild geranium. Just before beginning a gradual descent, the very observant will notice a small, stone-lined spring on the left. Beyond the spring the wide path enters a stand of hemlock sprinkled with large red oaks. An unmarked trail enters left as the main trail continues south.

To the right a small brook keeps you company until the trail swings left (west) and begins a moderately steep descent to the wetlands below. At the base of the hill a dirt road enters right as the main trail continues straight. With wetlands to both sides, the forest gives way to tangles of benzoin bush and witch hazel. In spring, benzoin bush lights up the leafless woods with tufts of fuzzy yellow flowers. In late summer the large aromatic leaves hide small green berries which ripen to a glossy red. Wood thrush and veerie particularly like the ripe berries, and years ago the berries were dried and used as a substitute for allspice, which gave this common wetland shrub its other name, spicebush.

Castle Craig atop East Peak, from the Metacomet Trail.

Marsh wrens dart about, as do vireos and warblers. In late fall white-throated sparrows stop by on the way south from their summer homes to the north.

The path continues along a level grade, passing a number of unmarked trails to the left before coming to Reservoir Avenue. Follow Reservoir Avenue across the dam at the north end of Meremere Reservoir. This long, narrow lake, embraced by red-brown, rocky cliffs on both sides, is one of the most beautiful bodies of water in the state.

At the far end of the dam turn left, leaving the road and scrambling up a short rocky ledge to the woods. The path climbs gently through a forest of oak and tulip tree, with lady-slipper and flowering raspberry beneath. The trail traverses the loose talus slope of the north shore, rising higher and higher above the water. The footing gets increasingly difficult in direct relation to the view over the water becoming increasingly beautiful.

After crossing a deep cleft where a small stream runs, the path veers away from the shoreline and follows the brook up the ravine. A brief but steep climb up a rocky cobble is the first of a series of climbs through alternating hemlock woods and stretches of bare bedrock. Eventually the hemlocks yield to a grassy woodland of hop hornbeam, hickory, maple, and oak. As the path slowly heads back toward the shoreline, it is time to be on the lookout for the black dog of the Hanging Hills.

According to local legend, a black dog haunts the forests that cloak the Hanging Hills. The black dog first appears behind hikers as they climb up the mountain. The animal gradually gains on the hikers, eventually passing them, and disappears into the woods along the trail ahead. Things get a bit spooky when it is noticed that the large animal fails to leave any footprints to mark its passing, and people farther along the trail usually report never seeing a black dog. The legend states that the first time the black dog is seen, good luck will follow. The second time it appears is a warning, and the third time means an untimely demise. The legend of the black dog makes good telling around the campfire, but I have yet to find anyone who has really seen it.

The trail soon comes to the edge of the Meremere cliffs, where a spectacular sight awaits. Hundreds of feet below are the cool, blue waters of Meremere Reservoir, with all of southern Connecticut stretching out beyond. Continue along the cliffs, soaking up the seemingly endless views. Around you grow bearberry, red cedar, common juniper, blueberry, oak, and hickory, all framed by the brown basalt cliffs.

Soon Castle Craig appears through the trees, the stone turret looking like a misplaced medieval fortification. Follow the path to the castle, where the views are wonderful. From the viewing area Sleeping Giant Mountain is to the south, with New Haven just beyond. On very clear days the broad sweep of Long Island Sound is faintly visible. To the north the city of Hartford fills the Connecticut Valley. As you enjoy the view, you might wonder just how this unique structure came to be.

At the turn of the century a man named Walter Hubbard owned most of the land around East Peak. The generosity of the Hubbard family was ultimately responsible for the creation of Hubbard Park, the signature park of Meriden's famous city-park system. In the winter of 1900, however, there was no castle atop East Peak, just beautiful basalt cliffs. But Walter Hubbard had a dream of putting a castle on his mountain, and hired a man named Stuart Douglas to build the stone tower. Construction began on April 30, 1900. Douglas and his crew of Italian stonemasons worked all that spring, through the summer, and into the fall to complete Hubbard's dream—and complete it they did. On October 29, 1900, the tower was dedicated. It has been a landmark of Connecticut ever since.

To return to the parking area just retrace your steps, keeping a watchful eye for the black dog.

COPPERHEADS

When I was about ten years old I used to walk through the wooded wetlands at the base of the Metacomet ridge. The columnar basalt cliffs rose hundreds of feet overhead like a massive sculpture left behind by an ancient civilization. Between the forests where I walked and the cliffs I gazed upon were the steep talus slopes composed of blocky boulders calved from the ridge above. It was on that talus slope, bathed in the warmth of the south-facing mountain, that the copperheads lived. That much I had been told. What I didn't know was that in summer the snakes migrated away from their winter den on the hillside, slowly making their way from the rocks to the cooler wooded wetlands below.

As I strode through the tangles of sweetshrub near a dried marsh, I broke through the brush into a more open area carpeted with tussocks of grass and shaded by tall red maples. I hadn't a care in the world at that moment, until I casually looked down at where my next step would land.

Copperheads are pit vipers, so called for the heat-sensitive organ, or pit, located between each eye and nostril. They are venomous snakes, injecting their poison via a pair of hollow fangs. So much for the scary part. In fact, copperheads are peaceful creatures that just happen to be heavily armed.

Copperheads have a pale, rusty-colored head leading to a thick, reddish orange body marked with darker, saddle-shaped diamonds across the back. Many snakes are mistaken for copperheads, but only copperheads have a pink tongue, scales that have a central keel, a single row of scales under the tail, and the pit between the eye and nostril. Their coloration makes them nearly invisible when viewed against a backdrop of fallen leaves and twigs.

The snakes pass the winter in rocky dens, usually on the south side of wooded mountains but sometimes on the edges of rocky talus slopes. In spring they disperse from the den site, wandering in a roughly circular loop a few miles long down to nearby low wetlands before returning, some four to five months later, to the den. They are not common snakes, and definitely prefer not to make your acquaintance. People who see them have a way of overreacting, to the detriment of the snakes.

What I saw that day many years ago made me freeze in my tracks. There, not two feet away, was a coiled, two-foot-long adult copperhead. I half-expected the snake to whirl around and strike my leg. What actually happened was completely different: The snake didn't move. Not even a twitch. For a few moments I stood absolutely still and gazed at the snake, then quietly backed away. When I had backed up a few feet, I stopped and admired the copperhead for a few minutes. It was lying on the leaves, rolled into a tight coil like a thick Italian sausage displayed at the market. Its head was resting on the ground, and for a moment I wondered what this beautiful, frightening creature was thinking. I was only ten years old, and the subliminal answer I received was to enjoy the experience but not dwell on it. With that in mind, I quietly circled around the snake and continued on my way.

Getting There

From Interstate 691 take Exit 5 to the Chamberlain Highway (Route 71). Go north on Route 71 to a stop light at the intersection with Kensington Avenue. Continue north on Route 71 0.4 mile to a pull-off on the right. A very small pull-off is sometimes available 0.2 mile farther north where the Metacomet Trail crosses the road.

—C.S.

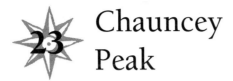

Chauncey Peak

Meriden

- Mattabesett Trail, Prospect Lake Trail
- 2.0 miles
- 377-foot elevation gain
- 2.0–3.0 hours
- moderate, with difficult sections

It is refreshingly rare to find a beautiful natural area within shouting distance of a city. Just such a place, called Giuffrida Park, is near the busy downtown section of Meriden. This hideaway has acres of woods, miles of trails, and a beautiful lake nestled against the talus slope of Chauncey Peak. There are spectacular views from the long, rocky summit ridge; interesting plants; water birds on the lake; and plenty of benches thoughtfully placed near the water's edge. If you wish to spend a few minutes, or a few hours, this is a place that exercises the body and soothes the spirit.

The walk over Chauncey Peak traverses a section of the Mattabesett Trail, which is blazed with light-blue markers. Turns are noted with two stacked blazes offset in the direction of the turn. The trails around Prospect Lake are marked with white blazes.

Look Forward To

- many, many views
- interesting plants
- lovely lake-side walk

The Trail

From the parking area near the rest rooms and caretaker's cabin, walk east through a grassy area in front of Prospect Lake dam. At the east end of the

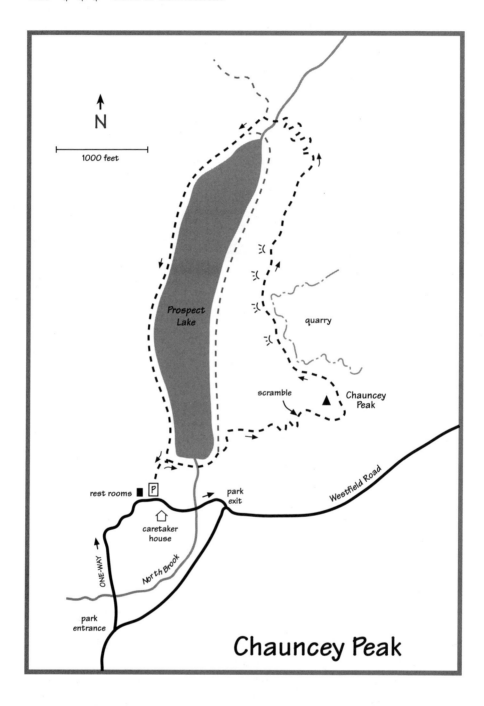

Chauncey Peak

dam a trail blazed with white markers heads left (north), and a blue-blazed trail continues straight ahead (north). Follow the blue blazes into a woodland of elm, maple, black birch, flowering dogwood, and arrowwood. The flowering dogwood is especially beautiful along the south flank of Mount Chauncey, where the blush-colored blossoms brighten spring afternoons.

After a moderate climb the trail levels out ever so briefly before turning right (east), and proceeds through increasingly rocky terrain. Soon the path swings left (north) and begins the short, but memorably steep, ascent of the southern buttress of the mountain. The treadway is paved with small, loose traprock stones which make the footing tricky. Near the crest of the ridge, large basalt ramparts appear which at first glance seem insurmountable. The trail negotiates the cliffs by threading through a narrow and exciting rock cleft. A brief scramble up the bare rock brings you to the top of this impressive ridge.

On reaching the top of the cliff, turn right along the ridge and climb the few paces to an impressive overlook. From the bedrock ledge there are beautiful views to the west, south, and east. To the west are the famous Hanging Hills of Meriden with Cat-Hole Mountain and East Peak, decorated with the stony silhouette of Castle Craig (see chapter 22). The Hanging Hills are also called the Lion's Paw, for the shape of the four eroded basalt ridges that comprise the stately rock formation. To the south, far beyond the hayfields at the base of the mountain, the skyline of New Haven is visible, with the sapphire-blue hues of Long Island Sound discernible on clear days. To the southwest is the Sleeping Giant, perhaps the most recognizable natural feature in Connecticut (see chapter 27). East of the overlook are the sheer traprock cliffs of Mount Higby (see chapter 24).

Follow the path along the ridge over traprock ledges dotted with staghorn sumac, red cedar, hickory, and oak. Staghorn sumac is a weedy little tree with soft, fuzzy stems and tropical-looking, pinnately compound leaves which turn bright shades of scarlet and orange in fall. Centuries ago Native Americans used the berries to brew a tart beverage that looked and tasted like pink lemonade.

Soon the trail leaves the ridge, swinging north into the woods and passing along the edge of a quarry. Use caution here as the trail comes close to the edge of some very precipitous cliffs. As you walk through scrubby woods of hickory, red cedar, and linden, watch for a strange little plant called feverwort which grows in the dry soil of the mountain. If you see it, you won't forget it. Feverwort has pairs of large leaves decorated with wings near their base that clasp the stem. In early summer small, yellow-

Looking south from Chauncey Peak.

ish purple flowers appear in the axils of the leaves, followed in fall by hairy orange fruit.

The trail wanders to the west side of the ridge, where it leaves the woods in favor of a series of overlooks high above the sparkling waters of Prospect Lake. Some people call Prospect Lake, Crescent Lake, which is fine. And those who don't call it Prospect Lake or Crescent Lake refer to it by the less romantic epithet Bradley-Hubbard Reservoir. Which is also fine. Regardless what name you tack onto it, it is a beautiful sight from high on the ridge.

The trail continues northeast along the ridge, past lovely, open vistas that just seem to beg you to stop and admire the view. Rock climbers sometimes practice on the cliffs below, and on crisp fall days Canada geese can be heard honking as they paddle in the waters below, while hawks soar overhead as they migrate to warmer winter climes.

The path then begins to descend the ridge through a picturesque forest of jutting boulders and bedrock mixed with evergreen hemlock. Brown creepers and kinglets mingle among the tree branches in fall and winter, providing welcome company.

In the hemlock grove the path turns steeply downhill, swinging left and crossing a stone wall before leveling off near a drainage at the base of the mountain. From here the blue-blazed Mattabesett Trail leaves right (north) and a well-worn path goes left (south) toward the lake. Turn south and follow the level treadway the short distance to the shore of the lake. A wooden bridge to the left escorts hikers onto a white-blazed trail that follows the rugged eastern shore back to the parking area. Continue straight ahead on the wide and easy path that follows the western shore.

The path stays close to the water, and thoughtful folks have placed many benches all along the way. This gives ample chance to linger and watch the geese and ducks, or just stare out at the water. Mount Chauncey and Prospect Lake are only a few minutes from downtown Meriden, but sitting here on one of the benches or resting atop the mountain, you would never know a city is nearby. It is that peaceful.

The shore-side path divides here and there into multiple trails. They all eventually find their way to the parking lot, but if you always choose the route closest to the water, the walk is much more rewarding.

SWEET BIRCHES

Wintergreen is one of the most popular flavors in the world, adding a cool, minty taste to everything from candy, teas, and medicines to soda and recipes. In the woods the charming fragrance of wintergreen can be found in three common plants; wintergreen, black birch, and yellow birch.

Wintergreen is a creeping evergreen plant that prefers the moist, acidic soils beneath pines and spruce or along the edges of bogs and swamps. The leaves are glossy green and always smell of wintergreen when bruised or torn. In spring, small white flowers appear, followed in late summer by red berries. The berries have a dry, white pulp and also smell strongly of wintergreen. Some people have mistaken young mountain laurel for wintergreen, but mountain laurel is poisonous and never has the distinctive smell of wintergreen.

Black birch is a tall tree of mixed hardwood forests preferring moist stream banks and cool upland woods. It is commonly found with hemlock, pine, aspen, maple, and oak. Black birch has dark, charcoal-colored bark that is smooth when the trees are young and breaks into irregular plates as the trees age. The twigs emit a strong wintergreen fragrance when bruised. Black birch is common in the woods of Connecticut, but this lovely tree has a surprisingly small range, extending from central New England to the eastern shore of Lake Ontario and southwest in a narrow band over the Appalachians. It was the black birch that gave candy and birch beer their flavor, the oil of wintergreen being distilled from the bark. The tender twigs can be steeped in hot water to make a subtly flavored herb tea.

A close relative of black birch is yellow birch. This tree, also called silver birch, grows in the same habitat as black birch, thriving in cool, moist areas including ravines and along streams, ponds, and marshes. The bark of yellow birch is quite beautiful. Young trees have smooth, golden-to-dark brown bark, while that of older trees is golden and glossy, peeling away in very thin, papery strips. The twigs of yellow birch also have a sweet, wintergreen flavor and can be used the same way black birch is used.

Getting There

From Interstate 691 in Meriden take the Broad Street exit. Turn north onto Broad Street and travel 0.4 mile to Westfield Road. Turn right onto Westfield Road, pass over the railroad tracks, and proceed to the junction with Wall Street, which enters on the right. Continue on Westfield Road, passing beneath Route 15 and coming to the intersection with Bee Street, which enters on the right. A golf course is on the left. Turn left and follow Westfield Road another 0.1 mile to the park entrance on the left.

—C.S.

24 Mount Higby

Middlefield and Middletown

- Mattabesett Trail
- 3.4 miles
- 610-foot elevation gain
- 2.0–3.5 hours
- moderate, with difficult sections

The Mattabesett Trail, which clings to the sheer basalt ridges of Mount Higby, is not a secret to Connecticut hikers. This long volcanic ridge has been a magnet to people seeking beauty amidst a stunning landscape for decades. In a state with many diverse wonders, from ocean salt marshes to summits in the Taconic Range, the cliffs of Mount Higby are special indeed. In addition to long walks along the lofty precipice, there is a host of plants and animals to enjoy. All only a few minutes' drive from the heart of Connecticut.

The Mattabesett Trail along Mount Higby is marked with pale blue blazes. Turns are noted by two stacked blazes, with the topmost blaze offfset in the direction of the turn.

Look Forward To

- beautiful views
- wildflowers
- long basalt cliffs

The Trail

From the pull-off where Route 66 becomes Interstate 691, a red-blazed trail enters the woods to the west. Follow the stone-covered path uphill about 100 yards to a flat area where the Mattabesett Trail, blazed in blue, and the

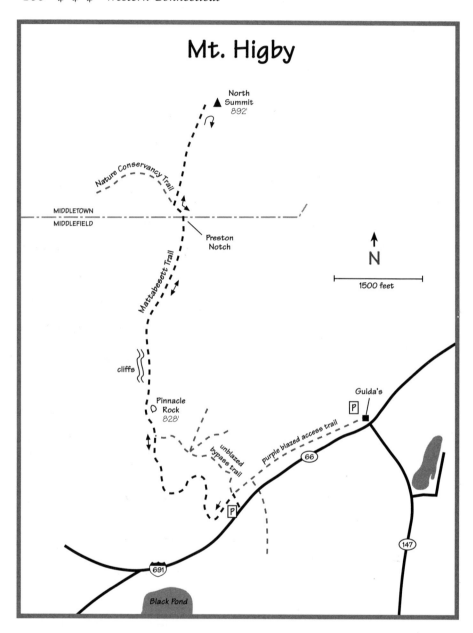

Mt. Higby

North
Summit
892'

Nature Conservancy Trail

MIDDLETOWN
MIDDLEFIELD

Preston
Notch

N

1500 feet

Mattabesett Trail

cliffs

Pinnacle
Rock
828'

Guida's

P

purple blazed access trail

unblazed
bypass trail

66

P

147

691

Black Pond

access trail from Guida's Dairy Bar, blazed in purple, enter on the right. Straight ahead is a largely unmarked trail which local folks use as a short-cut to the top of the ridge. It is shorter, but more difficult to follow and far less scenic.

Turn left onto the Mattabesett Trail, which runs parallel to the highway on the left, keeping the traprock talus slope of Mount Higby to the right. After a short walk the path turns sharply right and attacks the steep slope, using occasional switchbacks to ease the ascent. This is a moderately steep climb which slows you down enough to enjoy the many types of plants that grow here. Oak and maple are the dominant trees, with a few glossy green Christmas fern among wild sarsaparilla and creeping partridgeberry.

The path climbs over a series of small traprock ledges, passing a large boulder where Black Pond is visible to the south. The moist, well-watered valley forest of oak and maple now yields to the open, woodland savanna of the dry ridge tops. This area is dominated by grasses and blueberries growing among a rough landscape of rugged boulders. The open forest floor is shaded by widely spaced specimens of hickory, oak, ash, hop hornbeam, and red cedar.

As the trail crests a low rise, an unmarked trail continues straight while the Mattabesett Trail turns right and passes through a grove of stunted red cedar and hickory. It then descends into a small, steep-sided ravine carved by a vernal stream where hemlock thrive in the cool, moist soil. The path crosses the stream and ascends the opposite bank to the crest of Mount Higby's famous traprock ridge.

The trail proceeds north along the edge of the cliff, with peekaboo views to the west of Meriden and the Hanging Hills. Aster and goldenrod line the path beneath staghorn sumac, linden, ash, and red cedar. The shortcut trail encountered at the base of the mountain now enters on the right. Follow the blue blazes along the ridge a short way to the crest of Mount Higby. A brief scramble to the top of a house-sized outcrop (the south summit of Mount Higby called Pinnacle Rock) affords expansive views north, west, and south. To the south is the skyline of New Haven and the unique profile of Sleeping Giant Mountain in Hamden. Meriden and the four Hanging Hills (also called the Lion's Paw) are to the west, with Castle Craig and the huge American flag clearly visible atop East Peak. To the northwest are Lamentation Mountain, whose spine is studded with communication towers, and Mount Chauncey, with a large quarry devouring its eastern flank.

From the overlook continue north along the open ridge crest, which offers nearly continuous, spectacular views. Colonies of bearberry can be found hugging the exposed traprock ledges and colonizing the shady spots beneath stands of bear oak. Bearberry is a creeping ground cover that grows along the exposed ridges of the Appalachians as far south as Virginia and

The Mattabesett Trail as it weaves near the basalt cliffs of Mount Higby.

is hardy enough to thrive as far north as the Arctic. It has small, dark green, very glossy evergreen leaves and cinnamon-red exfoliating bark. Clusters of pendant, white-to-pale-pink flowers appear in spring and yield bright red fruits that look like tiny tomatoes in fall through winter. Wildlife, including birds and increasingly rare wood and box turtles, eat the fruit. Native Americans considered bearberry, or kinnikinick, a sacred herb and used it in religious ceremonies. Other plants growing on the ridge include bluestem grass, chokeberry, yarrow, wild mint, and butter-and-eggs, with snapdragon-shaped flowers in cream and orange.

As you walk along the bare basalt ledges, look closely at the stone's surface for long grooves etched into the rock. These scratches are called striations and were formed as the continental glacier advanced over the area during the last Ice Age. As glaciers move, they lift stones and boulders from the surface beneath them and incorporate them into the ice. The larger stones scrape over the bedrock as the glacier moves, leaving behind telltale grooves to mark their passing. The striations not only convey the message that the glaciers were once here, but record the direction the glacier was moving when it passed by.

This section of the trail hugs the edge of the cliffs and is wonderful to walk. It is easily one of the most spectacular paths in the state. The foot-way continually wanders teasingly close to the basalt cliffs, sometimes mere inches from the edge of the vertical precipice. As beautiful as this area is, hikers need to be very careful here, especially children. There is no restraining fence, and from the edge of the basalt cliffs it is a 100-foot drop to the bouldered talus slope below.

The path continues north, entering thicker woods before descending to a col called Preston Notch. Many years ago a coach road ran through here connecting Meriden and Middletown. Traces of the old thoroughfare still can be seen on the upland section of the notch. To the left of the trail is a stone marker that delineates the boundary between Middlefield, which you are leaving, and Middletown. From the notch a trail leaves left down the mountain. The path leads to Preston Avenue in Meriden through land owned by The Nature Conservancy.

From its intersection with The Nature Conservancy trail, the Mattabesett Trail swings right and climbs the northern section of Mount Higby into dry, woodland savanna. Along the path the bright scarlet-and-yellow blossoms of wild columbine bloom in late spring and summer, along with blue-flowered flax.

After a moderately steep climb the terrain levels out, following the cliff edge to a series of lovely overlooks with views north, south, and west. The northern summit of Mount Higby is the last overlook before the trail begins to descend. It is grassy and largely private, as most people stay on the southern section of the ridge. The north summit is a perfect place to linger and have lunch before heading back to the parking area.

TRILLIUMS

Trilliums are members of the lily family and are some of the best loved, most easily recognized of all wildflowers. There are three species of trillium native to the forests of Connecticut: large-flowered, painted, and purple.

Large-flowered trillium bears solitary icy-white flowers with overlapping, broad petals from mid- to late spring. It prefers the rich, slightly acid to slightly alkaline soils found atop limestone or marble bedrock. Look for them in open, mature hardwood forests near shrubby thickets or in areas sheltered by rock outcrops.

Purple trillium, also called wake-robin or red trillium, is the most common of the three Connecticut species. It flowers from April to June with solitary burgundy-red blossoms which often gently droop toward the ground. Though the flowers are beautiful to look at, they are less gentle on the nose. The plants are pollinated by flies drawn to the dark red color and rancid aroma of the flowers. Red trillium frequently occurs in colonies and thrives in a wide variety of shady woodlands, from well-drained hardwood forests to shrub-tangled wetlands.

Painted trillium is a delicate show-stopper with narrow-petaled, snow-white flowers splashed with crimson at the center. It prefers mature hardwood forests populated with such trees as beech and oak, whose leaves help keep the soil rich but acidic. It is most frequently found on slightly elevated cobbles or slopes near wetlands.

These flowers are as fragile as they are beautiful and do best when not disturbed. Picking flowers may seem like an innocent endeavor, but that simple act often kills trilliums. Be kind and leave the flowers behind.

Getting There

From Meriden take Interstate 691 toward Middletown. The interstate ends 0.5 mile east of the Meriden/Middlefield town line where the road becomes a two-lane highway and changes designation to Route 66. Follow Route 66 about 0.4 mile to the traffic light at the junction of Routes 66 and 147. Guida's dairy bar is on the left. You can park in the rear of Guida's parking lot and begin the walk by hiking along the purple-blazed trail, which merges with the Mattabesett. Or you can turn around at the traffic light and return west on Route 66. Travel about 0.5 mile west to the beginning of Interstate 691. Immediately after the road becomes a limited-access highway, there is a pull-off to the right. Park here and take the path the short distance to the Mattabesett Trail.

From Middletown take Route 66 to the junction with Route 147. Travel about 0.5 mile west to the beginning of Interstate 691. Immediately after the road becomes a limited-access highway, there is a pull-off to the right. Park here and take the path the short distance to the Mattabesett Trail.

—C.S.

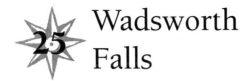

Wadsworth Falls

Middletown and Middlefield

Connecticut has many, many waterfalls to brag about, but some folks undoubtedly will say that if you've seen one waterfall, you've seen them all. Well, those folks are wrong. Wadsworth Falls is not just one waterfall, but two. And not only are there two, but they are completely different. The large falls displays a large volume of water pouring over a shelf of metamorphic bedrock. The smaller falls a short walk away cascades down a long series of sandstone steps. Together they make this walk in Wadsworth Falls State Park very memorable. In addition to the waterfalls, the trail passes wildflowers in spring and the giant laurel, one of the oldest and largest mountain laurels in the state.

This walk is along the Main Trail, blazed with orange marks; the Little Falls Trail, marked in blue; and the White Birch Trail, marked with white blazes. Most junctions on the Main Trail are signed, but junctions on the side trails are not.

Look Forward To

- big and little waterfalls
- the giant laurel
- wildflowers

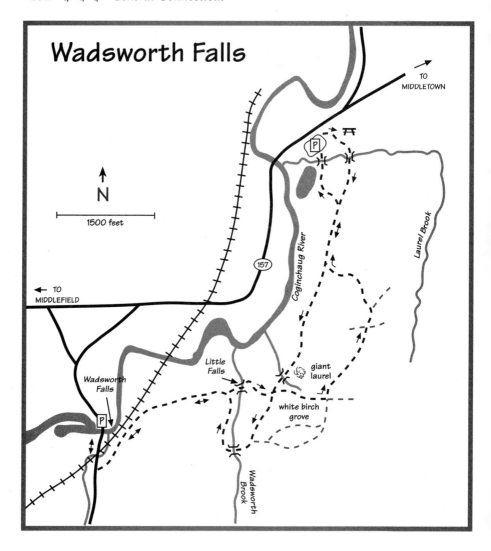

The Trail

To get to the trailhead from the parking area, proceed through the picnic area to the bridge that spans a small brook. The Main Trail, marked with orange, crosses the bridge shaded by hemlock trees and proceeds uphill into woods of birch, ash, apple, red cedar, and cherry, with an understory of burning bush scattered beneath. Leafy squirrel nests are a common sight in the treetops. An access trail that leads to the swimming area and the parking lot enters right a short distance farther.

The trail proceeds through the forest, coming to one of the treasures of Wadsworth Falls State Park, the giant laurel. This exquisite specimen is easily one of the largest of its kind anywhere. In colonial times large mountain laurel were fairly common and the extremely hard, durable wood was used to fashion a number of items, from tool handles to cooking spoons. But laurel grows slowly, very slowly, and once cut down, the massive plants of centuries past were never replaced. The giant laurel here has stems nearly a foot in diameter and a leafy evergreen canopy ten to fifteen feet tall and more than thirty feet wide.

From the giant laurel continue along the woods road, crossing an intermittent stream spanned by a stone bridge. Hemlocks grow along the shallow banks of the stream, shading red trillium in spring. From the bridge the woods become a blend of hardwoods including ash, oak, and beech interspersed with very large hemlock trees, some more than a hundred years old.

The Main Trail then passes the white-blazed White Birch Trail on the left and the blue-blazed Little Falls Trail on the right, descending into a wetland where red trillium, trout lily, and toothwort flower in spring, followed in late spring and summer by the pink blossoms of wild geranium. The spreading branches of beech trees arch overhead, giving the forest an ancient feel.

The trail crests a gentle rise, then descends into a grove of red pine recently killed by red pine blight. The straight, gray-barked skeletons stand in stark contrast to the expanse of green leaves offered by the healthy hemlocks surrounding them. Beyond the red pines, the forest again becomes dominated by hemlock, oak, and birch, with a few large, thick-trunked tulip trees. These beautiful trees grow very fast and straight, with some specimens reaching 100 feet tall. In spring the upper branches bear upright, greenish orange flowers resembling tulips.

The trail heads downhill, crossing a small stream on a wooden bridge. The path then climbs away from the brook, passing the terminus of Little Falls Trail before heading downhill toward Wadsworth Falls. The Main Trail tracks through the woods, following alongside the railroad tracks before ending at the roadway. To reach the falls, turn right onto the road and cross the railroad tracks and the Coginchaug River on a bridge. Reenter the park at a parking area. Cross the large grassy area to a series of stone steps leading down to the shore of the river. From the shore is a wonderful view of Wadsworth Falls pouring through a narrow bedrock gateway. The volume of water that crashes over this escarpment is exhilarating to experience.

From Wadsworth Falls retrace your steps to the terminus of Little Falls Trail. Turn left onto the trail, which almost immediately comes to a sandstone promontory at the top of a steep ridge. Below, Wadsworth Brook traces a slender course over the edge of the ridge, cascading in a lacy tumult down the rocks. The path swings left down the steep ridge to the base of the falls, where the best views of the water can be enjoyed. Unlike the fairly uniform rock of Wadsworth Falls, the sandstone of Little Falls is layered. This layering, called stratification, causes the rock to erode at slightly different rates. The result is a rock face that resembles a staircase, and a waterfall that trips down these stony steps with unmatched grace and beauty.

Graceful rivulets trip down Little Falls.

The trail then crosses Wadsworth Brook, briefly following it as it slides down a run of bare bedrock before turning uphill and away from the stream and its ravine. The path then passes through hemlock and hardwood forest dotted with red trillium, bloodroot, and toothwort, which bloom in early spring. At the end of the trail rejoin the Main Trail for a short way before turning right on White Birch Trail. ·

This path follows the course of an old abandoned road through waves of white birch trees into a wetland with many shrubs and vines, including benzoin bush, multiflora rose, greenbrier, maple-leafed viburnum, burning bush, barberry, and a little poison ivy. Jack-in-the-pulpit is a spring wildflower that grows here.

Continue through the woods to a multiple junction where a red-blazed trail leaves right (south), a yellow-blazed trail continues straight (east), and the White Birch Trail turns left (north). Immediately after turning left the trail forks, with the White Birch Trail following the right fork. The woods here are a mix of many trees including red cedar, maple, white birch, hemlock, and tulip tree. Wildflowers include red trillium and Canada mayflower, with its tiny spikes of white blossoms which smell like lily of the valley.

Many ski trails crisscross the White Birch Trail through here, and it is important to watch for the white blazes to be sure you remain on the correct trail. A green-blazed trail crosses and the White Birch Trail continues northwest. At the next fork turn left, following the white blazes west. After a short walk the White Birch Trail ends at the Main Trail. From here it is a short walk back to the parking area.

JACK-IN-THE-PULPIT

One of the more interesting plants that grow in Connecticut is jack-in-the-pulpit. Also called Indian turnip, jack-in-the-pulpit produces a one-to-two-foot-tall stalk topped by a large, three-part compound leaf which shades the greenish flower. Each blossom is composed of a curved hood (the pulpit) marked with vertical green and black (sometimes brown) stripes. Inside the pulpit, called a spathe by botanists, is a blunt, upright white-to-yellowish spike (jack). The flower spike, or spadix, produces either male or female flowers.

Jack-in-the-pulpits can change their sex from year to year. It takes much more energy to be a female jack-in-the-pulpit than a male. Male plants produce a flower and a bit of pollen and then go on with their lives. Females have to produce a flower, then spend the spring and summer nourishing developing seeds and berries. This is hard work and often weakens the female plants. To build their strength back up, the plants change sex. The result is that a jack-in-the-pulpit that bore male flowers last year may produce female blossoms this year, and vice versa.

A question that surrounds the jack-in-the-pulpit is, Who is Jack? There are several possibilities. Centuries ago the word "Jack" was used to refer to any man. Certain professions used it more than others, and it became common practice for sailors and laborers to refer to each other as Jack. When the word came to America with the English colonists, the word still referred to a man in general, but also became a synonym for the Devil. At first glance it doesn't make much sense to have the Devil in the pulpit, unless it was intended to illustrate good and bad existing in the same place. Which brings us to jack-in-the-pulpit's other name, Indian turnip.

Native Americans used the pulpy root of jack-in-the-pulpit for food. But the roots cannot just be dug up and tossed in the stew pot, for they contain large amounts of calcium oxalate, a chemical that causes, among other things, a severe burning sensation in the mouth. Even boiling doesn't disarm the compound. The roots are edible only if they are first thoroughly dried. So jack-in-the-pulpit was good (it was a source of food during hard times) and bad (if you didn't prepare it correctly, you paid dearly).

Getting There

From Middletown take Route 66 west to the junction of Route 157. Turn left onto Route 157; the park entrance is a few miles farther on the left. From Meriden take I-691 to Route 66 and follow Route 66 to the junction with Route 147. Turn right onto Route 147 and proceed to the junction with Route 157. Turn left onto Route 157 and proceed through the little town of Rockfall. After leaving Rockfall center, the park entrance is a short way down the road on the right.

—C.S.

Bear Rock

26

Durham

- Mattabesett Trail, unblazed snowmobile trail
- 1.1-mile loop
- 120-foot elevation gain
- 0.5–1.0 hour
- easy, with steep sections

There are no bears on Bear Rock. Well, not bears in the traditional sense, but that fact in no way diminishes the magic of the place. This rounded edifice of stone from which nature has carved the image of a bear's head has drawn me for many years. I have gone there in the company of family, and gone with only thoughts to accompany me. At first glance the rock does not seem unique. It is not overly high or difficult to climb, and the animals and vegetation can be found in many places. Yet it is unique in a most pleasing, completely undefinable way.

Bear Rock is in the town of Durham in the Cockaponset State Forest and lies along the Mattabesett Trail. The path is blazed with pale blue marks. Turns are noted by two stacked blazes, with the uppermost blaze offset in the direction of the turn.

Look Forward To

- wildflowers and spring peepers
- Bear Rock
- beautiful views

The Trail

From the pull-off on Harvey Road, near a small pond where spring peepers sing in April, head north uphill into a hardwood forest of oak, beech, and

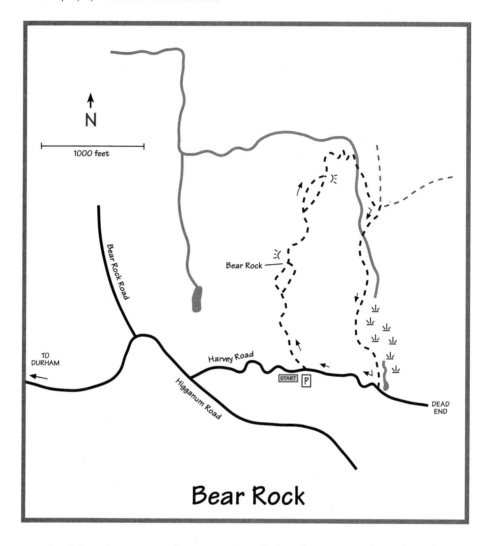

Bear Rock

maple rising above an understory of witch hazel, mountain laurel, and isolated specimens of yellow star grass. Related to amaryllis, yellow star grass forms tufts of narrow, dark green leaves from which rise slender stems topped with beautiful golden yellow six-petaled flowers from spring to summer. If it is not in bloom, chances are you will never notice this little plant. But if you see it in flower, the lovely, delicate beauty of yellow star grass will stay in your memory for a long time.

At the crest of a low hill the trail levels out and passes through a grassy woodland shaded by oaks and sprinkled with tall thickets of mountain laurel and a few wild azalea. In many parts of Connecticut mountain laurel is a shrubby plant which rarely grows above about six feet high. Along this section of the Mattabesett Trail, however, the laurel thrives, the twisted stems interweaving into tangles ten feet high. The path repeatedly slips beneath their canopies of glossy evergreen leaves, forming verdant, magical tunnels.

The trail gradually descends past rocky cobbles where sweetly scented Canada mayflower mingles with wild sarsaparilla, starflower, princess pine, witch hazel, and ground cedar. Soon the tallest and most magical grove of mountain laurel appears. Standing over fifteen feet high, the gnarled trunks look like a miniature medieval forest. In May and June, when the snow-white flowers decorate the tips of the stems, this place is enchantingly beautiful.

From the laurel thicket the trail sweeps through a moist woodland where summersweet grows and crosses a meandering stream. From the brook the path heads uphill through a well-drained woodland of white oak, chestnut oak, red maple, and beech. There are some rugged rock formations to the left and pink lady-slippers blossom here in late spring. Wild geranium and five-leafed cinquefoil flower in early summer along the trail beneath the spreading branches of flowering dogwood, which blossoms in spring.

As the path continues uphill it comes to a ridge where the trail forks. The left (west) branch wanders up the rocky face of Bear Rock. The last section of the ascent is a rocky scramble which will be difficult for some people. The right (north) fork circles around the back of Bear Rock, gaining the top with no steep scrambles. Take either fork to the top of a large, rounded rock formation called Bear Rock. Unlike some overlooks that offer only a limited view for your effort, Bear Rock consists of a large area of open terrain and many places to sit and admire the view. Twisted pitch pine, serviceberry, and bear oak forest the thin, rocky soil, and mountain sandwort blossoms among the wiry woodland grasses.

To the west is the shallow pass called Reed's Gap. To the right are the easily identified grassy slopes of Powder Ridge Ski Area. Between Reed's Gap and Powder Ridge are the distinctive traprock cliffs known as the Hanging Hills. To the far right (north) the skyline of Hartford is visible, while in the valley below lie the picturesque villages of Durham and Middlefield.

If you wonder why Bear Rock is named after an animal that has long since been extirpated from these woods, the answer is in the rock itself. A glance at the large outcrop and a liberal amount of imagination show that the cliff itself has been carved by nature to resemble the head of a bear.

Most people don't venture much beyond this overlook, but Bear Rock extends for a little way more. From the overlook the path rises to a rocky crest where mountain sandwort competes with pale corydalis in the infertile soil. The leaves of pale corydalis are similar to Dutchman's-breeches, but the flower is something all its own. In spring to early summer pale corydalis bears slender, pale-scarlet tubular blossoms marked with a spot of yellow. They are hardy little things, surviving in bright sun or dark shade and thriving in the dry, gravelly soil.

The path continues through patches of huckleberry and blueberry, chokeberry, and wintergreen to an open rock ledge with an easterly view over the tops of a forest of maples and tulip trees. The trail then follows the ledge a short way to another lookout before beginning to descend through lady-slippers, wintergreen, and hemlock.

Follow the trail down the steep slope, weaving through boulders and past a stunning rock formation that juts out over the trail. In spring and after a rain, the rock drips a steady stream of drops on passersby. In winter the trickle of water is transformed into a pillar of ice.

The path leads to a small stream bordered by a narrow wetland. The trail wanders back and forth through the wetland, where trout lily and dwarf ginseng grow. Dwarf ginseng is a bit of a wallflower, no pun intended. It has three glossy green leaves and a small puff of white flowers in April. Its cousin American ginseng has been nearly exterminated from the wild, but, through all the exploitation, dwarf ginseng lives on. If you happen to recognize the plant on your walk, admire it and, please, leave it be.

From the stream the path proceeds past more rock outcrops to the junction with an unmarked snowmobile trail. The Mattabesett continues straight ahead. Turn right onto the snowmobile trail and walk through a beech forest studded with old trees. A stream appears on the right where wetland plants thrive, including skunk cabbage and summersweet. A little farther on, the stream enlarges into a small pond—the peeper pond—where all sorts of water-loving creatures live. Snapping and painted turtles are here, as are great blue herons and mallard ducks. And in spring, from April right into May, the peepers sing from every available spot.

The pond borders Harvey Road. When you reach the road, turn right. The pull-off is only a few yards farther on.

SPRING PEEPERS

Nearly fifty years ago my mother and father built their home on the highlands above the Quinnipiac River in Cheshire. The area was once a farm but had long ago begun to revert to forest. The red cedar and barberry that dominated the pastures had slowly yielded to vast stands of red oak. As I grew up I watched this silent succession of landscapes change the land I thought of as home. Over the years, however, one thing about the place never changed: Each spring, usually in the first weeks of April, the spring peepers would begin to sing from the nearby marsh.

Peepers are really very small frogs that spend most of their life hopping through the woods looking for spiders and ants to eat. I know they are frogs, but there is much about these tiny creatures that seems unreal, making them more like phantoms or ghosts than amphibians. For example, these cold-blooded animals spend the winter under leaves and roots in the woods. They get so cold that their bodies freeze, yet come spring they thaw out and hop down to the nearest swamp to mate. In spring they congregate by the thousands in ponds and marshes, yet once they return to the forests even trained researchers have a difficult time finding them. In a way, they are a lot like happiness itself: easy to recognize but difficult to find.

Each spring I would hear the peepers, but I could never find any. I would try to sneak up on singing frogs, only to have them fall silent and seemingly vanish as well. Every time I searched for them, all I got was wet. One spring evening I convinced my father to don knee-high rubber boots and accompany me to the marsh. I figured there was strength in numbers. He carried the flashlight while I guarded the Mason jar with nail holes punched in the lid.

It took a long time for me to find any peepers careless enough to allow me to approach. Finally, however, I managed to capture one of the little guys and put him in the jar. As the flashlight illuminated his tiny body, I remember being amazed that I was actually looking at the source of such joyous song. I then rather selfishly took the peeper home and placed him on my dresser.

The anticipation was terrible. I lay in my bed with the lights out for hours waiting for the peeper to fill my room with the song of the outdoors. But the song never came. In the morning I realized a wonderfully important lesson: some things, no matter how beautiful, you just can't take home.

That morning I returned the peeper to the marsh and watched him swim away to hide among the sedges. That evening the peepers sang all night long. As I slowly fell into a peaceful sleep, the soprano chorus of hundreds of peepers slipped through my open bedroom window. And the empty Mason jar shone silent in the moonlight.

Getting There

From the junction of Routes 79, 77, and 17 in Durham take Route 79 south and almost immediately turn left onto Higganum Road. Go 1.4 miles to a stop sign at the intersection with Bear Rock Road. Turn right onto Bear Rock Road, then almost immediately left onto Harvey Road. Continue down Harvey Road about 0.3 of a mile to the small pull-off. The pull-off is located near light blue blazes that mark where the trail crosses the road.

—C.S.

Sleeping Giant

Hamden

- Blue Trail, Quinnipiac Trail, Tower Path
- 3.2-mile loop
- 620-foot elevation gain
- 3.0–4.0 hours
- difficult

Look Forward To

- rugged, rocky scrambles

- views and more views

- four-story summit tower

- wildflowers and Indian Rock

The Trail

From the parking area follow the narrow, paved road into the picnic area. As the road begins to swing from northwest to southwest, a blue-blazed trail leaves northwest. Follow the blue blazes around a moderately steep hill cloaked in evergreens to Axel Shop Pond. Turn right and immediately cross a small wooden bridge over a small stream. In a few yards the Blue Trail, now the Quinnipiac Trail, swings left (northwest) and tackles the short but steep climb up the giant's elbow.

Hemlock groves cloak the rocky hillside, along with a few chestnut oak. At the top of the hill the shallow soil yields to extensive patches of basalt, with fine views back over the pond below. From the elbow the trail follows the crest of the ridge through scattered clumps of red cedar, common juniper, oak, and hemlock. This has already been a challenging, pleasant walk, but it is about to become spectacular.

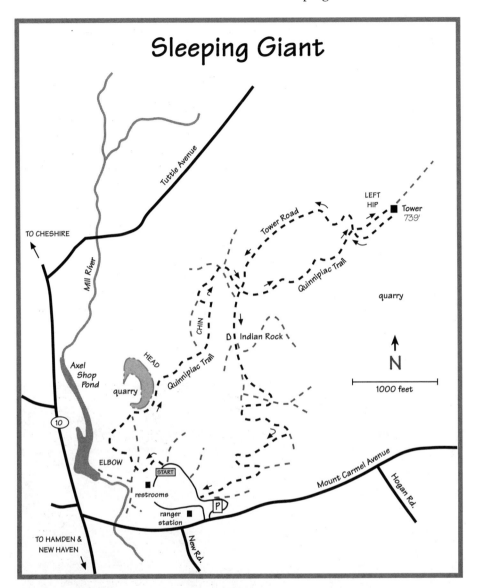

Sleeping Giant

TO CHESHIRE

Tuttle Avenue

Mill River

Tower Road

LEFT
HIP

■ Tower
739'

Quinnipiac Trail

quarry

N

1000 feet

CHIN

D ▮ Indian Rock

HEAD

Quinnipiac Trail

Axel
Shop
Pond

quarry

10

ELBOW

START

Mount Carmel Avenue

Hogan Rd.

restrooms

P

ranger
station

TO HAMDEN &
NEW HAVEN

New Rd.

At a cobble of boulders and bedrock the path makes a very steep descent through ancient faults in the rock to a shallow pass that separates the giant's elbow from the dome of basalt forming the giant's head.

The Quinnipiac Trail crosses the Red Trail in the col from which the massive buttress of Sleeping Giant is now in full view. Take a moment to soak up the scenery, for the trail ahead traverses some of the most difficult, and beautiful, terrain in Connecticut. In fact, the next mile of trail more closely resembles New Hampshire's White Mountains than a typical Connecticut state park.

From the col the footway climbs bare rock up the giant's head, at times coming only a few feet from the cliff and a sheer drop of 300 feet to the abandoned quarry below. Bypass trails swing farther away from the cliff where a few cedars cling to the rock, then rejoin the main trail near the top of the hill. Use caution on this trail, as many people have died or been seriously injured here. The rocks are especially dangerous in winter or when they are wet.

The path climbs over several scrambles before it levels out at the top in an area covered with wild grape vines, red cedar, bluestem grass, and bayberry. Juncos frequently hop among the grasses looking for food, and in summer blue-headed (solitary) vireos can be seen.

The trail wanders across the giant's head, passing numerous craggy overlooks and secretive hideaways in the rock before reaching an area known as the Giant's Chin. The chin is another sheer cliff of basalt which drops away to a bouldered debris field far below. The views from here are mesmerizing, and many hikers have idled away hours in this lovely spot.

Wild grapes grow along the Quinnipiac Trail.

From the chin follow the blue blazes downhill through a hardwood forest sprinkled here and there with mountain laurel. At the base of the slope the path crosses the Red Trail, then the comes to a junction with the Tower Trail in the shadow of the cliffs of the Giant's Chin.

Cross the Tower Trail and follow the blue blazes through rocky woods, passing over many forested cobbles. Follow the blazes carefully, for it is easy to lose the path among the boulders, trees, and laurel. After crossing the Tower Trail again, the footway wanders through deep thickets of laurel before emerging on the rocky scaffold called the Giant's Left Hip, where a four-story stone tower pokes into the sky.

The top of the tower offers a beautiful 360° view which includes the New Haven skyline and Long Island Sound to the south. On clear days the north shore of Long Island can be seen. To the north are the Hanging Hills of Meriden.

From the tower take the Tower Path back to the parking area. This is an enjoyable, easy walk through tall mixed hardwood forests and waves of laurel thickets. In spring there are loads of wildflowers to look for just off the path, especially near the wooded pass in the shadow of the cliffs of the Giant's Chin. Wild ginger, hepatica, and wild geranium are just a few of the flowers to be found here. A few yards farther on, as the path passes beneath the sheer cliffs of the giant's chin, there is a large boulder at the edge of the talus slope. This upright boulder could be mistaken at first glance for one of the grand statues of Easter Island. The stone is easily recognized as the profile of an Indian, with clean line and noble features. It was not carved or altered in any way. It is just there and speaks in its own way of the sacredness of this mountain.

SLEEPING GIANT AND HOBOMOCK

The Europeans who settled the land around this basalt mountain, and the people who now climb its impressive slopes, call it Sleeping Giant. When seen in silhouette from the overlooks of the Hanging Hills, Mount Chauncey, or Mount Higby, there is no mistaking this mountain for any other, for it has the exact full profile of a Sleeping Giant. But when viewed through the lens of those words, the mountain is colored in a European shade. A shade which does not adequately convey the essence of the place.

To feel the true emotion of this mountain you must know it the way the Native Americans who lived here knew it. To them the ridges were not a fairy-tale depiction of an extra-large reclining individual. No, to them the mountain was a living entity. The mountain was Hobomock.

The early colonists understood that the two most powerful spirits in Native American belief were Kichtan and Hobomock. Kichtan, also spelled Kiehtan, they believed was analogous to the Christian God, while Hobomock was seen as similar to the Devil. Convenient, but wrong. The beliefs of the Native Americans around New Haven did not fit into the linear thinking of the colonists, but the colonists just could not grasp the concept.

Hobomock is a spirit with powers far greater than any human or group of humans could possess. Like all things powerful, Hobomock was neither all good nor all bad, but a blend of the two. His power could heal the sick or destroy a village. He could summon earthquakes or bring a gentle rain. In short, Hobomock was a godlike figure, with human frailties. A healer and a destroyer. If you caught him on a bad day, look out.

In ancient times, thousands of years ago, the Native Americans believed the Connecticut River ran close to where the city of New Haven now stands. On one of Hobomock's bad days, he changed the course of the river, diverting it far to the east. Kichtan, who felt that diverting major rivers was stepping over the line of innocent fun, cast a spell over Hobomock, causing him to fall to the ground in a never ending slumber. So far it sounds like everyone is out of danger, but not quite. Remember that Hobomock is just sleeping. Tick him off and he'll wake up.

To keep Hobomock sleeping the people who live around him and climb his body must respect and care for him. If they do not, Hobomock will awaken and wreak catastrophes upon all people.

Some people think that such stories have little value in the modern world. Others—the wiser I think—see things differently. Remember that Hobomock is a transcendent, metaphorical entity. A representation of the light and dark sides of Nature. His lesson is simple: if we choose not to care for the world around us, then we deserve the consequences, regardless of what they are.

Getting There

From the junction of Mount Carmel Avenue and Route 10 (Whitney Avenue) in Hamden, turn onto Mount Carmel Avenue. The park entrance is on the left just past New Road.

—C.S.

28 Hezekiah's Knob and the Chestnut Grove

Hamden

- Violet Trail, Green Trail, Quinnipiac Trail, Horse Path
- 2.8-mile loop
- 500-foot elevation gain
- 2.0–3.0 hours
- moderate

Few places in New England are in the same league as Sleeping Giant State Park. The unique basalt mountain is home to everything from Indian legends to wildflowers to chestnut trees. It is a wonderful place, where each visit reveals something new and different. The walk to Hezekiah's Knob wanders through hardwood forests to a rocky cobble where lovely views await. On the way back, the path takes you to a place like no other in the state: a chestnut grove maintained by scientists from the Connecticut Agricultural Experiment Station at New Haven. The trees in the grove are an integral part of the effort to save the American chestnut from the ravages of the chestnut blight.

The Violet and Green Trails are marked with painted blazes. The Bridal Path is marked with painted U-shaped blazes, and the Quinnipiac Trail is marked with pale blue blazes. Junctions are not signed.

Look Forward To
- views from overlook
- rock outcrops and stone walls
- chestnut grove

The Trail
Near the parking area on Chestnut Road is an information kiosk that marks the junction of a number of trails. Trail maps, courtesy of the Sleeping Giant Park Association, are usually available here. From the kiosk proceed north-

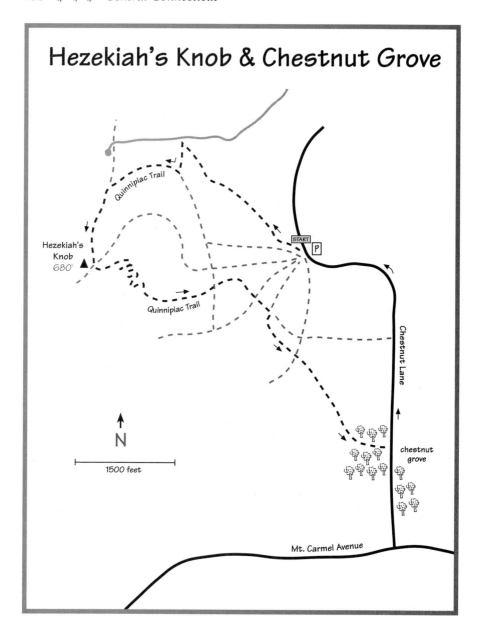

Hezekiah's Knob & Chestnut Grove

Quinnipiac Trail

Hezekiah's
Knob
680'

Quinnipiac Trail

START
P

Chestnut Lane

N

1500 feet

chestnut
grove

Mt. Carmel Avenue

west on the Violet Trail into a hardwood forest of beech, sassafras, maple, birch, red and white oak, and hickory. Near a large red oak the path crosses a stone wall where chipmunks live. Maple-leafed viburnum, a small, three-to-five-foot-high shrub with maple-shaped leaves, thrives in the dark, loamy soil of the forest. In spring maple-leafed viburnum's slender stems are topped with an open cluster of tiny white flowers. In fall the deep-green leaves turn a distinctive shade of reddish violet. Christmas fern and ground cedar also grow here.

As the trail penetrates deeper into the woods the forest becomes a beautiful woodland dominated by large red oaks. Northern red oak has dark gray-brown, richly furrowed bark. In early spring the trees are decorated with four-inch-long pendant tassels lined with tiny flowers. The acorns, which are about an inch long and egg shaped, take two years to mature. After crossing a second stone wall the path swings uphill, passing patches of princess pine, partridgeberry, and more ground cedar.

At a trail junction the Violet Trail turns right and crosses a small stream. Turn left (south) onto an unmarked connector trail. Follow the connector trail a short distance to its junction with the Green Trail. Turn right (north) onto the wide Green Trail, which proceeds gently uphill beside a stone wall before meeting the blue-blazed Quinnipiac Trail in a dense thicket of mountain laurel. Travel this path in late May and early June and it is easy to understand why mountain laurel is the state flower. The brushy evergreen landscape is crowned with tufts of its delicate white or pale blush flowers.

Turn left (south) onto the Quinnipiac Trail and continue uphill through tall woods of oak, maple, and hickory with witch hazel, red cedar, and laurel beneath. This section of the Quinnipiac Trail is an inspiring place, with huge, ten-foot-tall tangles of mountain laurel. The footway easily ascends over alternating bands of bare bedrock and soft earth, soon reaching a jumble of fractured bedrock outcrops. Like a prehistoric fortress dressed in shades of ghostly gray, this area is beautiful and haunting at the same time. The cracked stones are home to small colonies of polypody fern whose small, bright green fronds lend a bit of gaiety to woods. The trail wraps around the rocky cobble, climbing at an easy grade to the summit of Hezekiah's Knob.

Hezekiah's Knob is what New Englanders call a "cobble," a cluster of boulders and bedrock that pokes a bit higher than the surrounding hillside. Its exposed nature makes it a bit breezier than the nearby woods. Ash, hickory, red cedar, chestnut oak, linden, and white pine all crowd atop the knob, but still leave room for a view to the southeast. Small colonies of staghorn sumac produce crops of red berries in fall, and in summer the pliant stems of columbine wave their tiny yellow-and-crimson flowers. Also here is a shrubby tree called bear oak. This plant has leaves that look a bit like oak and a bit like holly. The acorns are small and gave the plant its name. According to tradition, the acorns were so bitter that the only animals that would eat them were black bears. Some people call bear oak, scrub oak, but there is no story in that.

The top of Hezekiah's Knob is crossed by both the Quinnipiac Trail and the White Trail. Stay on the blue-blazed Quinnipiac Trail and descend past isolated specimens of wild rose, with pure pink flowers in summer, to another overlook. From the second viewpoint the path proceeds through picturesque woods marked with stands of oak, pine, and hickory sprinkled here and there with grassy clearings. Soon the trail begins a serious descent of the knob, twisting down the hillside rather steeply. At the bottom of the hill the tall woods of oak, maple, and hickory return. Beneath the trees are small colonies of spotted wintergreen, with narrow evergreen leaves traced with white along the midvein. In spring a slender flower stalk rises, bearing a pair of small, waxy white blossoms which look like miniature street lights.

The Quinnipiac Trail then crosses the Green Trail and then the Orange Trail. To return to the parking area, turn left onto the Orange Trail. To continue to the Chestnut Grove, proceed through the junction with the Orange Trail a few yards farther to the junction with the Bridle Path. Turn right onto the horseback-riding trail, remembering that on this path large

Ground cedar growing on the forest floor.

hoofed animals have the right of way. Follow the path downhill and over a stone wall into a wide and grassy, easy-to-follow cart path which escorts you into the heart of the chestnut grove.

There are few places left in the country where a walk in the woods can lead you to a chestnut grove. This stand was grown by the Connecticut Agricultural Experiment Station for its research into Chestnut blight. The trees that grow here are mostly Chinese and Japanese chestnuts, though there are some interesting hybrids as well. In early summer the trees are decorated with long, pendant, greenish yellow flower clusters which have a sweet but mildly offensive odor. In fall the green burs, which look like sea urchins, gradually turn brown. The first few frosts open the burs, exposing a cache of mahogany-brown nuts. Come in fall when the chestnut burs cover the ground and you can get a small sense of what Connecticut was like a century ago. From the chestnut grove it is a short walk to Chestnut Road. Turn left onto Chestnut Road and walk uphill to the parking area.

SAVING AMERICAN CHESTNUTS

The American chestnut is one of the most majestic trees in the world. Its range stretches from the southern Appalachians to Maine and west through the prairies of Illinois. Before 1900 American chestnut constituted up to a quarter of all the trees in the forest. They grew to stand 100 feet tall and up to 10 feet in diameter. The oldest of these giant, straight-trunked trees were estimated to be more than 600 years old. Their small, sweet nuts were produced in such quantity that everyone who wanted them could harvest all the nuts they needed for roasting, stuffing, and eating, and still leave plenty for wildlife. That was a century ago—it isn't the same now.

In the mid-1800s it became fashionable to purchase and grow Japanese chestnuts in many places of the country. They were grown in New York, New Jersey, California, and Connecticut. What no one knew at the time was that some of these trees came to America infected with a fungal disease later called chestnut blight. It was first recognized in 1904 in New York City, but was probably also present, but unrecognized, in a number of other places along the East Coast at the same time. The blight, to which the Japanese chestnut was resistant, decimated the susceptible American chestnuts. Within 50 years virtually all the groves and forests of American chestnut were dead.

Since the beginning of the epidemic, the Connecticut Agricultural Experiment Station at New Haven has been conducting research to solve the problem and restore the American chestnut to the forests. For many years these scientists, led by Sandra Anagnostakis, have made great strides against the disease. In 1972 a weaker form of the disease, disabled by a virus that ironically infected it, was found in Europe. This weakened disease has made it possible to keep American chestnut trees alive long enough to conduct more-extensive breeding experiments—experiments aimed at instilling resistance in the American species. Today the Connecticut Agricultural Experiment Station has the finest collection of species and hybrid chestnut trees in the world. It is a tribute to the perseverance of the institution and its dedicated personnel.

The chestnut grove near Sleeping Giant State Park is an integral part of the effort to save the American chestnut. It is a very special place. As you stroll through the grove be sure to savor the moment. It is one of the few places in the world where you can still experience a walk beneath the spreading boughs of chestnut trees.

Getting There

From the junction of Mount Carmel Avenue and Route 10 (Whitney Avenue) in Hamden, turn onto Mount Carmel Avenue. Proceed to the entrance of Sleeping Giant State Park and continue down Mount Carmel Avenue another 1.9 miles to Chestnut Road. Turn left onto Chestnut Road and travel 0.8 mile to the trailhead.

—C.S.

29 Coginchaug Cave

Durham

- Mattabesett Trail
- 1.5 miles
- 100-foot elevation gain
- 1.0 hour
- easy, with steep section

The town of Durham is a small country village in a fast-paced world. Visiting here is akin to stepping back in time to another, more nostalgic age. A few minutes from the picturesque town green is a place where you can travel back even further, beyond nostalgic times to an era when Native Americans visited a place called Coginchaug Cave. Along the way you will travel through rocky forests of laurel, blueberry, and wildflowers, making this short stroll a lovely walk indeed.

The walk to Coginchaug Cave is along the Mattabesett Trail, which is marked with pale blue blazes. Turns are noted with two stacked blazes, the uppermost offset in the direction of the turn. The word "Mattabesett" comes from the Algonquin name for the area that is now called Middletown.

Look Forward To

- cliff-side cave
- rocky forests
- wildflowers
- blueberries

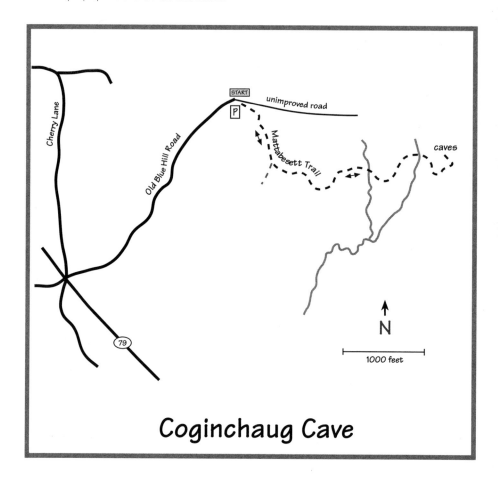

Coginchaug Cave

The Trail

From the parking area at the top of the hill, follow the dirt road about 100 feet to where the trail turns (right) into the woods. Continue through a scenic woodland of yellow and black birch, beech, and sassafras rising above a shrubby understory of witch hazel and sweet pepperbush. Sweet pepperbush, also called Indian soap and summersweet, is recognized by its slender spike of dainty white summertime flowers. The plant prefers the moist, rich soils at the edges of wetlands. When the flowers are rubbed between wet palms, the petals produce a light, white lather.

As the trail wanders south, watch the edges of the path for ground pine and Virginia creeper, two vining plants that intertwine among the glacial boulders and bedrock outcrops. Other plants that live here include polypody fern, which forms colonies atop the rocks, wild azalea, and trailing arbutus. Deer are frequent visitors, but most of the hoof prints here are from passing horses.

In a hardwood forest of hickory, red oak, and scattered clumps of mountain laurel, the bridle path continues straight (south) while the footway turns left (east). Slender stump sprouts of American chestnut mingle with patches of Christmas fern and false Solomon's seal. After passing through beautiful tangles of mountain laurel which provide a striking floral display in late spring, a jumble of boulders appears on the right. The path then swings south, skirting the cobble on the right and a small stream on the left where sensitive fern, skunk cabbage, and sphagnum moss grow. Cross the stream near a large boulder whose west face is covered with a lichen called rock tripe.

From the stream the path heads east and begins to climb up the hill, passing between ragged rock outcrops, before turning north. The footway becomes more rugged for a little way before reaching the ridge crest, a rocky plateau covered with blueberries, thorny vines of greenbrier, and groves of oak.

From the hilltop the path descends to another brook before entering a beautiful landscape of bouldered cobbles shaded by stands of tall, straight hardwoods. The trail twists through this stony labyrinth, gently rising through groves of laurel and past stony ledges. The terrain steepens and the footway passes through a rocky gateway which leads to the crest of another plateau.

Wild azalea, blueberry, serviceberry, and mountain laurel form a thick understory beneath plentiful maples and oaks. An unmarked path leaves left (northeast), terminating at the edge of a steep ledge. The Mattabesett Trail turns right (south) and immediately descends very steeply along the edge of the cliff. The descent is short but very slippery in bad weather. The path follows the contour of the ridge as it descends, soon coming to the massive rock overhang known as Coginchaug Cave.

Coginchaug Cave is a shallow recess carved from the bedrock by thousands of years of erosion. The cave is about twenty feet by twenty feet and provides a dry, fairly comfortable spot to linger and relax. The mouth of the cave faces a small drainage forested with ash, oak, yellow birch, and beech. As you sit here surrounded by walls of cold, gray rock, remember that this sanctuary has been used by people for thousands of years. Native Americans came here centuries ago, their artifacts still occasionally discovered in the dry, compact soil.

Pinkster azalea in flower along the Mattabesett Trail.

This place is special not only for its past, but for its present. From the cave you can watch and hear many types of songbirds in the spring and summer, including warblers, thrushes, veeries, and vireos. The birds are especially fond of the shrubby tangles along the stream.

To return to the trailhead, simply retrace your steps.

MOUNTAIN LAUREL

Every elementary school student in Connecticut learns early on that mountain laurel is the state flower. All too often the lesson stops there and the subtle wonders of this beautiful shrub remain unknown to many people.

Mountain laurel belongs to a genus of plants named *Kalmia* in honor of Peter Kalm, a Swedish botanist who came to North America for a brief time before the Revolutionary War. Although the plant is named for him, he didn't discover mountain laurel. The plant was known for centuries to Native Americans and was introduced into European horticulture in 1734, fourteen years before Kalm ever got here.

Mountain laurel is a plant of open woods and thrives beneath the canopies of deciduous trees such as oak, birch, and beech. It needs a well-drained, acidic soil with lots of organic matter, such as leaf mold, to grow best. In the dappled forest shade the emerald-colored evergreen leaves and irregular, twisted stems are welcome sights along any walk. It is spring, however, when the bushes display their enchantingly beautiful flowers, that the majesty of mountain laurel is most apparent. In May or early June clusters of rose-red buds atop the branches open to reveal snow-white, cup-shaped flowers. The inside of each blossom is marked with ten tiny red dots. These dots mark small recessed areas which hold the anther, the pollen-bearing portion of the flower, in place as the blossom unfurls. As the flower opens it puts tension on the filament, the thin, threadlike structure that connects the anther and the base of the flower. When a bee comes to the blossom it bumps the filament, which then releases like a taut bow-string. The anther pops out of its little pocket and dusts the visiting bee with pollen. The bee, completely oblivious to this neat display, gathers the nectar and flies off to another flower, where some of the pollen from the first flower is left behind.

Mountain laurel is native to a broad region of the eastern United States, from New England west to the Mississippi Valley and south to the Gulf and Atlantic coasts. The leaves and flowers are poisonous if eaten and should be kept away from children and overly curious adults. In Connecticut during colonial times, mountain laurel was called spoonwood because the very dense, hard wood made long-lasting cooking spoons.

Spoons and bees not withstanding, the most loved aspect of mountain laurel is its stunning spring floral display. In spring be sure to seek out walks that pass through especially thick stands of laurel. The masses of blossoms turn the evergreen thickets into ethereal, flowery clouds you will not soon forget.

Getting There

From the junction of Routes 79, 77, and 17 in Durham take Route 79 south 0.9 mile to Old Blue Hill Road. Turn left onto Old Blue Hill Road and proceed 0.7 mile. Park along the side of the road.

—C.S.

 # Bluff Head

North Guilford

- Mattabesett Trail, Mattabesett Loop Trail
- 1.8-mile loop
- 430-foot elevation gain
- 1.0–2.0 hours
- easy, with some steep sections

Bluff Head is the name of a steep traprock ridge that makes up the eastern slope of Totoket Mountain. From the valley below the sharp, wooded profile of the bluff is an imposing feature, like a ruined medieval castle given back to the forest. From a distance it seems unassailable. But Bluff Head is not as guarded as its outward features suggest. The trail up its flank is steep but manageable, and leads to beautiful views of southern Connecticut. The path skirts the edge of the cliffs for much of the way, the fragile precipice sheltering an impressive array of spring wildflowers. The return trip is even gentler, circling around the steep sections and passing through attractive woodlands dotted with more wildflowers.

The walk over the Bluff Head section of Totoket Mountain is along the Mattabesett Trail, blazed in pale blue, and the Mattabesett Loop Trail, marked with pale blue blazes surrounding a central orange dot. Bluff Head is protected and managed by the Guilford Land Conservation Trust.

Look Forward To

- rugged, rocky scrambles
- views and more views
- four-story summit tower
- wildflowers and Indian Rock

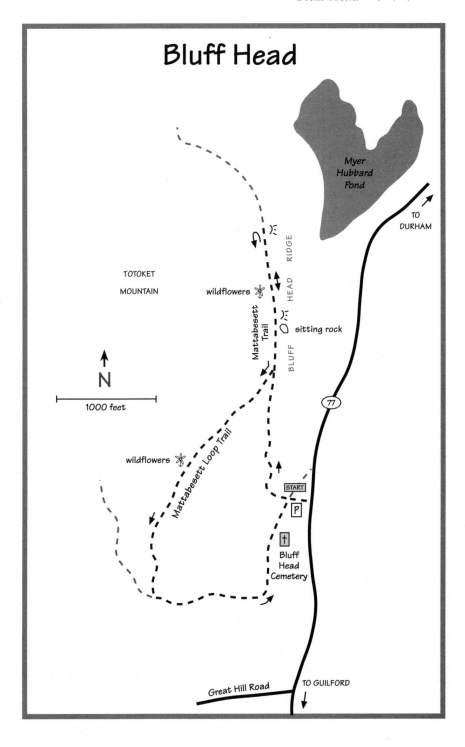

Bluff Head

Myer Hubbard Pond

TO DURHAM

TOTOKET MOUNTAIN

wildflowers ✳

HEAD RIDGE

Mattabesett Trail

sitting rock

BLUFF

N

1000 feet

Mattabesett Loop Trail

wildflowers ✳

77

START

P

Bluff Head Cemetery

Great Hill Road

TO GUILFORD

The Trail

Just southwest of the parking area on Route 77 the blue-blazed Mattabesett Trail intersects with the orange dot blazes of the Mattabesett Loop Trail. Turn right (west), following the blue-blazed Mattabesett Trail as it immediately begins to scale the steep eastern slope of Totoket Mountain. The path is shaded with tall trees of ash, maple, and white pine, with an occasional understory of benzoin bush. Evergreen Christmas fern and spotted wintergreen mingle with wild geranium on the forest floor. The steep, heavy-duty walking doesn't last very long, and the grade soon begins to moderate. The woods change as you climb closer to the top of the ridge, with beech, hop hornbeam, and hornbeam becoming more noticeable among the white, red, and chestnut oaks which predominate. Beneath the trees grow blueberry and a charming wildflower called pipsissewa. When not in bloom, pipsissewa can be recognized by its long, glossy evergreen leaves. In midsummer the plants bear small, pinkish white waxy flowers. Spotted wintergreen and pipsissewa are close relatives with similar-looking flowers, but spotted wintergreen has dark reddish green leaves marked in the center with a streak of white, while pipsissewa's leaves are solid green.

The trail hugs the edge of the cliffs as it continues uphill with peek-aboo views appearing through the trees. A small tree called serviceberry, or shadblow, thrives in the thin, rocky soil of the cliff edge. Serviceberry's delicate white flowers cover its slender branches in April. After a short, steep climb the path reaches an overlook at the junction with the Mattabesett Loop Trail, which enters left. Red cedar is the evergreen that clings to the rocks, and turkey vultures often soar on the breezes over the valley.

From the overlook continue north along the Mattabesett Trail. The path is wide and easy to follow as it skirts the edge of the ridge. A little farther on, the woods become dominated by beech trees which shelter thin clusters of mountain laurel. From the edge of the bluff Myer Hubbard Pond comes into view to the northeast. After passing a boulder on the left, which is a nice sitting rock if you are tired, there is a stretch of cliff that is home to a vast number of interesting wildflowers. Clumps of lyre-leaved rock cress and early saxifrage grow directly from cracks and crevices in the cliff face. Lyre-leaved rock cress has dainty white, four-petaled, sweetly scented flowers. Early saxifrage has short, very stout stems above a rosette of fleshy green leaves. The fragrant flowers are small and white with five petals. Along with the wildflowers are nice views to the east, toward Mica ledge. More wildflowers await the observant spring walker, including hepatica, with white or pink flowers, and Dutchman's-breeches with dangling white, pantaloon-shaped blossoms. Adding to the beauty are isolated specimens

Serviceberry clings to basalt cliffs at Bluff Head.

of flowering dogwood, with white-petaled (correctly called bracts) flowers in late April or May.

The trail then climbs a short steep section to a flat plateau and a lovely overlook. From here the waters of Myer Hubbard Pond are directly below. To the east is Mica ledge, while to the southeast are the bluffs called Broomstick ledges. Far to the south the waters of Long Island Sound are visible. Staghorn sumac, wild cherry, oaks, and wild strawberry all grow around the traprock outcrops. Garter snakes also like it up here, preferring the grassy areas away from the cliffs.

From the overlook turn back along the Mattabesett Trail and retrace your steps to the junction of the Mattabesett Loop Trail. Turn right onto the Mattabesett Loop Trail (blazed with orange dots). The trail heads west, then swings southwest through wide, open woods of hickory, oak, and maple. Many of the trees here are double or triple trunked. These trees arose from stumps left behind after the area was logged a few decades ago. As the path gently descends there are occasional clumps of hepatica and trout-lily flowers in spring, and the *thump, thump* of woodpeckers looking for food. In fall the squirrels are busy gathering nuts.

At a junction with an old road is a sign for the Loop Trail and mileages. Turn left along the dirt road, where the daisylike flowers of bloodroot blossom in spring. Wild onion also grows here, with cylindrical green leaves and a potent, oniony-tasting small white bulb. Continue along the trail, passing wet areas where benzoin bush grows and coming to the Bluff Head cemetery on the right. The parking area is a hundred yards or so beyond the cemetery.

ANTS IN YOUR PLANTS

In spring the woodland trails of Connecticut are often lined with clumps of blue, yellow, or white violets; painted and red trilliums; spring beauty; hepatica; and the pure-white, daisylike blossoms of bloodroot. Many times these clusters of flowers are near no others of their kind. They just appear here and there with no seeming pattern or sequence. Well, believe it or not, there are people who think about things like why flowers appear where they do. And after investigating this particular question, they have discovered some interesting things.

The seeds of plants get dispersed through many ingenious ways. In fall chipmunks stuff their faces full of maple and pine seeds, then bury their bounty in shallow holes in the ground called caches. They make so many of them that during the winter they forget where some of them are. In spring these seeds germinate and clumps of little trees poke out of the loamy forest soil. Other plants, such as greenbrier and bittersweet, rely on birds to disseminate their seeds. The birds eat the fruit and the seeds pass through their digestive tracts, to be deposited later on fertile soil and newly washed cars.

Springtime wildflowers have developed a way to spread their seeds around as well, and it is wonderfully original: Wildflowers rely on ants.

Wildflowers such as violets, spring beauty, trilliums, bloodroot, and hepatica produce very small seeds. Each of these seeds is coated with a substance ants find absolutely irresistible. Once attracted to the seeds, the ants carry them off to their colony, where the tasty outer portion of the seed is happily nibbled away. The seed is then unceremoniously dumped in the ant trash pile out behind the ant hill. These little trash dumps are just about the perfect place for a young wildflower to start life—better than the sweetest compost pile.

This type of relationship, where both species benefit, is called mutualism. Recently some scientists at Kenyon College in Gambier, Ohio, thought they would investigate the mutualism of ants and wildflowers more closely. As it turns out, the ants get more from the wildflowers than just a light lunch. Ant colonies that nibbled on wildflower seeds produced more than three times as many reproductive females as ant colonies that didn't eat wildflower seeds. So everyone involved benefits. The wildflowers get their seeds planted and off to a good start, and the ants get a gourmet treat and a stronger colony.

Getting There

From Durham center travel south on Route 17 to the junction of Routes 17 and 79. Stay on Route 17 and proceed south the short distance to the junction of Route 77. Turn left onto Route 77 and travel south 4.2 miles to the parking area on the right. From Guilford take Route 77 north and pass under Interstate 95 at Exit 58. From I-95 proceed north on Route 77 9.0 miles to the parking area on the left.

—C.S.

West Woods

Guilford

- White Trail, Green Trail, Blue Trail
- 3.3-mile loop
- 120-foot elevation gain
- 2.0–3.0 hours
- moderate, with some steep sections

West Woods is a wonderful surprise, in part for the array of natural wonders within its borders, and in part for its even being there. This sanctuary is along the south central shore, where tidy towns and homes have dominated the landscape for generations. Along the way to progress, however, people with foresight made room for West Woods, a 1,000-acre preserve of rocky granite outcrops and oak and hemlock forests. This walk travels along a scenic marshland; through a fairy-tale maze of seemingly endless rock formations; past the giant hemlock, whose story of endurance has a sad ending; and finally over a long boardwalk that bisects a marsh. It is great fun.

The system of trails at West Woods is daunting to the uninitiated, but it is actually easy to figure out. All north-south trails are marked with circle-shaped blazes. Other hiking trails, marked with square or triangular blazes, weave back and forth across the circle-blazed trails. A square-blazed trail and its connecting circle-blazed trail are always marked with the same color. Last are crossover trails, which connect trails of different colors. These are marked by crosses in the color of the circle trail they lead to.

Look Forward To

- fantastic rock formations
- the giant hemlock

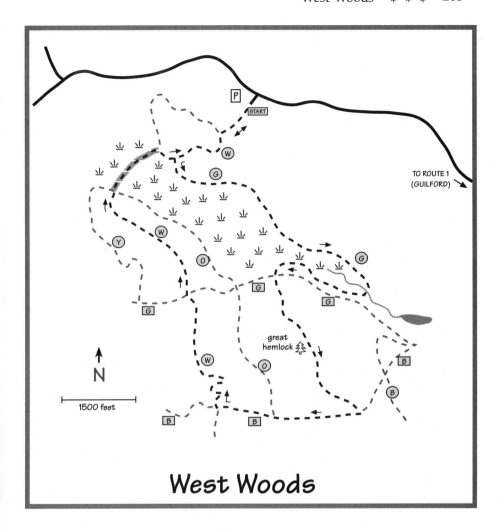

West Woods

• boardwalk through marsh

The Trail

From the parking area follow the path through a small wooded area into a
scrubby field where wild onion, daylily, wild rose, staghorn sumac, red
cedar, and honeysuckle grow. At the far end of the field reenter the woods
and skirt a rocky cobble covered with brambles and greenbrier. The path
heads downhill to the junction of the White Trail and the Green Trail. Turn
left onto the Green Trail and continue downhill toward the marsh. The forest here is typical of the woods that grow atop the metamorphic bedrock

found in central and eastern Connecticut. Types of red oak dominate, with shagbark hickory, maple, ash, beech, and birch also mixed in. At the shore of the marsh the trail swings to follow along its perimeter, winding through heavily bouldered woods. In the marsh grows a collection of common wetland plants, including marsh marigold, skunk cabbage, and a woody shrub called summersweet.

The path leaves the edge of the swamp to wander briefly along a bedrock outcrop, then drops back down to the marsh. In early spring the coarse but melodic song of red-winged blackbirds emanates from the wetland. The clear whistle of cardinals is also heard, as are chickadees and a variety of other songbirds. The trail passes through another very rocky stretch before crossing a small stream on steppingstones. Leaving the marsh yet again, proceed uphill into plentiful clusters of mountain laurel sheltered by high trees before heading downhill to a stone wall just above the swamp. Turn left along the stone wall. This is a lovely stretch of trail, with the marsh to the right and large boulders and impressive ridges of gray bedrock to the left. At the eastern end of the wetland, the marsh has been transformed into a small stream with defined banks and cool water the color of English tea. The brown color of the water comes in part from tannic acid, a natural byproduct of the trees, mosses, and other plants that grow in the swamp. After crossing the brook on a small log bridge, the path follows the brook upstream, weaving through a beautiful laurel thicket shaded by very large, hundred-year-old white pines.

The Green Trail, marked with green circles, is crossed here and there by paths blazed with green triangles. Follow the green circles up a short but steep rise and cross another hiking trail blazed with silver marks. Continue straight ahead, climbing a short, steep rise and entering a cool hemlock grove studded with weathered bedrock outcrops and boulders. Some of the rock formations here are spectacular, and you could spend many minutes wandering off the trail to explore them. A short way farther on, the healthy hemlocks yield to a large area of dead hemlock trees. Near the center of this area are the remains of the great hemlock, a massive tree which was 200 years old before its death in the late 1990s. The trees here, including the great hemlock, were killed by a small insect called the woolly adelgid. This aphidlike bug kills hemlocks by feeding on the trees. It doesn't usually kill the tree, but does weaken it enough to allow diseases or other pests easier access. Before 1985 the woolly adelgid was unknown in Connecticut but was found on Long Island. When Hurricane Gloria swept up the East Coast that year, her winds carried the insects across Long Island Sound to Connecticut.

Marsh marigold grow beside the boardwalk through the swamp on the White Trail.

From the great hemlock pass through a bouldered area, with some boulders as large as automobiles. Some of the stones here shelter small boulder caves. The trail climbs atop a bedrock ridge passing more spectacular boulders and rock formations. Leaving the ridge, the path passes over a rise and comes to the junction with a yellow trail marked with triangles and the Blue Trail marked with rectangles. Turn right (west), following a wide woods road that winds gently downhill to a tea-colored stream. Cross the brook on a wooden bridge and pass the intersections of an orange-blazed trail marked with squares followed shortly by an orange-blazed trail marked with circles.

Continue along the woods road to a junction with the White Trail (marked with circles). Turn right onto the White Trail and almost immediately enter a labyrinth of granite bedrock and boulders, hemlock, and mountain laurel. The path continues uphill, weaving through the rocky landscape shaded by hemlock and mountain laurel. This is a beautiful, if a bit rugged, stretch and worth the effort.

At the top of the ridge the trail passes over a length of bare rock studded with the skeletons of dead hemlocks. It then swings downhill into a rock-lined canyon called the natural monument. This area is like an enormous sculpture, with some parts of the cliff weathered into soft, rounded forms and other sections fractured into angled blocks. From the natural monument the White Trail proceeds through a mixed hardwood and hemlock forest, passing more rock formations along the way.

At the trail junction marked 22, where the path blazed with green squares crosses, continue straight, climbing to the crest of a hill marked by an extensive bald area composed of bare bedrock. This area is beautiful in every season of the year. Many people rest here, stretching out on the sunny rocks to idle away a few minutes. The bedrock continues gently uphill for about 200 yards. From the bald area descend into thickets of laurel before quickly coming to another, smaller bald area with limited views over the woods to the west. From the vista head downhill through laurel, passing a large rock outcrop on the right. The path crosses the Yellow Trail and comes to the beginning of a very long boardwalk which bridges a shallow, forested marsh.

The stroll over the narrow boardwalk is fun any time of year. Benzoin bush lights the wetlands with bright yellow-green flowers in very early spring, along with the shell-shaped blossoms of skunk cabbage. Later in the season the vivid yellow blossoms of marsh marigold bloom, followed weeks later by wild iris. Highbush blueberry grows here, with small, sweet fruit in summer. Ruffed grouse can be found on the drier sections, their drumbeat mating call a familiar sound in April. In fall yellow, red, and orange leaves float on the dark water as waterfowl fly overhead.

From the boardwalk it is a short walk along the White Trail back to the parking area.

TREETOPS

The rough terrain of rock outcrops, ravines, and wetlands that makes up West Woods is ideal habitat for tall oak trees. These trees can grow eighty feet tall with a canopy that spreads more than forty feet. As you walk the trails, the easiest thing to notice about these oaks is the wide diameter of their trunks and their rough, fissured bark. Less easy to discern is all the activity occuring high over your head.

In April, when the winter cold has retreated, the new leaves begin to emerge. At this same time the eggs of a number of species of moths begin to hatch. The larvae of these moths are called inchworms. These little guys are hungry right from the start and begin to eat the oak leaves. At the same time, however, warblers, vireos, and other migrant songbirds appear in the tops of the oak trees. The nexus of these three events is beautifully inter-related. The oak leaves appear in response to the changing seasons, the inchworms hatch when the nutrient-rich leaves are still soft and tasty, and the songbirds appear at the tail end of a six-week, thousand-mile journey north, in need of lots of easy-to-catch food.

The songbirds hop through the branches, eating hundreds of inch-worms each day. On years when the inchworm hatch is large, the branch-es can be quite crowded with many species of birds. As spring wears on and nesting begins, the tops of the trees are still full of life. In a typical spring and summer every 1,000 square feet of treetop environment supports about 100 nesting pairs of birds, well over half being migrant songbirds. In addi-tion to birds, the canopy is also a highway for many animals, including gray and flying squirrels. Even raccoons and chipmunks climb up once in a while. In short, the canopy above you is one of the richest, most diverse habitats in the state. Enjoy the view.

Getting There

From Exit 58 of Interstate 95 take Route 77 south toward Guilford to Route 1. Turn right onto Route 1. Proceed 0.7 mile to Peddlar's Lane. Turn left onto Peddlar's Lane and drive 1.1 miles to parking area on the left just past Den-nison Road.

—C.S.

 # Lost Lake

Guilford

- **White Trail, Orange Crossover Trail, Orange Trail**
- 1.5-mile loop
- **40-foot elevation gain**
- 0.5–1.0 hours
- easy

Lost Lake is a large, brackish pond which years ago was cut off from Great Harbor just to the south by railroad and highway bankings. Since then it cannot lay claim to being a part of Long Island Sound, or to being a freshwater lake. It is something unique, and its special nature is a boon to those who visit it. From the trails that creep along the shore, hikers can routinely view a number of water and wading birds, including great blue herons and egrets. In addition to the wealth of bird life, there are mysterious carvings in the bedrock and lovely walks through thickets of mountain laurel.

The walk to Lost Lake is part of the large, 1,000-acre reserve called West Woods. This natural area is webbed with a trail system that needs some explanation before people go off and explore. Here is a basic primer: All north-south trails are marked with circle-shaped blazes. Hiker-only trails, marked with square blazes, weave back and forth across the circle-blazed trails. A square-blazed trail and its accompanying circle-blazed trail are always marked with the same color. Lastly are crossover trails, which connect trails of different colors. These are marked by crosses in the color of the circle trail they lead to.

Look Forward To

- Lost Lake

- water and wading birds

- rock carvings

210

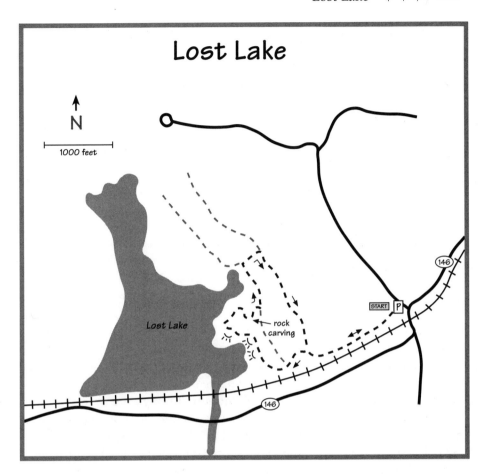

The Trail

From the parking area follow the White Trail into woods lined with thorny greenbrier and fragrant honeysuckle. The path parallels the railroad tracks and soon crosses a small wet area in a shallow swale. Climbing on a gradual grade with good footing, the junction of the White Trail and the Orange Trail is reached. Proceed straight on the White Trail a few yards to a second junction where the White Circle Trail swings right and the White Square Trail goes left. Follow the white squares down a slight grade to a massive stone outcrop with numerous boulders gathered near its base. Clusters of mountain laurel bloom here in May and June beneath the spreading branches of black birch.

From the rock outcrop the path heads downhill briefly before turning to follow a low ridge of bedrock. There are different ways to go from here, and old blazes mingling with newer ones make the treadway a bit difficult to follow. The path turns left, away from the bedrock ridge and toward a jumble of boulders near the shore of Lost Lake. The blazes lead you through a maze of large boulders and bedrock shaded by low-growing trees. Here rocky platforms reach like fingers out toward the shore, offering private views of Lost Lake. For the next 200 yards the trail skirts the shore with wide, beautiful views from a few selected rock outcrops. On quiet days it is pleasant to sit on the rocks and observe the many different birds that come to feed in the shallows.

The railroad tracks form the very straight southern boundary of the lake. Along this shoreline grow a mix of grasses, sedges, and other wetland plants. Many waterfowl and wading birds come here to feed, including Canada geese, mute swans, a wide variety of ducks, great blue herons, and great and snowy egrets. Great blue herons are very large birds, standing well over four feet tall with wingspans of five feet. They hunt frogs and fish along the edges of the lake by standing motionless for many minutes at a time, waiting for lunch to come closer. They stand so still that people often do not notice them until they leisurely fly off. Snowy egrets are smaller than great blue herons, reaching about two and a half feet tall with a wingspan of three feet. Their plumage is pure white, which contrasts with their black bills. Snowy egrets often congregate in small groups in the shallows, where they run after schools of minnows through the water. You can sometimes observe these groups from this section of shoreline, but you must be quiet and still or they will fly off to a less noisy section of the lake. So many species of birds come to the shore and waters of the lake that each trip holds the potential for viewing the extraordinary.

Follow the white blazes as they guide you along the shoreline through blueberry, greenbrier, and serviceberry. The rocks along the shore often hold clusters of mussel shells, trash piles left behind by seabirds dining on the tender shellfish. Here and there along the way the path slips down to the bouldered shore, where wide, beautiful views of the lake await. The rocks here are covered with large, blackish green lichens called rock tripe. These plants, part fungus and part alga, get most of their nutrients directly from the rock and do not need soil or much water to thrive.

The path climbs over bedrock and around boulders to a large outcrop of gray granite. Chiseled into a protruding section of the rock are molding patterns of the type used to decorate marble columns and stone buildings. Nearby the bedrock is punctuated with numerous punch marks. It is like bumping into a stonemason's doodle pad. But the mysterious isn't over yet, for a few feet farther on is another stone, this one nearly at ground level, which has been carved into a drinking trough.

Follow the trail downhill to where it rejoins the White Circle Trail in a wet area thick with laurel and tall oaks overhead. The path continues north through a dense jungle of evergreen laurel that often not only lines the trail but arches over it, forming a leafy tunnel. Just to the right is another impressive granite cliff which runs parallel to the trail.

In a wetland by a stream the Orange Crossover Trail leaves right. Turn onto the trail, which follows a lazy stream to the Orange Circle Trail. Turn right (southeast) onto the Orange Circle Trail. The woods are comprised of tall oaks, whose canopies amplify the sound of the wind as it blows in off the Long Island Sound. In June the pale white-and-pink flowers of mountain laurel are beautiful against the profiles of the many boulders and outcrops passed along the way.

The path continues south through stands of chestnut and red oak and waves of laurel. At the junction with the White Circle Trail, turn left and follow the White Circle Trail the short distance back to the parking area.

TRAILS

"The surface of the earth is soft and impressible by the feet of men," wrote Henry David Thoreau, "and so with the paths which the mind travels. How worn and dusty, then, must be the highways of the world, how deep the ruts of tradition and conformity. It is remarkable how easily and insensibly we fall into a particular route, and make a beaten path for ourselves."

Thoreau saw trails, whether through the woods or in ourselves, as habits that galvanize the mind and soul, turning them hard and thoughtless. It is easy to see paths that way, as things that cut through the seemingly unneeded and superfluous and make life more efficient. You see this attitude in many who walk through the woods—people who do not leave the outside world behind as they enter the forest, but bring their troubles and noise and lack of respect with them. What these people learn from their walks can be gleaned just as well from a stroll down a paved street or a visit to the mall.

It is true that the woodland trails we walk are substantive, defined things which lead from point to point. It is easy enough to see a trail as a way to get from point A to point B. Anyone can do that. But a path is much more, and, as the ancients said, the value of a journey is to be found not in its destination but in the journey itself. Today the trail is the avenue most used to journey through and to the world of nature.

In the fall of 1847 Henry David Thoreau left the shores of Walden Pond. "I left the woods for as good a reason as I went there," he wrote. He left to continue his life's journey in other places, having harvested from Walden lessons he would carry with him wherever he went. The woods had taught him that when mankind "simplifies his life, the laws of the universe will appear less complex, and solitude will not be solitude, nor poverty poverty, nor weakness weakness. If you have built castles in the air," he wrote, "your work need not be lost; that is where they should be. Now put the foundations under them." Come to the woods for as good a reason as Thoreau left them behind.

Trails are what we make of them. They can be ways to inject our world into nature, or entryways to nature's truths. It is our choice, and we make it each time we take a walk. As Thoreau wrote at the close of *Walden*, "Only that day dawns to which we are awake."

Getting There

From the center of Guilford take Route 146 east. Proceed east with the railroad tracks paralleling the road on the left for 1.3 miles. Just before Route 146 swings under the railroad tracks is an intersection on the right where Sam Hill Road intersects Route 146. Turn right; the small parking area is directly ahead and is so close to the intersection it seems a part of it.

—C.S.

Eastern Connecticut

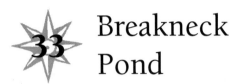

33 Breakneck Pond

Union

- East Ridge Trail, West Pond View Trail, Nipmuck Trail
- 6.7 miles
- 100-foot elevation gain
- 4.0–4.5 hours
- moderate due to length, with one difficult stretch

Breakneck Pond is a narrow, 1.6-mile-long body of water lying between two schist and gneiss ridges. The north end of the pond extends into Massachusetts. The advance of glacial ice widened and deepened the stream valleys that had existed previously in this far northeastern corner of Tolland County.

This is a region defined by alternating north-south-trending ridges and wetland systems. Numerous ponds, brooks, marshes, and swamps and even a few bogs are located in the hollows. Breakneck Brook flows northward from the pond to join the Quinnebaug River between Sturbridge and Southbridge, Massachusetts.

It is relatively wild, rocky country superbly suited to exploration on foot and by canoe. This walk originates in Bigelow Hollow State Park just south of Mashapaug Pond but then wends northward through portions of the 8,000-acre Nipmuck State Forest for most of its nearly seven miles. For most of that distance the trail follows along the laurel- and azalea-studded shores of Breakneck Pond, where interesting plant communities, including Atlantic white cedar and carnivorous sundews and pitcher plants, flourish.

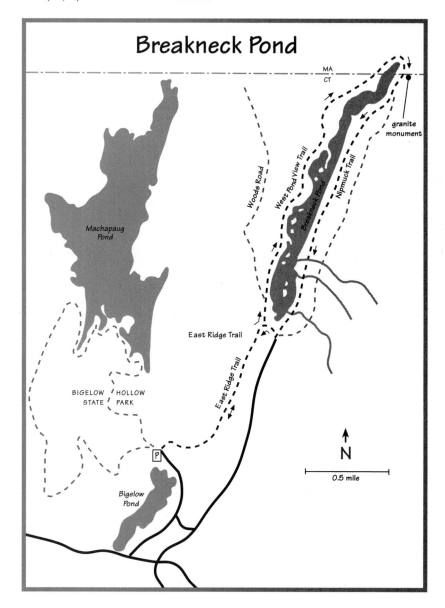

Although portions of the trail can be difficult to locate, the fine views of the pond from various compass directions and the luxuriant laurel blooms in early summer more than make up for the inconvenience of difficult-to-follow trails. With a little care, this relatively lengthy hike in a setting with a bit of a wilderness atmosphere will be a very enjoyable experience.

Look Forward To

- beautiful pond views

- interesting bog plants

- gorgeous mountain laurel

- diverse bird life

The Trail

Cross the paved park road and walk up a gravel bank to the trailhead, where a map is located. The trail options are well marked at a Y intersection from which you should walk right, onto the white-blazed East Ridge Trail. The southern end of Breakneck Pond is 1.1 miles distant. Walk under large white pine, eastern hemlock, black birch, and mountain laurel. Bracken fern does well in the sandy glacial soils. Soon enter a gravelly clearing that is regenerating to small white pine. On an early-summer visit my wife, Chris, and I found a handsome ringneck snake under a board in the clearing. These small serpents with orange bellies are harmless to humans and consume mostly insects. A tote road comes in from the right.

Enter shaded forest of hemlock, oak, and birch on a wide, pleasant roadway. Pass a small red maple swamp and cross a little stream. Male black damselflies with electric-blue abdomens flutter about the brook, and whorled loosestrife blooms yellow in summer. Reenter a hemlock stand (many young specimens line the roadway) and pass by a borrow pit situated on the right. Reach a Y intersection and follow the white rectangular blazes left. Note the near total absence of vegetation in the deep shade beneath the hemlock, but the wonderful aroma of needles permeates the air. Cross a railroad-tie bridge over a small brook. To your right is a small swamp thick with cinnamon fern, marsh marigold (actually a buttercup), and sphagnum moss. Green frogs call this home and tiny brown winter wrens frequent the forest as well.

Reenter hemlocks. Red and white oak and a few gray birch and American beech are also here, but the dominant tree is hemlock. Wintergreen, New York fern, starflower, striped wintergreen, and Indian cucumber-root grow along the roadway. The last blooms in early summer, and its small tubers were eaten by Native American peoples. The terrain rises gradually to the left; schist outcrops and boulders punctuate the slope. The summer woodland is alive with bird song as red-eyed vireo, ovenbird, black-throated green warbler, black-and-white warbler, and veery join the chorus. In June mountain laurel shrubs are bedecked with masses of white blossoms—the state flower of Connecticut. Massachusetts's state flower, trailing arbutus (a.k.a. mayflower), blooms in spring a little bit farther along the trail. It is tiny and rather inconspicuous in comparison to mountain laurel.

Reach a wetland about 200 feet left of the elevated old roadway and pass through former gateposts. At a Y trail split, stay left and come to a T intersection almost immediately at a shrub swamp. Shallow-rooted hemlocks along the wetland's edge have toppled into the swamp, where royal and cinnamon ferns and sphagnum moss flourish. Turn left to follow the West Pond View Trail, which is blazed blue with a white dot in the center. It is a walk of 4.4 miles around Breakneck Pond from here. Some trees show cutting by beaver. Shortly come to the narrow, orange-blazed Pond View Trail on the right, which skirts the water's edge. Walk among fragrant white pine and through blooming laurel in June and early July. Some hemlock have been girdled by beavers.

Walk gently uphill, turn right, and swing left under more laurel shrubs, again toward the shoreline. The blooming laurel are very pretty. A large white pine leans out over the pond, which is dotted with bullhead lily pads. There are also white-flowered fragrant waterlilies. Birds associated with water, such as red-winged blackbird and yellow warbler, frequent this area. Reach a more open view of the south end of the pond; more sign of beaver-cut and girdled hemlock. Hemlock are surely not among the beaver's preferred food plants, indicating perhaps that more-desirable species are in short supply. Look for painted turtles that may be sunning themselves here. Tiny, creeping partridgeberry creates bright-white, four-petaled twin flowers in early summer which later produce red berries.

Red squirrels accumulate refuse piles, or middens, of discarded pine cones from which they have extracted the nutritious seeds. Rejoin the blue-blazed trail at the T, turning right and walking over planks through a boggy area. Deep-pink-blooming sheep laurel adorns both sides of the plank bridge. It is a much smaller shrub than mountain laurel. A beaver dam is situated on the left close by, and the pond surface behind the dam is coated with floating duckweed. In summer dragonflies patrol the pond shores and intercept prey insects in midair. Shiny black whirligig beetles gyrate in masses on the water's surface like old bumper cars at an amusement park.

The white-on-blue-blazed trail swings right to continue along the shoreline. *Follow this wide tote road for only a short distance before turning right, immediately past a big hemlock located on the right and onto a narrow trail that follows the pond shore very closely. This spot is easy to miss, as the blazes are obscured. Do not continue walking uphill on the roadway.* This is the most demanding portion of the walk, requiring you to climb over fallen trees and boulders. It makes one wonder whether this was what gave the pond its name!

A steep, boulder-strewn slope rises up on the left. You are now walking just below the parallel roadway from which this trail is virtually invisible. In early summer the unassuming six-inch-tall cow-wheat plant produces pale-yellow snapdragon-like flowers in sunny patches along the trail.

Note the old beaver lodge situated about 150 feet out into Breakneck Pond and the trees cut years ago by these rodents on shore. Some hemlock that were not totally girdled have healed. The shriek of escaping young green frogs may startle you as you proceed. A small island of partially submerged white cedar comes into view. Watch for wood ducks in the vicinity of nest boxes erected for them here; tree swallows also utilize them. Climb easily for a short distance away from the pond through a laurel thicket. The forest, in addition to hemlock, includes red maple, red oak, and black birch. At three boulders the trail turns right and heads down toward the water rather steeply. A few small striped maple appear, as well as black and white oak and lowbush blueberry. Another islet of white cedar appears near shore where a tiny least flycatcher spits out his unmusical, clicking *che-bek* "song." Curious, carnivorous pitcher plants growing on the islets send up their parasol-like maroon-and-yellow flowers.

Come to a vernal pool on the left at the base of the rocky slope. Only the mounded trail ridge separates it from Breakneck Pond. The trail leads directly to the pond edge and swings left. Beautiful swamp white azaleas bloom along the shore in late spring and early summer, and azaleas emit a wonderful floral fragrance. Reach open oak woods with signs of camping use. A few black spruce, which may be much older than their size would indicate, stand with the white cedar on the islets. Black spruce is a denizen of cold bogs, as are pitcher plants. This glacier-gauged hollow, a relict of the ice ages, acts as a cold-air sink within which such northern species can survive. In contrast you'll also find a few bayberry or wax myrtle shrubs, more characteristic of the mild coastal region, growing on shore. Continue walking on the white-on-blue-blazed path through dry oak woods with bracken fern, sheep laurel, and a few highbush blueberry shrubs. The mountain laurel shrubs you walk up through are eight or nine feet tall.

Back in the hemlock along shore, you are proceeding along a small ridge from which you gain a nice view of the pond below. The trail swings left to a wooded swamp where little common yellowthroats nest. The males sport black masks. Cross a wet spot easily on logs, rocks, and a short beaver dam. Turn right to follow the shore. Blue-headed (formerly called solitary) vireos sing their measured, burry phrases from the hemlock. These six-inch-long bespectacled insect eaters build lovely cup nests woven partially of thin birch-bark strips at the fork end of a branch. An impressive clump of mountain laurel, heavy with mounds of nickel-sized blossoms, may well tempt a photo or two when they are in bloom in mid-June to early July. Laurel flowers employ an ingenious way of smacking visiting bees with their spring-loaded pollen-bearing anthers.

The pond now is more open. The white cedars have disappeared, replaced by larger islands bearing more-substantial white pines. Skirt a damp spot along the pond edge and come to oaks gnawed by beaver. While beaver generally cut trees with softer wood, they will tackle dense and heavy oak as well. Continue through a shaded hemlock stand and reach a narrow waterway between the mainland and an island; continue straight on the white-on-blue-blazed trail. From here looking back south, you have a very scenic view of the pond. Climb gradually through somewhat stony oak, hemlock, and laurel woods to a point nearly fifty feet above the water. There are a few small gray birch but abundant mountain laurel.

Pass some big gneiss boulders to your left. Polypody fern and leaflike rock tripe, a lichen, obscure the gray rock surface. Rock tripe is brown when dry, becoming green when wet, as its component algae begin photosynthesizing again. This appears to be a fairly young forest of black and gray birch, red oak, chestnut, mountain laurel, and a few white pine. On the left, pass more massive rock-tripe-encrusted boulders which create a tiny "cave" between them; you can explore this crevice. Scarlet tanager, an oak woods species, and black-throated blue warbler, partial to building its nest in laurel thickets—both breed in these mixed woodlands. The trail skirts this glacially deposited boulder field, gently proceeding uphill through laurel. An outcrop on the left has a small black birch growing out of it.

Drop down gradually through more laurel growth and lichen-covered boulders. Flashy five-and-a-half-inch-long, orange, black, and white American redstarts fan their tails as they flit among the boughs searching for caterpillars to feed to their hungry brood. A bit farther along, a large boulder resembling the prow of a ship stands on the right. More angular, slanted chunks of rock come into view as you continue along the west side of Breakneck Pond. This line of glacial debris is known as a boulder train. Interspersed as the boulders are here with mountain laurel, it makes for a very pretty scene. On a tiny ledge of one boulder we found an eastern phoebe's nest. Phoebes are among our earliest spring returnees, arriving back on the breeding grounds by the end of March.

Descend along boulders. A small duckweed-covered pool is visible through hemlock below the steep slope on the right. Come closer to the pond and reach a tote road labeled Horse Trail. The gurgling of flowing water alerts one to a stream crossing on the right. Turn right and cross the brook on steppingstones where black damselflies flutter. Continue on the

*Aromatic swamp azaleas display their white blos-
soms along the shores of Breakneck Pond in late
spring and early summer.*

tote road through dense young hemlock lining the roadway. Walk through
a wide sandy area where the skeleton of an old truck rusts. Pass a wooded
swamp on the left, screened by trees, and arrive at a T intersection and follow the old road right, along the shoreline. You are now at the northern tip
of the pond in Massachusetts.

A Louisiana waterthrush, a ground-dwelling warbler that builds its
nest along the banks of clear streams, teetered along ahead of us before flying into the forest. A fencelike growth of young hemlocks lines the shore.
Come to a granite monument marking the Massachusetts/Connecticut
border on the left just beyond the hemlock. The white-blazed East Ridge
Trail splits off here, climbing up the ridge. Remain on the roadway, following the blue rectangles. Hemlock boughs overhanging the road make for a
pleasing scene. In spring, blue flag irises bloom along the shoreline. After
passing a big white pine, the trail deviates from the road by bearing right.

The path can be difficult to locate near the shore. It becomes narrower, crosses a small flowing stream on steppingstones and goes gradually up the slope among hemlock and gray and black birch.

Red squirrels have left middens of pine cone cores and scales, and the path is cushioned by the thick hemlock needle duff. Pass a small vernal pool to the left. The path undulates through attractive forest, made even more appealing by bountiful displays of laurel, as more white pine join the hemlock. Mountain laurel tends to produce more flowers in well-lit locations. This is now pine-oak-maple woodland where black-capped chickadees, ovenbirds, and red-eyed vireos nest. Pass a gneiss outcrop situated on the left, while on the right a four-inch-diameter hemlock emerges from the top of another outcrop. Walk downhill through outcrops; on the left is a damp area with moss-covered rocks and cinnamon fern. Islands with tall pines lie offshore. Cross a tiny trickle flowing through a dip surrounded by laurel shrubs.

You are now on a hemlock ridge above the pond; to the left a boggy area lies in the crease between ridges. The cheery notes of an American robin, the state bird, ring through the woodland. Walk gradually downhill now, closer to the water, and cross feeder rills, the second larger and rockier. While following the shoreline closely here I made an interesting discovery during a late-June outing. A small antique glass bottle lying on the forest floor had been totally engulfed by mosses and fine hemlock roots so as to be all but invisible. It seems that given enough time, the work of human beings can be totally obliterated by the hand of nature.

Pass an ancient rough-barked hemlock and then a hemlock snag riddled with deep pileated woodpecker excavations. Beautiful black, yellow, gray, and white magnolia warblers nest in these conifers, and tiny, mouse-like winter wrens sing their loud bubbly songs in the shaded hollows. Descend the slope toward the pond, then curve left past an impressive straight-boled white pine. Cross another little feeder brook on stones and reach a level spot along the shore where clumps of sticky-tentacled sundew plants sit passively trapping unsuspecting insects. Like pitcher plants, these bog specialists supplement their nitrogen intake by absorbing nutrients from insects lured to their modified leaves. A nice view of the cedar islets situated along the far shore is possible from here.

Pass through a small clearing where a leaning outcrop has been used as a fireplace by unauthorized campers. Continue walking through hemlock, birch, oak, maple, and laurel woodland. One large red maple along the trail displays very shaggy bark. As you continue near the shoreline, note trees that beaver have chiseled the bark off of. They consume the nutritious inner bark, or cambium layer, which enables trees to grow. If the trunk is completely girdled the flow of nutrients and water from the roots to the crown is cut and the tree perishes. Come to an open grove of pine and hemlock showing more signs of unauthorized camping. The trail swings left and passes through a swampy hemlock-maple outflow area on stones. Walk over another tiny feeder stream. Long beech fern, which has its bottom pair of leaflets pointing downward, does well in the moist rocky soil here.

Recently felled small hemlock indicate that beaver are indeed still abroad. Another wetland denizen, a female wood duck, giving its characteristic squealing alarm call, flew off at our approach. Come to another woodland clearing under white pine where the wonderful aroma of pine resin hangs thick in the warm air. Looking out toward the pond, you'll notice that you are now opposite the tall pine islands. Yellow warblers, our only all-yellow birds, are common summer residents near water on this side of the pond as well. The trail bears left through laurel and brings you to another pond viewpoint clear of underbrush below white pine and hemlock. The pines must have colonized this once open ground first, since their seeds require full sun for germination. Hemlock, on the other hand, are extremely shade tolerant. Black-throated green warblers sing their buzzy songs in the pine boughs from May through July.

On the left a hemlock-covered slope rises at a low angle. The waxy white blossoms of pyrola bloom under the evergreens. Cross a rock-strewn feeder brook and then walk over two sections of bog bridge, where green frogs reside. A few witch hazel shrubs grow here as on the opposite side of the pond. Pass a small clearing on the left. Later, spinulose wood and New York ferns add splashes of green to the forest floor. Walk through a boulder field vegetated by yellow birch and hemlock. Eastern chipmunks scamper over the woodland floor, seeking shelter from weasels and other predators among the rocks. An open view of the south end of the pond is possible here, and as you gaze in that direction note the leatherleaf shrubs—another bog plant. Our largest frogs, bullfrogs, bellow from the shallows.

The trail swings left, passing the end of a stone wall on that side. Come to an orange-blazed trail on the right and turn onto it; this junction is difficult to see. Amble left along the swamp border, and in a short distance reach a T junction with the white-blazed East Ridge Trail; this closes the pond loop. Walk straight ahead and retrace your steps 1.1 miles back to the parking area where you left your vehicle.

BOG CARNIVORES

The Venus' flytrap, the one "meat-eating" plant known to almost everyone, is not native to and cannot survive the harsh climatic conditions of New England. But two other insect-consuming species—pitcher plant and round-leaved sundew—are reasonably common in the proper habitats:

glacial relics known as bogs. Bogs represent a nonrenewable natural resource in our landscape. The acidic conditions within bogs reduce decomposition of plant and animal matter to a very minimal level; the nitrogen plants require for survival is thus not readily available to them. This leaves bog plants with a major "vitamin deficiency." Insectivorous plants have overcome this dilemma by means of several ingenious strategies.

Pitcher plants are aptly named, as their basal leaves are fused into a tall urn lined with downward-projecting bristles. Rainwater accumulates in the pitchers, while sweet secretions from the plant lure insects to their doom. Flies and other six- and eight-legged creatures easily follow the downward-projecting hairs into the depth of the pitcher, but find it virtually impossible to climb out. Exhausted by their struggles to escape, they fall into the pool and drown. Digestive juices released by the plant soon reduce the insect's proteins to its constituent parts, including nitrogen, which the plant then absorbs.

Sundews have taken a different tack to reach the same end. Sweet droplets exuded from the tips of their reddish tentacle-like leaf projections attract a wide variety of insects to the plant. Once the bugs alight, the extreme stickiness of the clear substance makes escape all but impossible. As the insects struggle they become ever more mired in the sweet embrace of the sundew's leaf. In time the leaf curls inward and then goes about digesting the soft portions of its prey. Upon closer inspection, I discovered that one of the sundews growing in a small colony along the eastern shore of Breakneck Pond had ensnared a small damselfly as well as several gnats and flies.

These highly specialized plants cope very successfully with the limiting conditions of bogs and sandy, acid soils by having evolved remarkable anatomical and behavioral adaptations. I always get a thrill out of seeing these carnivorous plants in the wild because they are such a wonderful example of the infinite variety and adaptability of nature.

Getting There

From Exit 73 off Interstate 84, travel north on Route 190 for 2.3 miles to its intersection with Route 171 in Union. Bear right onto Route 171 eastbound and drive for 1.5 miles to the entrance for Bigelow Hollow State Park on the left. Enter the park, pass the entrance kiosk, and travel 0.65 mile to the Bigelow Pond Picnic Area parking lot on the left. The trailhead is on the opposite side of the paved road. Please note that hikers are asked not to park at the boat-launch area.

—R.L.

Trail Wood Sanctuary

Hampton

- Ground Pine Crossing Trail, Beaver Pond Trail, Far Northwoods Trail, Old Woods Road, Boulder Field Trail, Colonial Road Trail, Shagbark Hickory Trail
- 2.3-mile loop
- 120-foot elevation gain
- 2.0 hours
- easy

In the summer of 1959 Edwin Way Teale, the acclaimed nature writer, and his wife, Nellie, moved into a refurbished 150-year-old farmhouse set on 156 diverse acres in the Windham Hills of northeastern Connecticut. The abundance of walking trails on the property led the Teales to name their new home Trail Wood. It was at Trail Wood that Ed Teale, the first nature writer in 50 years to win the Pulitzer Prize for literature in 1966, worked on many of his beloved books, including *Wandering through Winter*, *A Naturalist Buys an Old Farm*, and *A Walk through the Year*.

Ed and Nellie Teale explored every nook and cranny of their special piece of the earth, chronicling the comings and goings of the seasons and the myriad creatures large and small associated with each habitat. Their beloved Trail Wood, now owned and managed by Connecticut Audubon Society, offers the same stimulation, the same solitude, the same inspiration to visitors that drew the Teales to its fields, woods, ponds, streams, and stone walls.

The trail system is extensive and takes in a wide variety of natural communities given the relatively small size of the sanctuary. And if you are familiar with the beautiful and evocative prose Edwin Way Teale set to paper, a sojourn across the landscape of Trail Wood will mean all the more to you.

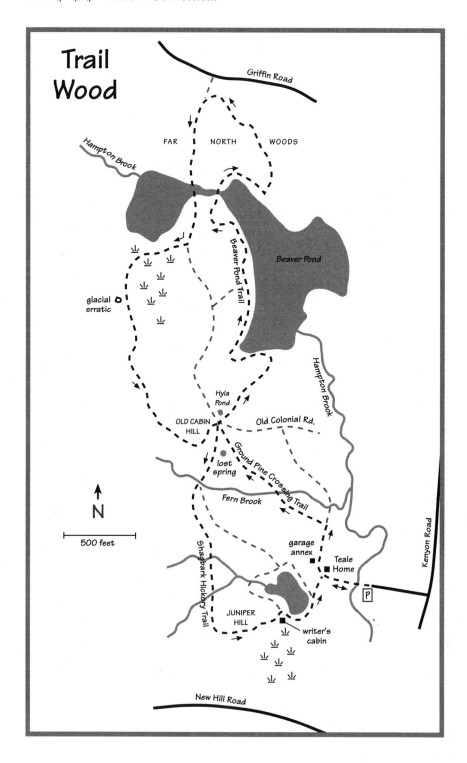

Trail Wood

Griffin Road

Hampton Brook

FAR　　NORTH　　WOODS

Beaver Pond Trail

Beaver Pond

glacial erratic

Hampton Brook

Hyla Pond

OLD CABIN HILL

Old Colonial Rd.

Ground Pine Crossing Trail

lost spring

Fern Brook

N

500 feet

Shagbark Hickory Trail

garage annex

Teale Home

P

Kenyon Road

JUNIPER HILL

writer's cabin

New Hill Road

Look Forward To

- wildlife-rich beaver pond

- an abundance and variety of ferns

- picturesque stone walls

- Teale's writing cabin

The Trail

After parking in the grassy lot left of the farm lane, turn left onto the lane and walk toward the white farmhouse. Cross Hampton Brook, which hosts fish, crayfish, and green frogs, on a stone bridge and continue up the gentle slope to the house. This old gravel lane is bordered by stone walls; the one on the right is draped with grapevines. Hay-scented fern grows thickly along the lane and wall. A flower garden densely populated with showy blossoms in July attracts a myriad of butterflies, including elegant eastern black swallowtails. Pass hickory trees on the left and curve right around the house. Trail maps and a visitor registry are housed inside the garage annex to your left.

The effervescent song of the house wren celebrates the summer season as you follow the mowed path in spring and summer through what the Teales knew as the Starfield. Here they marveled at the depth and clarity of the rural night sky. Uncut fields of wildflowers—Queen Anne's lace, black-eyed Susan, and spotted knapweed—provide sources of nectar for dainty and colorful American copper butterflies. Oriental bittersweet, an invasive exotic plant, is unfortunately invading these fields. Come to a trail intersection and turn left; you are now walking on Ground Pine Crossing Trail over Nighthawk Hill. Significant amounts of poison ivy edge the mowed path.

The field to your left is known as Woodcock Pasture and is bordered by black oak, red maple, and quaking aspen. It is patrolled on summer days by dragonflies, while field crickets produce their soothing, if monotonous, chirping amid the rank grasses and wildflowers. The trail now curves right, entering moist deciduous woods of green ash, black oak, and red maple. Cross intermittently flowing Fern Brook on steppingstones. Skunk cabbage, interrupted fern, the club mosses ground cedar and princess pine (which give the trail its name), New York fern, royal fern, highbush blueberry, mountain azalea, and abundant spicebush shrubs thrive in the moist soils. Skunk cabbage, one of our earliest-blooming native plants, is remarkable in that it produces its own heat in winter, which allows this plant to melt its way through the snow cover.

Woodland butterflies such as the northern pearly eye, whose wings are bordered with eye spots which may fool predators, alight on leaves in patches of dappled sunlight to bask. Chestnut saplings growing from the still-living roots of American chestnut trees appear. Chestnut blight effectively wiped out this once dominant tree of eastern forests hereabouts in the 1920s. Small sinewy ironwood trees grow beneath the ash and white and red oak. Large cinnamon fern are common amid the abundant fern cover, which now also includes shiny dark green Christmas fern. A rock wall stands on the left as the trail undulates very slightly. A usually damp depression on the right is often dry in summer. Oak, ash, and hickory shade the path, while enchanter's nightshade blooms on the darkened forest floor. Its white flowers have only two petals.

Come to rock-lined Lost Spring on the left as the trail begins to rise slightly. The spring feeds the see page area thick with skunk cabbage in the depression at the right of the trail. Join Old Colonial Road Trail on the right and two trails on the left, creating a wheel-spoke configuration. Proceed straight ahead to a sign for Hyla Rill/To Beaver Pond at a Y fork. Turn right toward a beaver pond and pass Hyla Pond on the left, a vernal pool where salamanders and frogs play out their annual breeding rituals before the heat of summer dries their pool. An oak-covered slope rises gently on the right. Fall-blooming witch hazel and the much shorter maple-leafed viburnum are two common shrubs here. Black birch, ash, black and red oak, and chestnut saplings lead up to a stone wall parted by the trail, which now swings left.

Ferns, of which there are twenty-six native species at Trail Wood, continue numerous. Christmas, hay-scented (which thrives on rocky ground), interrupted, and New York (whose fronds are tapered at both ends) fern provide an attractive, feathery ground cover. Scarlet tanagers, unseen despite their brilliant red-and-black plumage, sing their deliberate, throaty phrases from the oaks overhead. Some stones of a rock wall built long ago of flat Hebron schist flagstones glisten with mica. The trail swings right, providing the first glimpse of the beaver pond through trees to your left. Red maple, Juneberry (shad), ironwood, white oak, black cherry, and highbush blueberry vegetate these open woodlands. Eastern wood pewees perch and wait for flying insect meals to happen by.

Arrive at the rather extensive pond created by North America's largest rodents in the early 1960s. Much of its surface is now covered with the floating pads and strikingly large white blossoms of fragrant waterlilies. The stillness is broken by the amusing gulps of green frogs proclaiming their territorial rights. A portion of the beaver dam, across Hampton Brook, is visible to the right. The creation of this pond was a big surprise to the

Teales, who chanced upon it one fall day. The green mounds of tussock sedges poke out of the water, and superabsorbent sphagnum moss grows in patches along the shore. A belted kingfisher rattles and flies with jerky wing beats across the pond, while a crow-sized green heron stands motionless and hunched over on a dead stump, totally absorbed in its quest for frogs. You may want to linger for awhile, alert for some of the myriad life forms that reside here, or just drink in the serenity of the place.

Turn left to follow the trail along the pond shore. It bears right to cross a boardwalk over a tiny brook. This is the Teale's Hellebore Crossover. In summer ferns steal the show—hay-scented, New York, royal, interrupted, and chest-high and taller cinnamon fern are abundant and eye-catching holdovers from the Carboniferous era, long before the age of dinosaurs. As you continue along, you are now treated to a nice open view of the pond on the right. We spotted an eastern phoebe, a six-and-a-half-inch-long olive-gray flycatcher feeding insects to its two nearly full grown fledglings on a red maple limb above us.

Sections of stone wall dating from perhaps the eighteenth century and which once kept livestock out of planted fields, border what is now a beaver pond over whose placid surface dragonflies on gauzy wings capture insects. Pass a trail junction on the left that leads up an oak-hickory slope to Old Woods Road. Stay straight and continue paralleling the shoreline. Large rosettes of gray-green lichens, some likely older than the forest trees, dot the stone wall on the right you soon pass through. The wall is now on your left as you skirt woods of maple and hickory with considerable undergrowth. Pass through fern, huckleberry, and maleberry shrubs. Colonists regarded maleberry as the male blueberry shrub, which of course it is not. Maleberry's fruits are clusters of small dry capsules.

A glance at the pond in summer may reveal the small yellow pea-like flowers of bladderwort protruding above the water's surface on slender stalks. Below the surface the plant's bladders suck in passing minute life forms if the creatures are unlucky enough to touch a triggering bristle. An old overgrown and probably unoccupied beaver lodge is visible also. Pass by the end of a stone wall on the left and bear away from the pond. Climb gradually into oak woods with a black birch and witch hazel understory. Wild sarsaparilla, sessile-leaved bellwort, and princess pine grow in the rich soil below the trees and shrubs. Now swing down and right, with stone walls on both sides of the path. Some sugar maple appear. Woodland wildflowers include rattlesnake plantain, whose attractive green leaves are graced by a network of fine white veins, starflower, and Canada mayflower.

Reach flowing Hampton Brook, the source of the pond, and cross it on stones. Jewel-like black damselflies flutter on ebony wings as you cross the brook. A large yellow birch with four trunks stands on the left just before you come to a T junction. Turn right toward the Far North Woods and cross a dry (in summer) seep where the presence of skunk cabbage plants betrays the hidden moisture. Pass through a stone wall. Ghostly white Indian pipes push up through the rotting oak and maple leaves, taking their nourishment from decaying plant matter. Enter a small sunny clearing where some trees show recent beaver gnawing. A few bayberry bushes, more characteristic of the coast, grow here, as do the eye-catching, upturned, fiery orange flowers of wood lily. The gorgeous lilies bloom in midsummer.

Watch for the intersection of the Far North Woods Trail on the left where a red maple tree stands near a red cedar; this is easy to miss. Follow this trail left and then through a gap in a stone wall. If you go straight, by mistake, you will soon come to the end of the path at the beaver pond's edge. These are young woods of black cherry, red maple, black oak, spicebush, and Japanese barberry, an exotic invasive shrub which is a sure sign of prior disturbance. Ground cedar, one of the nonflowering club mosses, thrusts candelabra-shaped, spore-producing fruiting stalks above its flattened leaves, and poisonous jack-in-the-pulpit grows in rich damp soil along the wall itself.

The trail now passes through maple-oak-hickory woods which also feature black birch trees and huckleberry shrubs. Striped or spotted wintergreen, handsome both for its pendant white blossoms and its boldly patterned dark-green-and-white foliage, blooms in summer. The two and three blossoms per plant may glow brightly in the dappled but intense sunlight like tiny lanterns. The trail then rises gradually to drier oak-hickory forest, with hazelnut and lowbush blueberry below. Red-eyed vireos, one of the most common eastern deciduous birds, sing from the tree canopy above. Climb very gradually and follow the trail as it bears left and then goes lazily downhill. A vigorous growth of lacy New York fern may be spotlighted to the right when the sun is shining.

Walk amidst ferns and continue through another stone wall, to a junction with a trail on the right. Turning right takes you to Griffin Road. Continue straight instead. Shortly come to a flowing brook giving life to sizable skunk cabbages and cross it on flat stones. Reach an alder shrub wetland on the right where horsetails, primitive green raspy stalks without leaves, and red maple also thrive. Big coarse bracken fern stands thigh high along the edge in the sun. Climb gradually now into dry oak woods where huckleberry bushes, hay-scented fern, Canada mayflower, and starflower are found. Come to a T junction on the right. Turn right and walk down a very modest slope through oak, black birch, and chestnut sprouts. In late July there are already some ripe fruits on the highbush blueberry shrubs.

As you walk over bog bridges through wetlands with skunk cabbage, spicebush, and jewelweed, listen for the lovely *ee-o-lay* song of the wood thrush. Spicebush has very aromatic egg-shaped leaves with a definite citrus odor when crushed. The foliage sustains the larvae of the beautiful blue-hued spicebush swallowtail butterfly. The bright red fruits appear in late summer. From this low, damp spot walk slightly up and then across a rock wall where white ash rise up tall. Proceed uphill and pass a big black oak on the right; the slope drops away to the left. The songs of tufted titmouse, red-eyed vireo, and rose-breasted grosbeak floated to my ears. These are just a few of the more than 144 species of birds recorded by the Teales during their years at Trail Wood.

Large oak trees, widely spaced, are interspersed with smaller trees—hickory, ironwood, oak, and yellow birch. A glacial boulder, or erratic, sits where it came to rest more than 10,000 years ago on the right as the trail swings left. Look closely and you'll notice that it has been partially split. Three- to four-inch-long drilled holes along its edge indicate where iron rods were inserted to split it. As you walk down the slight slope of the North Boulder Field, come across more, smaller glacial boulders. Where the path levels off, remnants of barbed wire, indicating former pastureland, can be seen. The trail swings left. A stone wall is to your right, and the privately owned land beyond it is partially cleared of trees.

Continue straight ahead past the informal trail junction on the left. An L-shaped foundation remnant of a former cabin sits on the same side. Follow the path through oak-hickory-hazelnut woods as it bears left and downhill along Old Cabin Hill. A perfectly camouflaged comma butterfly whisked by rapidly in erratic flight during our summer visit. When at rest, the raised undersides of its wings blend in uncannily with bark. Arrive again at the major six-way intersection. Take the first spoke to the right, which is Shagbark Hickory Trail. Patches of Christmas, hay-scented, and New York fern enliven the forest floor under the oak, hickory, and ash. Cross the dry (in summer) bed of Fern Brook. The dainty two-toed prints of a white-tailed fawn, perhaps two months old, pockmarked the bare mud between the leafy skunk cabbage plants during our mid-July visit.

Come to an unmarked Y junction almost immediately and take the right fork to West Woods. This fork is easy to miss. Delicate and lovely maidenhair fern, regarded by many as the most beautiful of all ferns, spreads airy fans above its shiny dark stalks. Plenty of Japanese barberry grows here as well amid the hickory and oak. Continue gradually down and cross a dry stream bed. A red-bellied woodpecker, which, like the wild turkey, wood duck, blue jay, and chipmunk, is fond of acorns, called *churr-churr-churr* loudly as it hitched up the trunk of an oak. Arrive at a trail intersection on the left that goes downhill. Stay straight and walk through an area where sharp-hooked raspberry canes and prickly barberry shrubs predominate and Virginia creeper spreads its leafy runners over the ground.

Continue leisurely downhill under oak, hickory, and ash, by knee-high maple-leafed viburnum, and past jack-in-the-pulpit and Christmas fern, then climb gradually into drier oak-hickory woods where pole-sized and smaller black cherries are common. Head slightly downhill again. The loud, very insistent refrain of the ovenbird rings through the forest, where poison ivy is again common. Soon reach a T intersection at a stone wall. Turn left and walk downhill adjacent to a low stone fence which once bounded a pasture to your right. Oak, hickory, ash, and maple long ago replaced the grasses and wildflowers. The modest shoulder of Juniper Hill rises to your left as you walk uphill. There are few junipers (a.k.a. red cedars) left now on Juniper Hill. Junipers are sun-loving, pioneering trees that can't tolerate being shaded out by later arrivals.

Step through a gap in yet another stone wall, bearing right. Ed Teale once estimated that their 156 acres held nearly five miles of old stone walls! Abundant barberry, oriental bittersweet vines which encircle and literally strangle their host trees, and euonymous shrubs, all exotics that indicate former disturbance, are in great evidence here. Arrive at Teale's hand-hewn log writing cabin overlooking an artificial pond. This is where the author did much of his reading and writing during the warmer months of the year. A small wood stove provided heat during chilly spring and fall mornings. The cabin is usually open for visitation.

Just outside the front door of the cabin I photographed a very impressive black-and-yellow female giant ichnuemon wasp with exceedingly long antennae and a five-inch-long "tail" as it rested on a leaf. With its long antennae it feels vibrations from a tunneling horntail larvae beneath the bark. Horntails are themselves wasplike in form. The ichnuemon uses her tail, actually an ovipositor, to penetrate the bark of a decaying tree in which the horntail larvae are feeding. The parasitic wasp then deposits an egg in the horntail's tunnel. When it hatches, the ichnuemon larva consumes the horntail larva and pupates.

Turn right to head back toward the Teale home. The one-acre pond was constructed in 1963 by human digging and damming. Above the far end of the pond stands a screened gazebo known as the Summerhouse. Cross the pond's outlet stream on a wooden bridge. Purple spikes of pick-erelweed decorate the shoreline in summer. Recent beaver activity in the

A female giant ichnuemon wasp, sporting five-inch-long antennae, rests on a leaf just outside Teale's former writing cabin.

form of a small dam immediately downstream of the pond is an interesting juxtaposition in the making of human versus animal pond building. Alder grow thickly now along the pond shore to the left. After crossing the bridge the trail bears left and continues as a mowed path up through Firefly Meadow. Come to a four-way intersection just below the Teale home. Continue straight up through a stone wall to the lane. We watched as a chimney swift flew down the red brick chimney of the house and then back out again, probably just having fed a nest full of young. Turn right and follow the lane about 400 feet back to the parking area on the right.

A MAN FOR ALL SEASONS

Edwin Way Teale (1899–1980) was a meticulous and gifted observer and recorder of nature, a wonderfully insightful naturalist, and a gifted writer. I had admired Teale's writing for years, after reading such now classic works as *North with the Spring* and *Autumn across America*.

One excerpt from *A Naturalist Buys an Old Farm;* in which the author describes some of what he experienced while observing nature from a hollow brush pile of his own creation; reads as follows:

There was the humming of bees among the mountain mint, the liquid monologue of the waterfall, the steely chorus of the meadow insects, the rushing of wind among the summer leaves. In the hot still days of August, the shrill cicada's song would soar above me among the treetops to end in a descending buzz and a dying sizzle.

Teale had a great gift in that he could explain in very understandable but at the same time evocative prose the extremely complex workings of the natural world. Usually his books dealt with the wilderness that lies just beyond our back doors. A world populated by creatures every bit as fascinating, albeit not as large and glamorous, as, say, African elephants and lions.

Teale's philosophy of life on the land are summed up by these passages from the same book:

We have experienced surprisingly little feeling of possession, of ownership. The deed is ours. But in our minds the trees own the land almost as much as we do. We are one with the robin among the wild cherries in the sunshine. We own Trail Wood together, we and every other wild creature that shares with us these country days.

In our minds the sense of guardianship, of responsibility, surpasses that of ownership. Our title to the farm gives us the power to protect this small fragment of the earth, these woods, these streams, these fields, and all the inhabitants they contain.

Inside the desk of his writing cabin is this quote from a gravestone in Cumberland, England: "The wonder of the world. The beauty of the power. The shape of things. Their colors. Lights and shades: These I have seen. Look ye also while life lasts."

Ed Teale certainly followed this admonition throughout his long and fruitful life. It was his credo, and it seems to me to be a fitting epitaph for him as well.

Getting There

From Exit 91 (Route 6) of Interstate 395, take Route 6 east for approximately 10.0 miles to its intersection with Route 97. Turn right (north) onto Route 97 and drive for 2.6 miles through Hampton to Kenyon Road on the left. Turn left onto Kenyon Road and travel north for 0.35 mile to the lane on the left leading into Trail Wood Sanctuary. A grassy parking area is located 0.1 mile down the lane on the left. A pit toilet is located here also.

—R.L.

Rock Spring
Wildlife Refuge

Scotland

- white-blazed trail, white/yellow-blazed side trail to lookout
- 3.6-mile loop
- 240-foot elevation gain
- 3.5 hours
- moderate

The 445-acre Rock Spring Wildlife Refuge in northeastern Connecticut is a gem. This Nature Conservancy property is off the beaten path and combines lovely upland woods, a scenic vista, and the tranquil Little River valley and its flood-plain forest into a wonderful mix for exploration and wonder. Indeed, Rock Spring is among my true favorites.

This glacier-sculpted landscape, removed from major population centers, was once farmed and pastured like most of the region. In the century and a half since its abandonment, the forest has reclaimed and reclothed the rolling north-south-tending ridges. Black bear, bobcat, wild turkey, and common raven, all forest dwellers, inhabit the area once again while beaver, otter, and mink have repopulated the river valley.

The refuge's trails are well maintained and easy to follow. Parking is limited and there are no sanitary facilities, but if anything, this adds to the sense of adventure you'll experience when visiting this wonderful preserve.

Look Forward To

- variety of habitats
- wonderful vistas
- scenic Little River valley
- striking fall foliage

235

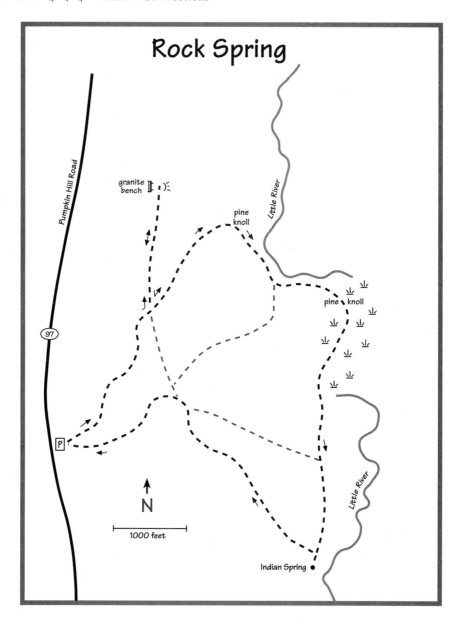

Rock Spring

granite
bench

pine
knoll

Pumpkin Hill Road

Little River

97

pine knoll

P

N

1000 feet

Little River

Indian Spring

The Trail

Enter the maple-ash-oak woods and walk gradually downhill through an old stone wall to a kiosk on the left, where a map of the trails is posted. Another stone wall appears on the left as the trail curves right. Christmas fern is always green, as is the attractive variegated foliage of rattlesnake plantain. In fall, woodland asters bloom white. Private property borders the stone wall to the left. At the point where both the wall and the path jog left, lowbush blueberry and shinleaf grow. You'll walk easily now downslope through patches of hay-scented fern. Red maple, bitternut hickory, black oak, white oak, and black birch, some quite large, are dominant trees. Most trees are of young or moderate age. The abundance of stone walls shows that colonial farmers were very serious about keeping livestock out of their crops as well as those of their neighbors. Today they make great lookouts and cover for scampering chipmunks.

Pass through a stone wall. The rocks are mica schist. As the soil dampens, red-fruited spicebush appears, as does cinnamon fern. The latter grows in waist-high clumps of three to ten stems. Ruby-throated hummingbirds use the reddish fuzzy covering on the stems to line their walnut-sized nests. A Japanese barberry thicket on the left indicates former soil disturbance; an effort to remove some of this invasive shrub is underway. Cross a rocky intermittent brook bed. The rocks here appear to be of another metamorphic type—gneiss. Gneiss tends to show gray and white banding. The slope you are walking along, especially to your right, is solidly fern covered. Christmas, cinnamon, and hay-scented species all grow where a tiny drainage way crosses the white-blazed path.

The path turns right when you reach a stone wall. Spicebush shrubs now line both sides of the trail. The crushed foliage has a very pleasing citrus aroma. Some of the oak here are sizable. Another stone wall begins on the right and also crosses the path, which is littered with the golden leaves of black and yellow birch in autumn. The trees are mostly eight to twelve inches in diameter. The wall veers away to the left, the slope becomes steeper, and the trail bears left. The abundant hay-scented fern are transformed to light yellow after the first frosts. Ground cedar, one of the non-flowering club mosses, spreads by runners and forms rows of tiny plants. Even in fall the loud, ringing voices of spring peepers resonate through these rather open woodlands.

Yet another rock wall begins on the right. There is an abundance of sapling growth in the midst of the larger trees. Thick patches of dark-green Christmas fern thrive near the lower end of the slope, perhaps being fertilized by nutrients washed down from higher up. Hickory becomes more common. These are tight barked and have seven to nine leaflets, making them the bitternut species. Some ledge stone is visible at the top of the ridge. Reach the end of the wall where it and the path meet an old woods road. Turn left and walk gradually uphill in the direction of the overlook. The white-blazed trail picks up again on the other side of the road about thirty-five feet after you turn left. Continue straight on the road for now; you will return to pick up the trail here later.

The golden hue of the frost-killed hay-scented fern was striking under the dark trunks of the black birch during one early-October visit. The deep green of Christmas fern also created a nice contrast with the yellowed fronds of hay-scented. Big-tooth aspen make an appearance while woodland goldenrod blooms yellow in fall. The old roadway veers left, while the trail to the lookout continues straight. Be sure to follow the trail. The white-and-yellow-blazed path traverses dead bleached and brown skeletons of New York fern, which are tapered at both ends. Begin easy downhill walking, with stone walls on the right. A small American toad, virtually the same shade as the decaying leaves it sat upon, caught my eye only when it hopped. Small sassafras saplings with green stems and waist-high maple-leafed viburnum shrubs with blue-black berry clusters grow here.

Bear right, pass through a stone wall, and then swing left. Descend to cross an intermittent brook bed where spicebush reaches nine to ten feet in height. The trial curves right after climbing out of the hollow. The birch-maple canopy is golden as sunlight passes through the fall foliage. New York fern, although no longer green, are lovely shades of rust, pink, yellow, and tan. Cross a drainage bed, curve left, and climb gradually over gneiss outcrops. Tufted titmice were scolding noisily as I passed through another wall, while the distant ridge began to be visible through the burnished foliage. One last short climb to the viewpoint and an imposing gray granite bench.

Black, white, and red oak shade the overlook, while huckleberry (red foliage in fall) and lowbush blueberry soften the outcrop. There are also hickory (golden yellow), red maple (scarlet), ash (maroon) and black birch (bright yellow) contributing brilliant hues to the autumnal spectacle. The view eastward at any time of year is very nice. The *chur-chur-chur* notes of a red-bellied woodpecker emanated from a nearby oak. I later watched this bird insert an acorn into a crevice in the top of a decayed snag and pound away at it. He appeared to eat some of the acorn and then flew off with the rest.

After drinking in this splendid scene, retrace your steps back to the old road and continue about 100 yards to where the white-blazed trail turns left. Turn left onto it and cross over a stone wall. This is rocky oak-hickory-birch woodland carpeted with fern. Walk easily downhill with the slope dropping away to the right. Cross an old overgrown roadbed. Easily recognized shagbark hickory are present, while small black-and-white, spiny abdomened spiders hang from silken threads. The feathery plumes of maidenhair fern are held aloft by their slender ebony stems. Continue through a thick Christmas fern growth and a fair amount of spicebush shrubbery. The white orbs of white baneberry, or doll's-eyes, are indeed reminiscent of the porcelain eyes of twentieth-century era dolls.

The trail bears right at a point where boulders sit to your left, and continues very gradually downhill. A stand of blue cohosh straddles the path. In fall they bear attractive but poisonous clusters of deep blue berries above their leaves. Cross a drainage way (a big ash stands on the left) and then another intermittent brook bed. Walk over a stone wall amid oak, shagbark hickory, maple, and ash, and then reach some white pine with two-foot-plus-diameter furrowed trunks. Where the trail bears left a mourning cloak butterfly flew rapidly and erratically by during my October walk. Climb easily up the knoll dominated by white pine. Tiny princess pine grows thickly below its namesake and is joined by ground cedar (another club moss), lowbush blueberry, and some poison ivy. Ghostly white Indian pipes bloom amid the pine duff. As they age, the pipe "bowls" turn upward. There are also tiny seedlings of white pine.

The trail then turns right and descends the knoll. Beaver-cut logs on the knoll seem absurdly out of place until you discover the wetland at the base of the hill. Husks of shagbark hickory nuts litter the path where a red squirrel has opened them. Continue downslope and bear left under pine and oak, and pass a very large multitrunked white pine where the path levels out. You have reached the Little River. Along the banks grow cinnamon fern, winterberry, highbush blueberry, ironwood, and red maple. Red maple are especially common in this flood-plain forest. Azaleas, winterberry shrubs, and New York ferns border the path as it follows the river. Green frogs call and leap to safety at one's approach until hard frosts send them into winter dormancy. Another red-bellied woodpecker churred, the fourth one heard on that October day.

Some of the trees along the river produce exquisite foliage in autumn; one fluorescent-orange sugar maple is especially memorable. My camera was kept busy that sunny day. A fish-eating belted kingfisher flashed upstream, a sure sign that the river was flowing clear over its gravelly bottom. It flows swiftly with a pleasing gurgle. Small, gnarled ironwood trees, whose nickname aptly is "musclewood," are common in the flood plain. The shrub-lined path emerges from the trees and follows closely along the stream banks. Bank erosion and storms have caused large trees to fall across the river. I watched a comma butterfly alight upon the blue fruit cluster of a nannyberry shrub, while the shrill screams of a red-shouldered hawk resounded through the valley.

The river makes a sharp turn to the left and then back around to the right to create a peninsula covered with broad-leafed deer-tongue grass.

One can access the river at this location where the trail curves right. The foliage of autumnal red maple may be a brilliant red here, while the burnished gold of dead royal fern line the path. Cross a tiny feeder stream on a sturdy wooden bridge, from which a picturesque view of the colorful wetland is possible to the right. Winterberry shrubs loaded with coral-red berries are visible on the other shore as the trail curves left. Old beaver cuttings are evident as well. Photo opportunities abound. Come to a trail junction on the right; this is a shortcut trail that leads back toward the parking. Continue straight along the river. A tree-mounted sign reads No Horses Beyond This Point.

The woodland is composed of pine, hickory, maple, and oak. Wild sarsaparilla is the common herb. A giant oak has fallen across the river and serves as a convenient bridge for small mammals. The trail now curves right, climbs away moderately steeply from the river onto higher ground, and then curves right to the top of a pine-oak knoll. A very fine view of the river is yours from this vantage point. The trail very gradually continues down the knoll's other side. The wooded river wetlands to the left are thick

Red or swamp maples produce brilliant autumnal foliage along the banks of the scenic Little River.

with dogwood and nannyberry shrubs. The ground drops off eight to ten feet just left of the trail, which skirts the wetland edge. More fine views of the river valley greet you as you follow the path within the flood plain. An old fallen oak tree serves as support for a beaver dam the big rodents have constructed partially against it.

Emerge into a sunny clearing from which another, lower dam is visible. It was here that a green female katydid came flying along and, to my surprise, alighted on a greenbrier stalk. Its curved, brown ovipositor was clearly visible upon close inspection. Continue walking past the end of the beaver dam and parallel with the river. The woody vegetation consists of hickory, red maple, ironwood, nannyberry, and beaked hazelnut. New York and cinnamon ferns are common too. Pass a big broken white pine, part of which has fallen into the river. You can examine the river from a pebbly bank here. Katydids produce their rhythmic *katy-did, katy-didn't* refrain from the trees. Cross a fallen red maple from which two branches have grown upward to become surrogate trunks for the prostrate tree.

The path is very close to the cut bank and no doubt will have to be moved as flood waters continue to carve away this side of the channel. More bright clusters of winterberry and many ironwood trees appear just before you reach a wooden bridge over a mostly dry feeder stream that enters the Little River from the left. The trail now bears right, away from the river and the flood plain, and enters a narrow red pine plantation. Virtually nothing is able to grow in the constant shade below the pines, which are spaced six to nine feet apart. After 100 yards of walking between straight rows, reenter natural woodland as the trail bears right, then left and uphill. A smaller trail splits off to the right. Continue straight up the gravelly knoll, another gift of the glaciers. Lowbush blueberry and a few pink lady-slippers grow in the acidic soil below the pine and oak.

Emerge into a gravel clearing with young white pine, quaking aspen, prickly dwarf juniper, and little bluestem grass. The trail turns left and leads along the top of a gravel and sand ridge (actually a glacial esker) covered with oak, aspen, and pine. Reindeer lichen forms cushiony mats in a sunny clearing regenerating to white pine and oak. There is also little bluestem, dwarf juniper, and shining sumac, whose deep-red fall leaves glisten in the sunlight. Reenter oak woods with ground cedar club moss as you continue along this glacial spine. Another small, sandy opening hosts sweet fern. Curve left over gravel and enter oak, black birch, and white pine woodland with abundant lowbush blueberry as well as dwarf juniper clumps. There is even bayberry, usually found only in coastal areas, here in the poor soil.

Walk downward, curve left, and enter another cobbled clearing with little bluestem, a common midwestern prairie grass; reindeer lichen; bayberry; and in fall, violet-blooming stiff asters. A large ant mound in the clearing may also catch your attention. Reenter the woods, continuing downward and to the left, and reach a trail junction on the right. You will turn here to head back to the trailhead, but first walk the 100 feet straight ahead to Indian Spring. A raised, round, stone springhead with a concrete lid contains an inscribed stone that reads Old Bar One Indian Spring. A sign warns against disturbing the soils or stones around the spring. Note the water welling up in a depression and flowing away.

Return to the white-blazed trail and turn left. Ignore another small, unblazed side trail and walk steadily uphill into a young white pine grove, with lowbush blueberry and princess pine below the conifers. The trail curves gently right and leads to a stone wall on the left. Begin climbing to the top of the hill over a path of loose, glacially deposited pebbles and cobbles. Pass through a small grassy opening and shortly reach the crest under oak and white pine. A few skeleton red cedar remain, shaded out by the broadleaf trees. From this low ridge the land falls away on both sides. Come to an informal trail on the left, but stay straight on the white-blazed trail. This is open oak woodland rejuvenated with the new growth of white pine.

The path bears right at a small grassy clearing filled with lowbush blueberry, princess pine (some with spiky spore-emitting strobules) and ground cedar club moss. Huckleberry shrubs are also common below the oak and red maple. Pass through a stone wall that has a huge magnificent spreading and leaning white oak alongside it. It must have been spared by a farmer who favored it for shade and the acorn bounty it produced. Continue right, over high ground under oak and birch, once again in the haunt of the vocal red-bellied woodpecker. The trail undulates gently over a forest floor softened by grasses, Christmas and hay-scented fern, and wild sarsaparilla. It then curves right and takes you through an imposing stone wall which was originally four and even six feet wide in places.

From here the level path follows an old woods road to a four-way intersection. Turn left onto the white-blazed trail and walk steadily uphill under oak and black birch. Make a sharp turn to the left and pass through a rock wall where a big white ash stands on the left. Bits of rusty barbed wire embedded in the trees represent what was once a major technological leap from stone walls for enclosing livestock. The path is mostly level now, but bears right and climbs in a switchback, turning left. Pass through another stone wall, cross a damp swale, and continue climbing through lots of hay-scented, New York, and Christmas fern; spicebush; red maple;

ash; hickories; and oaks. Pass through yet another wall and then bear right, paralleling a well-built chest-high rock wall on the left back to the kiosk and the roadside parking straight ahead.

FALL FINERY

In late summer, as the days gradually shorten, tree leaves halt their production of green chlorophyll as if on cue. The diminishing daylight brings about this change, and gradually, as the chlorophyll dissipates, the other pigments contained in the leaves assert themselves visually. In New England, the maples, both sugar and red, produce some of the most glorious autumnal foliage known anywhere on earth. Weather conditions leading up to this time can influence the quality of the show, but even during so-called poor foliage years, the pageant put on by Mother Nature has few rivals anywhere.

Only after the first frosts do the leaves reveal their most intense colors. Some leaves become a golden yellow, while others, usually the red, or swamp, maple, take on a scarlet-red hue as early as late August. Ashes are transformed into an odd but attractive maroon. The signature bright-yellow and fluorescent-orange foliage of our sugar maple is the most renowned among all the trees and the primary reason that the annual fall foliage spectacle in New England has spawned a multimillion-dollar tourist industry.

The trees, of course, are simply and elegantly preparing for the drought winter will bring by hoarding most of their water and nutrients in extensive root systems below ground. When the hard frosts finally come, a layer of cells located at the attachment point of leaf stem and twig gives way, sending billions of spent leaves cascading to the ground and into waterways, where they will eventually be broken down by bacteria, fungi, and a host of other microorganisms and soil invertebrates. The nutrients, far from being lost, are reduced to their basic building blocks and made available for incorporation into the tissues of other plants and animals, the ultimate recycling plant.

Getting There

From the convergence of Interstate 384 and Routes 6 and 44 east of Manchester, take Route 6 east for 25.4 miles to the junction with Route 97. From the junction of Routes 97 and 6, turn south (left) onto Route 97 and drive 3.6 miles to the entrance of the refuge on the left. There is parking space for several vehicles off the pavement.

—R.L.

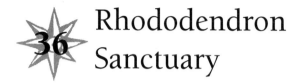

Rhododendron Sanctuary

Voluntown

- Rhododendron Sanctuary Trail
- 0.5-mile round trip
- 10-foot elevation gain
- 0.5 hour
- easy

The Rhododendron Sanctuary is one of the most uniquely beautiful places in all of Connecticut. Nestled in the temperate climate of the southeast corner of the state, this botanical wonder is in the middle of a swamp forested with hemlock and Atlantic white cedar. Beneath the trees are immense tangles of native rosebay rhododendrons ten to fifteen feet tall with leaves up to ten inches long. Spectacular.

The walk to the rhododendron sanctuary is in Pachaug State Forest in the H. H. Chapman Recreation Area.

Look Forward To

- wild rosebay rhododendrons
- Atlantic white cedar swamp
- boardwalk through swamp

The Trail

The trail to the Rhododendron Sanctuary begins in a dry forest of birch, pitch pine, red cedar, and hemlock. The soil in which these trees are growing is sandy and well-drained, with low fertility. The trees that grow here are well adapted to surviving in these difficult conditions. Beneath the trees are more plants that do well in difficult sites, including sheep laurel and highbush blueberry.

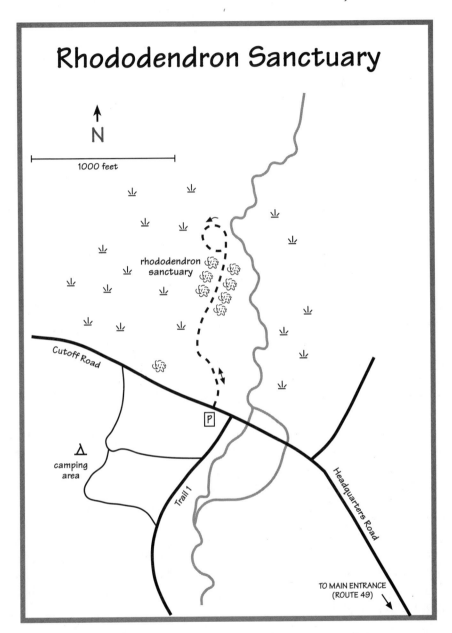

The trail is blazed with pale blue markers and was once part of the Pachaug Trail. Along the path patches of shining club moss grow next to princess pine. Shining club moss, also called running pine, is a slender, glossy evergreen plant with hundreds of scruffy little leaves. The plant looks like a little green bottle brush. Princess pine is also evergreen but looks like a small, four-inch-tall pine tree growing on the forest floor. As different as these plants look, they are actually closely related, different species of the same group of plants called club moss. Mingling with the running pine and princess pine are clumps of wintergreen and colonies of Canada mayflower.

The path descends the short way to the cedar swamp and begins to traverse the wetland on a raised gravel walkway. To either side wild iris, skunk cabbage, and sheets of sphagnum moss grow in the tea-colored water. Two types of trees predominate in the waterlogged soil; Canadian hemlock and Atlantic white cedar. Hemlock has small, flat, dark green needles marked with two white lines beneath. It thrives in the cool climate of the wetland, but the standing water atop its roots does have an effect, inhibiting the passage of oxygen to the roots and slowing growth. The result is that even some fairly small trees in the swamp are actually very old. A six-inch-diameter hemlock in well-drained soil is probably 20 to 30 years old, while a tree of equal size in the cedar swamp can be 100 years old or more.

The other tree growing here is Atlantic white cedar, a beautiful tree with a strong, straight trunk and smooth, fibrous bark. The evergreen leaves are thin, scaly, and arranged like miniature fans. The wood of Atlantic white cedar is famous for being very resistant to rot. Untreated wood can survive for decades in swamps without rotting.

As you proceed farther into the swamp, the first rhododendrons appear mixed in with highbush blueberry and mountain laurel. As you continue to walk, the magnificence of these plants surrounds you. The gnarled trunks reach up to fifteen feet tall with deep, glossy evergreen leaves from six to ten inches long. Crowning each branch is a large flower bud that opens in late June to early July, revealing a showy truss of white to light-pink flowers. Gorgeous.

About midway through the swamp the gravel walkway yields to a boardwalk that guides you the remainder of the way. Near the looping turnaround at the end of the trail is a section where a patch of rhododendrons and the large hemlocks above them have died. They were killed, ironically enough, by too much water.

For the last few years beaver have been busy constructing a dam downstream from the swamp. As the water built up behind the dam it raised the water level of the swamp. At first glance, it may seem that such a change would do no harm, but a swamp such as this one is a very fragile thing. The conditions are so difficult that many of the trees and shrubs are under stress all their lives. Even a modest beaver-induced flood can push these plants over the edge and destroy large areas of the sanctuary. The beaver dams are removed when they threaten the sanctuary, and park personnel are monitoring the damaged area to see if the rhododendrons and hemlock return.

The trail makes a short loop near the damaged area. Retrace your steps to return to the parking area.

ROSEBAYS

The rosebay rhododendron is the largest rhododendron of eastern North America, with some specimens reaching thirty-five feet tall. It is native from the coastal plain of Maine through southern New England, and from the Catskills through the Appalachians to northern Georgia. In the northern part of its range the rosebay is uncommon, forming isolated and often widely separated colonies in swamps and marshes. Farther south it thrives in the cool climates of the higher elevations of the Appalachian and Great Smoky Mountains, where it can form dense, impenetrable stands in damp forests. It is one of the most spectacular plants you will see in the wild and lends a touch of the exotic to wetland forests.

Rosebay rhododendron growing in the Rhododendron Sanctuary.

Rosebays are one of two large rhododendrons of the eastern states, the other being the catawba, or mountain rosebay. Catawbas are smaller than rosebays, growing to twenty feet tall with six-inch-long evergreen leaves as opposed to rosebays' ten-inch-long evergreen leaves. While rosebays sport blush-white blossoms, catawbas display trusses of deep-rose to purple-lavender flowers. Catawba rhododendrons grow in a narrow belt in and around the Great Smoky Mountains.

As beautiful as these rhododendrons are in the wild, chances are you don't have to venture past your backyard to appreciate them. Many very popular rhododendron varieties are derived from these native plants. Catawba varieties include 'Roseum Elegans', 'Cunningham's White', 'English Roseum', 'President Lincoln', 'and Charles Dickens'. Rosebay varieties include 'Album', and 'Purpureum'. Any and all of these plants can bring beauty as well as a touch of the wild to your garden.

Getting There

From Voluntown center take combined Routes 138/165/49 east 0.4 mile to an intersection where Route 49 leaves left. Turn onto Route 49 and follow it the short distance to the main entrance to Pachaug State Forest on the left. After entering the forest proceed along the main road 0.9 mile. Turn left at the fork, cross a small bridge, and enter the Chapman Recreation Area. Parking is straight ahead.

—C.S.

 # Mount Misery

Voluntown

- Combined Nehantic, Pachaug Trail
- 1.7-mile round trip
- 170-foot elevation gain
- 0.5–1.0 hour
- moderate

Mount Misery is a pair of rocky promontories in Pachaug State Forest. Its low elevation (441 feet) allows many people who could not climb higher ridges access to the twin summits and their beautiful panoramic views. Along the way are songbirds and interesting wildflowers which give ample reason to pause and enjoy blossoms and melodies.

The walk to Mount Misery is along the Pachaug Trail, which is marked with pale blue blazes. Turns are noted by two stacked blazes, with the upper blaze offset in the direction of the turn.

Look Forward To

- beautiful views
- wildflowers
- songbirds

The Trail

From the Chapman Area parking lot walk down Cutoff Road past the trail to the Rhododendron Sanctuary. Continue northwest down the forest road to the green gate. Pass through the gate and cross a small stream in a hemlock grove. Just beyond the stream the combined Nehantic, Pachaug Trail enters the woods on the left. Follow the blue blazes into the grove of hemlock and white pine. The shady evergreens and the soft

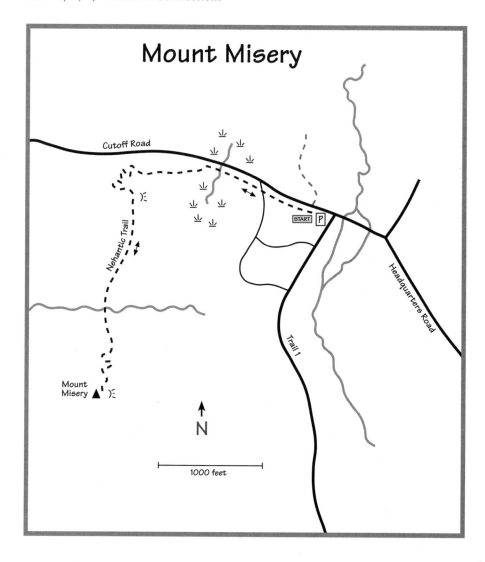

Mount Misery

Cutoff Road

Nehantic Trail

START P

Headquarters Road

Trail 1

Mount
Misery ▲

N

|———————————————|
1000 feet

feel of needles underfoot make this section of trail especially inviting in summer. In winter the grove is a refuge for such wintering birds as chickadees, titmice, downy woodpeckers, nuthatches, and brown creepers. Sometimes small groups of kinglets also spend time in the shelter of the hemlock branches.

Beneath the trees are thickets of laurel and one or two Atlantic white cedars. As the path begins the climb up the north slope of Mount Misery, the cool evergreens increasingly give way to oaks. The treadway becomes rocky as the path weaves up the hill using a series of switch-backs. From May to late summer warblers and thrushes sing in the woods.

As the trail crests the hill, it turns sharply left (east) and proceeds through woods of white pine, hemlock, and oak to a bare rock shelf with a nice easterly view. This is a great spot to stop and rest a bit. The frequent breeze here discourages bugs from bothering you too much in summer. In fall the colorful foliage makes the view even better. An old windfall lies across the ledge, while wild cherry trees ring the bare bedrock.

From the rock shelf the trail follows the contour of the ledge south, offering peekaboo views through the trees. In winter this is a pleasant walk, with broad vistas available through the bare branches. The forest along the ridge is typical of rocky woodlands in southern Connecticut, with white pine, oak, and pitch pine. Colonies of lowbush blueberry blossom in late April and produce small but tasty berries in late July and early August. Wintergreen is another plant that grows along the path. This trailing woody plant has glossy evergreen leaves about an inch or two long. In spring small white flowers appear, followed in late summer by bright red berries. Wintergreen is easy to identify because the leaves and berries always smell of wintergreen.

Soon the trail begins a gentle descent, passing isolated plants of spotted wintergreen and pipsissewa. Both these wildflowers have evergreen leaves and springtime waxy, whitish flowers with five petals. The path then comes to a small brook that marks the low point between the north ridge and the summit of Mount Misery. Cross the stream on a plank bridge and begin the climb to the top of Mount Misery. The path becomes steeper as you pass through woods of beech, oak, and white pine. Isolated specimens of highbush blueberry offer tasty treats in late summer.

The grade steepens as the terrain becomes studded with boulders and rock outcrops. The last section of trail becomes steep and passes by a large rock from which there is a pleasing view before gaining the crest of the mountain. The summit area of Mount Misery is mostly bare rock ledge with scattered white pine, bear oak, and pitch pine. Thorny strands of greenbrier snake through the brush. The views from the bedrock ledges are more than worth the climb, with a panoramic vista to the south, east, and north which includes parts of Connecticut and Rhode Island. One of the birds that frequents the ridge is the Eastern towhee. The male has a black head and back and chestnut-colored sides, while the female has a gray head and back and chestnut sides. Towhees are frequent ground feeders and have a habit of searching for meals by quickly hopping forward and backward in dry leaves to uncover prey. These little birds make a great deal of noise while looking for food, which can frighten the heck out of people unfamiliar with the woods. A little investigation, however, reveals the innocent nature of the disturbance.

To return to the parking area, simply retrace your steps.

MY LITTLE CHICKADEE

Many people limit their woodland walks to the warmer months, when the forest is replete with the diverse songs of warblers, thrushes, vireos, and other migrant songbirds. An increasing number of people are finding the simple pleasures of hiking in winter, however. In the colder months the migrant birds have gone, abandoning the northern landscape for warmer climates. But those who walk in winter are not alone. Keeping you company along the way are birds that live here all year long. And they have developed an interesting, inventive way to survive the New England winter.

Most of the year flocks of birds are made up of members of the same species, blackbirds or starlings, for example. In winter, however, a number of different species team up to make what ornithologists call a mixed flock. The primary members of such flocks here are chickadees and titmice. Birds of many other species join the mixed flock now and then, but are not central members. These other birds include downy and hairy woodpeckers, nuthatches, and brown creepers.

Each morning the chickadees and titmice group together and begin to forage their territory. Within that territory they search the trees for insects trying to pass the winter months in the relative safety of bark crevices and tucked into tufts of pine needles. Other groups of chickadees and titmice are kept out of this foraging territory, but the other species are let in and out of different groups as they please.

If danger threatens, such as a prowling hawk passing by, some of the chickadees and titmice let out alarm calls. This helps all members of the flock, whether they are chickadees or woodpeckers, find shelter before they become someone's supper. As it turns out, chickadees are especially good at detecting danger and quickly letting others know about it. So good that birds of other species, such as woodpeckers and nuthatches, can spend more time looking for food than they would if they were hunting alone. They get fatter because they rely on the chickadees to warn them of danger.

The next time you see a group of chickadees, remember that they are more than cute little birds. They have developed a survival strategy that benefits not only themselves, but many other of our favorite winter birds as well.

Getting There

From Voluntown center take combined Routes 138/165/49 east 0.4 mile to an intersection where Route 49 leaves left. Turn onto Route 49 and follow it the short distance to the main entrance to Pachaug State Forest on the left. After entering the forest, proceed along the main road 0.9 mile. Turn left at the fork, cross a small bridge, and enter the Chapman Recreation Area. Parking is straight ahead.

—C.S.

38 Laurel Loop

Voluntown

- Nehantic Crossover Trail, Laurel Loop Trail
- 3.3-mile loop
- 130-foot elevation gain
- 2.0–3.0 hours
- moderate

This is a walk for mountain laurel junkies. There are literally miles of laurel thickets to stroll through, many tangles reaching over ten feet tall. In spring when the bushes are in full bloom, the trail is as beautiful as any botanical garden. In addition there are forested marshes with interesting plants and birds and old stone foundations and walls.

The walk along Laurel Loop is in the Green Falls Area of Pachaug State Forest. The Nehantic Crossover Trail is marked with a red dot in a pale blue rectangle. The Laurel Loop Trail is marked with a yellow dot in a pale blue rectangle.

Look Forward To

- mountain laurel
- old stone foundations
- more mountain laurel
- forested marsh

The Trail

From the parking area walk down the road to the tollbooth at the road junction. Enter the woods on the east side of the tollbooth and pass through a forest of white pine, oak, and laurel. Get used to the view, because this oak

254

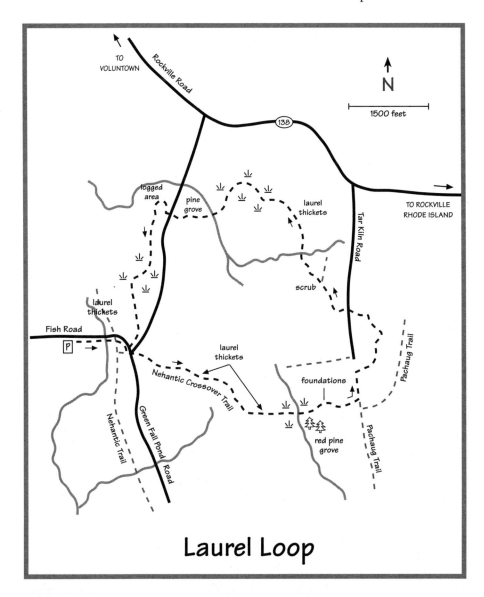

Laurel Loop

and laurel forest, so typical of many parts of south and central Connecticut, seems to go on for miles. The trail proceeds gently uphill through a nonstop sea of evergreen laurel leaves. In June this walk is spectacular, with frothy clouds of whitish pink blossoms floating on glossy green leaves. These woods are home to many creatures as well as beautiful plants. Garter snakes are common in the dry woodlands and enjoy sunning themselves in the dappled light beneath the oaks. Deer come through from time to time, and even the odd coyote and fox are here.

After crossing a small wetland the path levels out. What follows is one of the nicest stretches of trail anywhere. For a long while the laurel creeps up to the edges of the trail, touching your arms and shoulders as you pass by. The tall shade of the oaks is omnipresent, and together they afford a wonderfully relaxing serenity. Sometimes the laurel is only waist high, while at other times it towers over your head like an emerald-colored arch. In spring and summer the migrant songbirds can be heard from the trees or within the evergreen thickets near the path.

The trail eventually begins to head downhill to a shallow swale where a small stream meanders. The laurel yields to brambles and greenbrier, that nasty vining plant with the grabby black thorns and clusters of blue-black fruit that persist from fall to spring. Greenbrier is by nature a scratchy thing, but it is not all bad. It has another aspect to its personality besides inflicting thorny misery on passersby: it is actually a tasty spring treat, the young shoots gathered and prepared like asparagus.

Besides greenbrier and tall oak trees, ruffed grouse like this swampy area. They like to hide from predators (to a grouse, a hiker is as much a predator as a coyote is). They have a habit of waiting until you are almost on top of them, then bursting out of the scrub with a thunderous flapping of wings to scare the life out of you. Folks who often walk the woods eventually get used to it, but I know some people who have been hikers for years and still jump every time a grouse flushes nearby.

From the stream it is a short walk through a dead red pine grove to a complex of stone foundations which are truly interesting sights. The stones are arranged in a Stonehenge-like pattern of walls alternating with open spaces. They are unlike any foundations I have run across elsewhere in the state.

From the foundations the woods are open and lovely. The path is level at first, then begins a gradual climb to a scrubby clearing where the Nehantic Crossover Trail meets the Laurel Loop. *Caution:* The Nehantic Crossover Trail is well maintained; such is not always the case with the Laurel Loop Trail. It can get seriously overgrown. If the trail becomes difficult to follow, turn around and take the sure way back. If the trail is maintained, it is a delightful walk.

At the grassy path the red-dot Nehantic Crossover turns right, while the yellow-dot Laurel Loop turns left (north). Turn onto the Laurel Loop and follow the grassy road through scrubby blueberry, laurel, and sheep laurel. Just before a rock barricade near private land, the trail turns right, into the woods. Follow the path through more waist-high scrub, passing a rock outcrop before coming to paved Tar Kiln Road. Cross the road onto a wide grassy woods road which is easy to follow. Highbush blueberry here affords a nice nibble in late summer.

Laurel Loop proceeds through a scrubby area before turning left where an unmarked path proceeds straight ahead. This junction can be easily missed and is not signed. Look for a blaze on a tree to the left. The path then heads downhill into more thick laurel and crosses a small stream. The laurel is very thick through here, often growing well over your head. From the stream continue through a patch of tall trees before again descending to a marshy area overgrown with greenbrier. A privately owned field is just to the right.

The trail then passes through a long section of mixed pine and hardwood, eventually coming to a stream spanned by a quaint wooden bridge. Cross the bridge and proceed to a pine grove which provides welcome cool shade on a hot summer's day.

The Laurel Loop trail, framed by a tranquil pine grove.

From the pine woods it is a short walk to the junction with a dirt forest road. Cross the road and follow the path into a logged area. Continue downhill, crossing several wet, swampy areas beneath the shade of dark-green hemlock trees. Laurel Loop then passes through waves of laurel, crossing more small streams before emerging from the woods near the toll-booth. From the tollbooth it is a short walk back to the parking area.

GARTER SNAKES

One summer when I was a very little kid, my much older brother kept a garter snake in a glass terrarium in the living room. He was going through what my parents called the "snake phase" of adolescence, and he was allowed to keep the snake for a couple of days. The condition was, of course, that the animal have plenty of food and water. That is where I came in. I was hired to procure the snake's diet, which was assumed to be little toads. When I caught one, I could put it in the terrarium where the snake awaited, and my brother would give me a nickel. Now, I liked snakes, but I liked toads too, and I had a battle with my conscience about knowingly depositing hopping amphibians in harm's way. After some thought, I arrived at a solution, and went out to hunt toads.

Garter snakes are the most common snake in Connecticut. If you bump into a snake along the trail or in the backyard, chances are it will be a garter snake. Both males and females have alternating yellow and black or yellow and gray stripes along their backs and a red tongue tipped with black, which makes them easy to recognize. The females are decidedly larger than the males, with adult females reaching three feet or more while their male counterparts are most often eighteen inches or less.

Garter snakes are perhaps the hardiest of all New World snakes, living nearly as far north as the Arctic Circle and being active well into fall. I once came upon a garter snake slipping through the grass in mid-December. They live in forests, fields, and wetlands and hibernate from midautumn to March. They mate in spring and the young are born in late summer. In the warmer months they become creatures of routine, returning to the same places at the same times just about every day.

Their favorite food is small frogs, with insects, salamanders, and earthworms rounding out their die—which brings us back to toads. It took me a little while, but I caught a toad I thought suitable and put it in the terrarium with the snake. My mother's patience wore out very soon after that, fearing for the snake's health, so the garter snake was released where my brother had originally found it. By the way, the toad was released as well. I had put the biggest toad I could find in the terrarium, and the snake never bothered that big boy one bit.

Getting There

From the center of Voluntown proceed to the south junction of Routes 138/49. Turn south onto Route 49 and travel 0.9 mile to Fish Road (sign says Green Falls Entrance). Turn left onto Fish Road and travel 1.1 miles to a pull-off parking area on right. Park here and walk 0.2 mile farther on Fish Road to a junction where a tollbooth is placed in season. The walk begins on the Nehantic Crossover Trail, which enters the woods near the east side of the tollbooth.

—C.S.

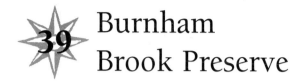

Burnham Brook Preserve

East Haddam

- unnamed blue blazed trail
- 1.7-mile loop
- 175-foot elevation gain
- 2.0 hours
- easy, with moderate sections

The 491-acre Burnham Brook Preserve has a magical feel about it. This Nature Conservancy property, located a short distance southeast of Devil's Hopyard State Park, has all the rural charm and atmosphere not readily found at more heavily visited properties.

Here you'll walk along well-built stone walls bordering a sunny hayfield; through rocky, open woodlands of towering hardwood trees under which verdant patches of ferns flourish; and along a lovely hemlock ravine through which courses clear Burnham Brook.

Some places possess a certain inherent magic. Burnham Brook Preserve is a place where the solitude so rare today is palpable. The solitude and the elegant beauty of the natural world, now left virtually undisturbed, combine to make a great impression on the psyche. This is just such a place for me—a place I want to return to again and again.

Look Forward To

- well-built stone walls

- hemlock ravine and brook

- ledge outcrops

- huge glacial erratic

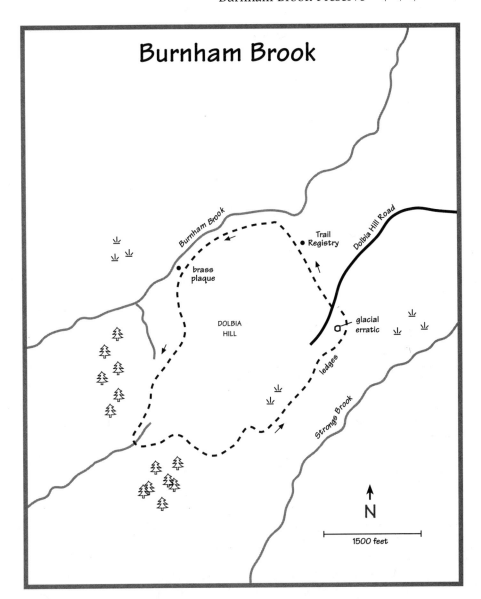

The Trail

Walk around the end of the three-rail barway and into the woods on a wide lane bordered on both sides by sturdy stone walls. Oak, hickory, and sugar maple shade the entryway. Red cedar trees, now in the process of being shaded out, border the lane on the right. To the left on the crest of Dolbia Hill are privately owned hayfields. Wooden nest boxes mounted on metal pipes in the large field host nesting bluebird broods in spring and summer. The level path is bordered by hay-scented fern which take on a honey color in fall. The mosaic of forest canopy is composed of red maple, whose scarlet leaves are stunning in fall against a cobalt-blue sky, black cherry, and black oak. Red cedar and sassafras form a second, lower tier while highbush blueberry dominates the shrub layer.

Come to a trail junction on the right at an opening in a stone wall; continue straight and begin walking downhill very gradually. Beyond the three wooden rails of a barway on the left, there are bucolic views of the field. Periodic cutting keeps it from regenerating to forest. Pass a second gap in the stone wall; large dark mica crystals are very apparent in the rocks at your feet. Pinkish feldspar crystals are also noticeable. Two oak species join the mix—white oak and chestnut oak—while black (or sweet) birch and sassafras are common. Ironwood and red maple are also present.

Reach a sign and trail register at the corner of a stone wall that was used as a convenient repository for additional rocks cleared in subsequent springs, after the wall was initially built. Proceed straight, downhill; the rock wall on your left continues. Pass a gap in the wall. A stout grapevine with brown, shredding bark climbs high into a supporting white oak here. In fall, the foliage display is gorgeous. A low stone wall now begins on the right, bounded beyond by a sea of hay-scented fern. A few boulders sit on this gradual slope among the ferns, also known as boulder fern. Common birds of the oak woods—bold and raucous blue jays and impudent tufted titmice—add their voices to the sounds made by fluttering leaves.

Pass a twin-boled white oak on the left with impressive poison ivy vines climbing up it. A few small eastern hemlock appear, and then tulip trees. Dark-green Christmas fern, which requires rich, moist soils, pokes up through the earth tones of the leaf litter. On the left sits a boulder sporting very visible mica and quartz crystals, two of the three minerals that make up granite; the third is feldspar. New York fern commences as the slope continues gradually down. This species has fronds that are tapered at both ends, making it easily recognizable. It, along with hay-scented fern, forms a veritable carpet on the forest floor. Wild geranium blooms along the path in spring.

At a yellow birch, the trail jogs right as the stone wall to your left bends away in that direction. A brook that flows only during wet seasons is reached. Spicebush shrubs indicate the moister soil. Cross the drainageway and follow blue blazes, more numerous now, steadily but comfortably downhill. Both highbush and lowbush blueberries, ironwood, young American beech, and black cherry grow under the canopy of chestnut, red, and white oaks; red maple; black birch; and tulip tree. Chestnut oak seedlings, which do well on dry, well-drained sites, are numerous. Their leaves are wavy edged and not oaklike. Huckleberry, whose leaves are covered with minute resin dots, unlike those of the similar blueberry, appear.

Bear left at the base of the slope. You are walking on a terrace now, with the slope dropping away to the right down to the brook which is as yet not visible. The trees—many of them beech—appear quite young, with few trunk diameters greater than ten inches. The impression is one of rather open woods with little undergrowth. There are many ironwoods, whose rippled gray trunks have a muscular appearance. Hop hornbeam, an understory tree with thin, flaky brown bark, first appears here, while red maple is still very common. Pass under a fourteen-inch-diameter hemlock, the largest so far, and then spot on the left one that is a full two feet across. The timber is definitely getting larger as you pass around the end of an old fallen tree, some of the black birch and maple being especially large.

Walk through an intermittent drainageway; along its margins a few Christmas fern as well as spicebush and New York fern have found sufficient moisture. In autumn the sugar maples' golden foliage is gorgeous. The dark green leaves of mountain laurel shrubs stand out as if polished, sunlight reflecting very brightly off the upper leaf surfaces. At a sugar maple the trail turns right and proceeds downhill gently. A few small flowering dogwood trees, which blossom in May, stand on the right near two large ash. Yellow birch becomes more numerous and a thicket of mountain laurel, with gnarled trunks, comes into view. Pass through a stone wall and bear left toward a large hemlock. Katydids, sounding far bigger than they are, call their names rhythmically from the foliage high above. Sometimes they shorten the verse simply to *did...did.*

Enter laurels just above Burnham Brook and follow the path diagonally downslope amid the chirp of the katydids. Hemlock and yellow birch are much more common in this cool ravine. Reach rocky, permanent Burnham Brook, a tributary of the Eight Mile River, which flows directly into Long Island Sound approximately eight miles south. Outcrops of gneiss rock are visible on the far side. *The trail now turns left and parallels the brook; it may be difficult to distinguish after leaf-fall.* Interrupted fern and creeping partridgeberry line the path. Some yellow birch are quite large. This is one of my favorite trees—the burnished-brass look of the curly metallic bark is unique; in winter, low-angle rays of sunlight reflecting off the yellowish trunks make these trees stand out in a most pleasing and easily recognizable way.

Cross a small feeder stream where leafy liverworts grow on the damp stones. Walk under a fallen but still living hemlock whose root ball is covered with moss and shining club moss. Hemlock is especially numerous on the north-facing left slope, while deciduous trees predominate on the opposite, sunnier side. Tiny golden-crowned kinglets flit and briefly hover among the hemlock needles in search of insects and spiders in fall and winter. A summer resident, hermit thrush, bathes in the brook and then preens its feathers. At a boulder on the left, the trail begins to climb above Burnham Brook. One old red maple trunk is blackened by fire. As you climb, the ravine becomes deeper and more clothed in hemlock.

A very large (two feet in diameter), straight, and tall American beech stands at the point where the trail bears left, then right. Come to a brass plaque mounted on a boulder which commemorates the establishment of the preserve in 1960. It is dedicated to John Ide, a donor and one of the founders of the preserve. Horizontal ledge rock outcrops emerge from the forest floor and poke out just beyond the brook, exposed by water erosion. The trail now swings left and upslope, away from the brook, through open woods. A rotting piece of wood hid a two-and-a-half-inch-long red-backed salamander on a late-October visit. Bear right under hemlock, beech, birch, and red oak. A rock wall comes into view above you on the left. The trail undulates left and right as it continues along the shoulder of the modest slope.

Turn left toward a stone wall, skirting the end of it. A low rock wall, reduced to rubble, trails off at a sharp angle to the right. Pass a grapevine climbing up a hemlock just before you enter a stand of hardwoods—red maple, yellow birch, oak, and tulip tree—with patches of New York fern beneath. Walk by some tulip trees that have two-foot-plus diameters. Winterberry shrubs are adorned with bright red fruits. Grapevines with stringy bark hang down on the right from small trees, including hop hornbeam. Continue under a low overhang of winterberry. Another rock pile sits in the right angle of a stone wall on the left as you walk gently uphill. The stone wall to your left is formidable—chin high to an adult of average height.

Make a right turn at a young yellow birch displaying a double blue blaze. In fall the ground is uniformly covered with a blanket of fallen leaves, except where turkey and deer have been foraging for acorns. Plenty of young hemlock grow below the oak, maple, and birch. Walk gradually downslope amid the excited alarm cries of blue jays. Small rock piles are numerous on the forest floor. It is difficult to believe that this woodland once produced livestock rather than yellow birch and eastern hemlock. Where sunlight penetrates the canopy, ferns flourish. The path turns left at a double-blazed black birch and continues through shady hemlock, oak, birch, and maple woods, with mountain laurel below. Gray squirrels gather acorns on the forest floor in preparation for the oncoming winter.

Ledge outcrops are visible up the slope to the right. Dead hemlock stand on top. I heard the laughing call of a pileated woodpecker, a large bird which requires extensive mature forest, one October here. Bear left in laurels and pass through a seasonally damp area. If you visit during dry periods, listen carefully and you may be able to hear water flowing beneath the rocks when you reach the brook bed. *The trail, however, turns right just before you reach the brook's bank. This is easy to miss, as there are no blazes here.* Turn right and follow along the bank. A double blue blaze now comes into view ahead as the land rises up on both sides of you. Turn left at the double blaze, cross the brook bed, and bear right along the shoulder of a rocky talus slope.

Gray gneiss ledges rise up above the rocky brook channel downstream. Crusty greenish gray lichens hold ever so tightly to the rocks of the slope, joined by green mosses. Evergreen wood fern also pokes up among the boulders. With a little imagination the dark-green mats of moss appear like a forest as seen from an airplane high above. Some of the moss has a furry quality and looks like a green version of the forehead hair of a Hereford cow. Pass a four-trunked red oak on the left and continue uphill, soon reaching the top of the ledge outcrop. Virginia creeper vines decorate some boulders. From here you'll be treated to nice views of the forest below, especially after leaf-fall.

The trail now bears left and squeezes you through a cleft in the rocks. A quartz vein is evident at the top of one boulder on the left, immediately beyond the cleft. Follow along the top of the ledge as it bears left; there are many dead hemlock here. Pincushion-like masses of silver mound moss line the rocks along the path. This is a scenic area and a fine place to relax and have a snack. The trail continues to climb and curves left, away from the cliff face, and then bears right under picturesque mountain laurel shrubs whose foliage is higher than your head. Pass an isolated boulder on the right and note that most hemlock are dead in this area. Continue on rather level ground under white oak, red maple, and more laurel bushes. The slope drops away to the right.

One of our most vocal woodpeckers, the beautiful "zebra-backed" red-bellied, has a churring call which is easily recognized once you learn it; listen for it in oak woodland like this. Another woodland singer here is our familiar eastern chipmunk, whose clucks and chirps are surprisingly bird-like to the uninitiated ear. Just below the ledge on the right is an old cedar fence line, the wire long ago having disintegrated. Descend very gradually as the trail parallels the outcrop.

Turn sharply right at a point marked by double blazes just before reaching the end of a stone wall on the right. Walk down to the old cedar-post fence line, bear right, and cross it diagonally. To the right are fine views of the ledge just crossed. Walk toward a large windfall that was chain-sawed where it fell across the trail, but be sure to turn left just before it. *The trail splits at the log; do not follow the right fork. Instead turn left and walk past the root ball of the fallen tree, up the slope under hemlock, black birch, and oak. This turn can be easily missed.* When the path reaches the top of the ledge cliff, bear left and follow along the outcrop. Oak and young beech trees predominate as the outcropping drops off sharply to the right. A white-breasted nuthatch gives its nasal *yank-yank* call as it clings head down to the rough bark of a white oak.

Huckleberry grows in profusion here. Continue walking near the cliff edge, where a nice view of the forest below is to be had. A screened view of a wooded ridge beyond is enhanced by leaf-fall. You are headed northeast now, over the top of these forty-foot-high ledges. The rocks are covered with the rosettes of gray-green leafy lichens. Thirty feet beyond a pair of trees (an oak on the right and a hickory on the left), the path turns right and heads with moderate steepness downhill off the ledge. To the right rocks line the path.

Before reaching a stone wall ahead, turn left at a blazed oak and walk gradually downhill, adjacent to the ledges on the left above. You're progressing along the edge of a hemlock stand now. On the left side Christmas fern dots the forest floor under a cover of hardwoods. Notice the contrast between the sunny black birch, oak, and hickory forest and the shaded hemlock stand on the right. Skeletons of red cedar indicate that this was once pastureland. Pass through a small stand of flowering dogwood trees and curve right. An enormous truck-sized glacial erratic rests off the trail to the left up ahead. Several other large boulders are also present where the ice sheet dropped them.

Below the hemlock and witch hazel are mica-filled rocks which sparkle as you walk over them. More flowering dogwood and some ironwood make an appearance. Dogwood, in fact, becomes quite numerous; its large, four-petaled, white blossoms are a lovely sight in spring. Boldly patterned striped wintergreen plants pop up through the leaf litter trailside. Sweet pepperbush, common in coastal regions, grows thickly in the slightly moister ground, and tulip trees, which also require a fair amount of soil moisture, reappear. The hillside to the left below the ledge is adorned with

Christmas fern. An interesting fallen beech has rotted off at the tip but lives as three live, tree-size shoots which grow vertically from its prostrate trunk. Pass through a boulder field, where spicebush shrubs with red fruits grow among the rocks, and reach a rock wall; pass "through" it.

Tulip tree, birch, and lots of fragrant spicebush grow in the damp area on the right. Walk under overarching witch hazel shrubs which produce straggly yellow but welcome flowers in fall, and begin heading steadily uphill. White oak becomes common as you reach a stone wall halfway up the slope. A big chestnut oak stands on the right. Hickory and more dogwood appear now. Lifeless in the shade of the hardwoods are long-dead red cedar. The trail bends left and climbs gradually along the base of the hill, which you soon crest. Reach Dolbia Hill Road, turn left, and walk about 200 feet back to your vehicle.

FENCES IN THE FOREST

Perhaps Connecticut should be known as the stone wall state. Given its very modest size, this state had an incredible 20,505 miles of stone fences in 1871, fully one-third of all fences in the state at that time. I've come to marvel at these byproducts of Yankee agriculture. Having grown up in the Midwest, I never actually took them for granted, but I never fully appreciated them either, until reading about what went into their construction.

Stone walls—more accurately stone fences—served as real barriers that prevented grazing livestock from getting into one's neighbor's or, for that matter, one's own cornfields. And this was not taken lightly during the colonial era, when nearly everyone's livelihood depended upon subsistence agriculture. It was each farmer's solemn responsibility to keep his walls in good repair, lest he court the wrath of both his immediate neighbors and the community. To a far lesser extent, they also served as boundary markers.

It took two strong individuals one long day to build ten feet of well-constructed stone wall. That included collection of the raw material the glaciers were so generous in providing, and building a foundation which had to begin two feet below the surface to ensure that the wall would not be damaged by frost heave. A properly constructed wall was at least four feet high. The heavy stones—one cubic foot of granite weighs 150 pounds, for instance—were hauled by oxen (and later by plow horses) on wooden sledges known as "stone boats."

But why *stone* for fences? Stone was an abundant building material and wood was scarce, especially right after the Revolution. Every household burned thirty to forty cords of firewood each year—a huge amount by today's standards. New England was, as a result, only 20 percent forested back then. Stone was a last choice, really, but these fences lasted forever if properly maintained.

Each spring the action of freezing and thawing ground water brought a new "crop" of tough gneiss or granite stones to the surface which had to be cleared before planting could commence. Is it any wonder, then, that New England's rocky ground was abandoned for the thick, fertile, black prairie soils of the Midwest in the 1840s?

Today these walls, so seemingly out of place now, remain as picturesque reminders of a bygone era and as an important part of our shared agricultural heritage.

Getting There

From the north, follow Route 2 and then Route 11 and take Exit 5 (Witch Meadow Road), turning right at the bottom of the ramp. Follow Witch Meadow Road for 0.5 mile, and then turn left onto West Road and drive 2.5 miles to Dolbia Hill Road. Turn right and travel 0.55 mile up Dolbia Hill Road to the entrance on the right (to the second barway). Pull off the road; there is room for a limited number of vehicles.

From the west, follow Interstate 95 to Old Lyme, Exit 70, and turn left at the bottom of the ramp onto Route 156. Follow it for approximately 9.0 miles to its terminus and turn right onto Route 82. Continue for 2.5 miles to Woodbridge Road, turn left, and drive 1.0 mile; then turn left onto Dolbia Hill Road. Follow it 0.55 mile to the entrance on the right.

From the east follow I-95 to Exit 77, turn right onto Route 85, and drive approximately 10.0 miles to the traffic light at Route 82. Turn left onto Route 82 and drive 2.3 miles to Woodbridge Road. Travel for 1.0 mile on Woodbridge Road and turn left onto Dolbia Hill Road. The entrance is 0.55 mile down on the right.

—R.L.

40 Devil's Hopyard State Park

East Haddam

- Vista Trail
- 2.5-mile loop
- 300-foot elevation gain
- 2.0 hours
- easy, with moderate sections

Flowing water and its dramatic effects are the chief features at Devil's Hopyard, an 860-acre park with a fanciful name and an extensive trail system. Chapman Falls, on the cold-running Eight Mile River, is the major attraction. It cascades over three tiers capped with erosion-resistant schist rock in a picturesque fall totaling sixty vertical feet. Potholes varying in diameter from a few inches to several feet pockmark the bedrock below the falls.

The falls are located some fifteen miles north of the shores of Long Island Sound in a long-dormant fault zone which separates the Windham Hills region of the state from the coastal slope to the south. They once powered both a gristmill (until 1854) and a sawmill (until about 1895).

After descending the falls, the Eight Mile flows south toward the Connecticut in a shaded valley between rugged hills clothed with a thick forest of hardwoods and hemlock. Steep hillsides rise up dramatically from the clear, fast-flowing trout stream. The river forms a natural migration corridor for birds. This nearly idyllic setting seems hardly appropriate for tales of sorcery, witchcraft, and other works of the Devil. Quite on the contrary, this popular state park offers the walker fine paths through charming woodlands and beside gurgling streams bounded by rocky hillsides, to a sunny vista point studded with mountain laurel bushes and views of the Eight Mile River valley.

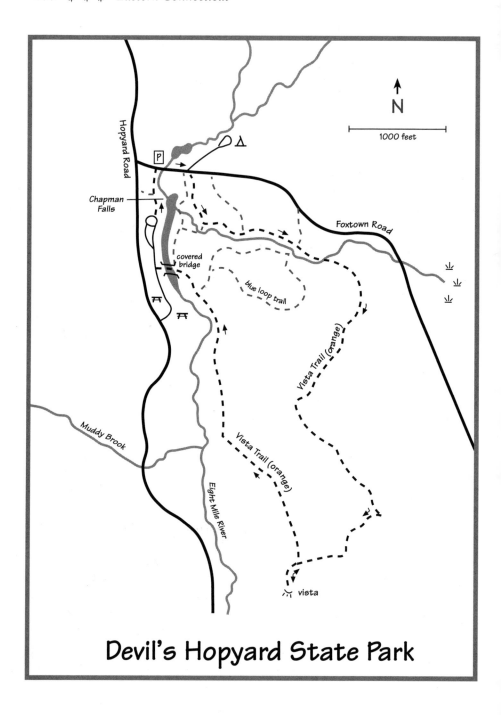

Hopyard Road

P

Chapman
Falls

covered
bridge

blue loop trail

Foxtown Road

N

1000 feet

Vista Trail (orange)

Vista Trail (orange)

Muddy Brook

Eight Mile River

vista

Devil's Hopyard State Park

Look Forward To

- Chapman Falls

- swift-flowing river and brooks

- a fine vista

- huge hemlock trees

The Trail

After parking in the lot located across Foxtown Road from Chapman Falls, turn left and walk along the road about 300 feet to the campground entrance on the left. There will be time for exploring the falls at the end of the walk. Cross the road opposite the campground entrance road and reach an unmarked trailhead. Walk over exposed bedrock, go downhill, and come to a trail junction just before a wooden walkway over a brook.

Orange blazes mark the Vista Trail; turn left to follow the path upstream along the boulder-strewn brook on your right. Pass through tall mountain laurel shrubs with gnarled trunks and shiny green leaves only at their tops, as you make your way up the gradual slope under the shade of red maple, yellow birch, and red oak. Here the clear stream is but four feet wide as it flows through sun-dappled woods. Caddis fly larvae drag their protective, inch-long stick cases about on the brook bottom, taking refuge under stones from brook trout. Hemlock appears on the darker north-facing slope of a small ravine to your right. Pass a large boulder as you begin walking uphill. Listen for the emphatic sneezelike song of the olive-green Acadian flycatcher as he gives his distinctive territorial and breeding vocalization from the shaded ravine.

Pass a big twin hemlock on the right and soon come to a fork; stay right (straight) on the main trail. The other fork goes downhill for a short distance to the brook. Many of the mature American beech trees here are disfigured with the blackish scars of graffiti carved into their smooth gray bark years ago. The path is well worn, and shallow beech roots cross the trail. Beech are prolific root sprouters, and the understory here is dominated by sprouts, which are all clones of their parent trees. Come to a stream crossing on rocks and begin a modest ascent. The brook now flows below you to the left as you turn right and walk under large white pine and then eastern hemlock and black birch, continuing uphill. A small yellow birch, the tree with peely metallic bark, grows seemingly right out of a boulder just before the trail levels off.

Rock walls stand as reminders that this was once open pastureland. Some of the large white pine are spreading, with multiple trunks, a sure indication that they grew to maturity in what was then an open, sunny environment. Notice that even a few red cedar, whose seeds germinate in sod, are still hanging on. But most of the woodland is now composed of white, red, and black oak, as well as black birch. Pass through a rocky, wet area under hemlock where skunk cabbages grow. These plants are named for the fetid odor of their crushed foliage. A massive white ash stands right of the trail. Recognize ashes by their tightly crosshatched bark.

After entering the dense shade of a hemlock stand, come to a T intersection. An impressive frilly mass of fluorescent-orange sulfur mushroom growing on the rotting hulk of a fallen oak caught my eye. It fairly glowed in the gloomy forest. Now turn right and pass a huge hemlock snag on the right, a portion of which is still alive. Another trail enters from the left, but stay straight and follow the orange blazes gradually downhill. A slope rises to your left and a stream trickles down on your right. Pass through an area of naked, dead hemlock where sunlight striking the ground creates an anomalous dry spot. Some of the dead trees are of considerable girth—two and a half feet across. A tiny insect called hemlock woolly adelgid has killed many of the state's hemlock during the past decade.

Walk through another seep area on stones, and then almost immediately cross the flowing trickle of a stream issuing from the left slope. Cross it also, on stones where tall cinnamon fern and skunk cabbage find the soggy conditions to their liking. The underside of one skunk cabbage leaf provided a stage for reflected sunlight as it bounced off the flowing water, creating a magical, dappled light effect. Reach another T intersection. Turn left and follow the trail rather steeply uphill (the other direction leads downhill). Continue uphill through dead hemlock and living white oak and red maple. The rocks sparkle with mica, an abundant mineral in schist. This is the highest section of the route. Come to another flowing (at least in late spring) stream with deciduous woods on the far side where red-eyed vireo, scarlet tanager, wood thrush, and ovenbird all nest.

After passing a fallen tree, approach a ledge outcrop on the left. The trail turns right at a big dead hemlock snag. Black birch, which contain a good amount of fragrant oil of wintergreen, are numerous here. Grassy-looking sedges carpet the forest floor on both sides of the trail. A prostrate, but still living, sugar maple lies on the left and the deep-green fronds of Christmas fern decorate the woodland. Come to another T intersection. Both directions are blazed orange. Walk left and downhill a short distance to the vista, staying straight.

Emerge from the forest onto sunlit granite ledges with a fine southerly view down the shallow valley of the Eight Mile River. The valley is bounded on opposing sides by densely wooded hills, narrowing to an apex in the distance. The southern exposure gives rise to updrafts of warm air which enable turkey vultures to gain altitude. Three big black birds did just that as we stood on the warm bedrock gazing up at them. The abundant sunlight also causes mountain laurel to bud and put on a striking floral display in June. Sassafras, scrub oak (with woolly white leaf undersides), and black and white oak also border the sunny clearing.

Nearly 300 feet below and about two-tenths of a mile to the right, an almost rectangular pond, backdropped by Hopyard Road, bucolic pastures, and tree-covered hills, lies placidly along the course of the river. While eating lunch, a tufted titmouse called *peter-peter-peter* and a black-and-yellow tiger swallowtail butterfly alighted upon a mass of pink laurel blossoms to sip nectar.

The swift-flowing Eight Mile River cascades over three tiers of erosion resistant schist rock to form Chapman Falls.

You'll probably want to linger here. When ready to push on, return to the intersection and this time continue straight, uphill, then turn left and follow the path downhill. Pass by more rotting hulks of deceased hemlock. Sunlight, now able to penetrate to the forest floor, induces a rich growth of ferns in the clearing. An eastern wood pewee whistles its melancholy tune—*pee-a-wee*. On the right, above the trail, sits a ledge nearly high enough for a person to stand up straight under.

Now enter the deep shade of a hemlock grove and continue downhill. One immense hemlock on the right is fully three and a half feet in diameter. Cross over water flowing down from a rock outcrop on the right in this area of numerous old fallen trees. Reach Eight Mile River, its water stained root-beer brown by tannin. Hemlock bark contains significant quantities of tannin, once used in the hide-tanning industry. The trail swings right and soon crosses a small feeder stream on a log bridge. Cliffs crown the rocky slope to your left. Again reach the river, which has been stocked with trout and salmon, and turn right. An exquisite male black damselfly, with an electric-blue abdomen, flitted over the bubbling stream and alighted on a royal fern growing on a little rock "island" when we were there. The water makes a soothing, gurgling sound as it flows over the rocks.

A jumble of boulders, topped with rock-loving polypody fern, jut from a talus slope on the right. Follow along the stream and past a large uprooted hemlock which has fallen into the river. Here you can stand on bedrock at the water's edge and enjoy the cool air of the valley on a hot summer's day. Walk among sizable hemlock, some dead, others living, just before beginning to climb a rocky slope. Tree roots lie exposed amidst the mass of stones. A picnic table is in view on the opposite shore. Follow along the rock ledge where the rock has fractured in 90° planes, then reach its crest. A nice view of the river below presents itself as you peer through the hemlock boughs.

Join a larger, orange-blazed trail on the right under the hemlock and bear left to enter deciduous woods of oak and red maple, with mountain laurel below. Meet the blue-blazed loop trail on the right, but continue straight on the orange trail. A yellow-throated vireo enunciated its burry phrases above me as I passed by. Proceed through two cemented stone abutments with culverts but no water through them and come to a covered bridge over the river. Nearly every bridge in the Northeast has its resident eastern phoebes. These olive-gray flycatchers, among our earliest spring arrivals, are partial to bridges over streams. Here they construct their mud nests, covered with green mosses, on ledges of rock, metal, or wood. This bridge is no exception.

Cross the bridge and enter the picnic area, which is especially popular with visitors on warm weekends. Turn right and follow the wide dirt path, past a wooden log gate, then uphill. Come to a wooden fence on the right where steps go downhill, then take the dirt path toward the left to obtain a fine view of Chapman Falls. The falls descend the sixty-foot vertical distance in three measured steps. Return to the main path and walk along a red cedar rail fence back toward your vehicle. Reach a trail intersection on the left, but stay straight to return to the parking area. Cross a wooden bridge and come to a kiosk where a trail map and other information about the state park are posted. Cross Foxtown Road to return to your vehicle.

HEMLOCK UNDER ASSAULT

The eastern, or Canadian, hemlock is an important and very beautiful member of Connecticut's upland forests, where it becomes especially common on cool, moist sites such as those found in the shaded ravines and Eight Mile River valley of Devil's Hopyard State Park. Hemlock is exemplary in many ways. It is extremely tolerant of shade. Its tiny cones open only when dry, remaining closed when wet. The winged seeds they release thrive in deep shade, unlike those of white pine, which require plenty of sunlight to germinate.

With a life span that may stretch to six centuries or even longer, eastern hemlock is also one of our longest-lived trees. As the tree ages and matures, its bark cracks and furrows deeply, eventually revealing a characteristic cinnamon hue in ancient individuals. Old-growth specimens of such girth are often 300 or more years of age.

But even towering hemlock have very shallow, albeit wide-spreading, root systems which make them vulnerable to wind throw. The shallow roots snake across the park's trails in many places, and toppled trees are quite evident along the Vista Trail route.

This stately tree, one of our largest and most majestic species, is also unfortunately very susceptible to fire and insect pests. While fire has been largely eliminated as a major concern these days, insect pests continue to pose a grave threat to the welfare and perhaps even the continued existence of southern New England's hemlock. The tree is now under serious attack from one of the tiniest insects, the hemlock woolly adelgid. This minute sap-sucking insect is related to the more familiar aphid. Its arrival in our region not only coincided with Hurricane Gloria in 1985, but seems literally to have been precipitated by that storm. Gloria, as you may recall, smashed into the Connecticut coast only fifteen miles southeast of Devil's Hopyard. The adelgid had previously been unknown on this side of Long Island Sound.

This insect in its multitudes feeds on the sap of young hemlock branches, eventually killing the tree. A heavy infestation of the tiny creatures is capable of killing a massive hemlock in only one year. So far no effective means of combating the adelgid has been found.

Getting There

From the south on Interstate 95, take Exit 70 (Old Lyme). Go straight ahead at the end of the exit ramp and follow Route 1 0.8 mile to its junction with Route 156. Turn right onto Route 156 west and drive (actually north) for 8.5 miles to the junction with Route 82. Turn right onto Route 82, travel 0.2 mile, and turn left onto Route 434 (also known as Hopyard Road). Drive 3.2 miles to the park's main picnic area and parking lot. The parking lot is located on the left 0.35 mile after you turn right, off of Hopyard Road.

—R.L.

41 Chatfield Trail Caves

Killingworth

- Chatfield Trail, Alternate Trail
- 2.6 miles
- 175-foot elevation gain
- 3.0 hours
- moderate, with rocky stretches

The Chatfield Trail traverses a small portion of the Cockaponset State Forest. Here you are only six miles north as the crow flies, but a world away, from busy Hammonasset Beach State Park (see the chapter # 42) and Long Island Sound.

This rocky region was far less suitable for farming than much of the rest of the state, and what land there was under cultivation was abandoned rather early on—circa 1800. You encounter but a few of the omnipresent stone walls along these trails that are such an integral part of the state's landscape elsewhere. Thus the overall feeling is almost that of an untamed wilderness.

True caves, which nearly always form in rocks of marine origin such as limestone or marble, are quite rare in Connecticut. Since this part of the state contains no marble bedrock, you might expect that the Chatfield Trail "Caves" are not true caves—and you would be correct. Instead, the caves are actually crawl spaces—nooks and crannies shielded by overhangs of gneiss rock.

Even so, the resulting scene is pleasing to the eye and makes for very enjoyable exploring on foot, since much of this excursion takes you along imposing ledge faces, under rock overhangs, and over and through crevices in the ledge outcrops.

Look Forward To
- imposing ledge cliffs and outcrops
- "caves"
- perched glacial erratic

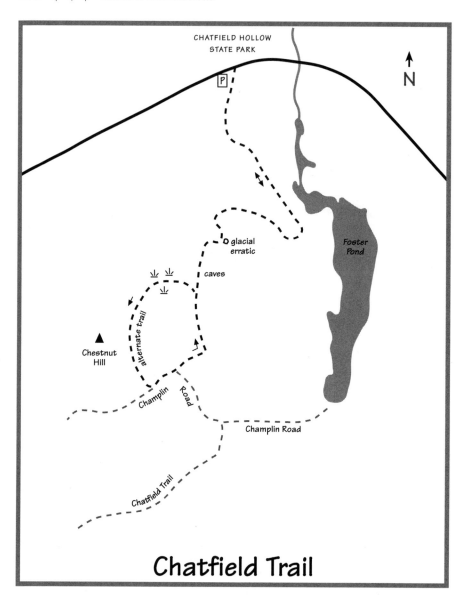

Chatfield Trail

The Trail

Follow the blue-blazed Chatfield Trail over a rocky old forest road paralleling a stony brook bed on the right. To your left a ledge outcrop appears—the first of many. The forest dominants are yellow birch, red oak, and sugar maple. Witch hazel and the evergreen mountain laurel are the common shrubs. The trail leaves the road shortly and heads up toward the gneiss ledge. Pass the end of the outcrop and climb into a woodland of American beech and chestnut oak. Here the shrubs are sweet pepperbush and high-bush blueberry; soon they are joined by huckleberry and maple-leafed viburnum. Solomon's seal, common polypody—a small fern—and mosses soften the rocks. In midsummer the mechanical buzzing of cicadas fills the warm air. The high-pitched, unhawklike *pit-teee* call of the crow-sized broad-winged hawk, which nests in these woodlands, is often heard as well.

The trail climbs gradually and reaches an outcrop of flat boulders over which you walk in staircase fashion. The rocks are dotted with the greenish doilies of lichens, while at the other end of the plant spectrum, white oak trees appear. Cross up over the bedrock mound, which is hori-zontally fissured. Laurel is common and small red maple are present. Swing left at the top of the outcrop among stunted oak and birch. Huckleberry shrubs are numerous as you enter dry oak woodland. Walk easily downhill past lichen-covered outcrops, and then swing left around an outcrop past hickory and a few low sassafras.

Come to a small sunny opening atop the gray rock ledge, where the trail makes a sharp turn to the left. Foster Pond is visible at a distance through trees. After crossing the ledge follow a switchback in the trail to the right and descend. Cross a stone wall at the end of the outcrop and then follow downhill along its face. The flat-faced cliff, its horizontal slabs seem-ingly placed one on top of another, rises above you. As you descend, the cliff grows higher, until it towers thirty-five or forty feet over your head near its end. Black birch saplings and false Solomon's seal have found footholds in the rock. Hermit thrushes nest in the woodlands, slowly rais-ing and lowering their rust-colored tails when agitated.

The gradual descent past the cliff face continues, and then you walk through a boulder field where beech, sugar maple, and New York and Christmas ferns grow between the glacially deposited stones. Rattlesnake plantain plants grow near the trail. The unmistakable bluish green leaves of this small orchid are marked with attractive white veins. Note a few dead hemlock snags. The pond again becomes visible at a distance as you pick your way through a boulder field. Climb up and over an outcrop past live hemlocks. There are dead trees too, and some that don't appear healthy. These may have been killed by a minute insect known as the hemlock wool-ly adelgid (for more about it, see pages 275–76). The leaves of pink lady-slipper, the other orchid in these woods, protrude from the acid soil. Princess pine, or tree club moss, adds its dark evergreen foliage to the scene.

Drop down momentarily from the raised, hemlock-topped outcrop-ping and cross a rivulet, dry in summer, which feeds lily-covered Foster

Pond. Climb back into hemlock woods with hay-scented fern in open spots created by fallen trees. Despite the fact that dead hemlocks are common on this slope, hermit thrushes still sing beautifully here. Pileated woodpeckers have chiseled cavernous holes in the decaying trunks to reach the insects inside. Other birds that reside here in summer include black-and-white warbler, blue-headed (formerly solitary) vireo, and eastern wood pewee. Active black-capped chickadees and tufted titmice enliven the scene year-round.

Indian tobacco blooms pale blue along the trail in summer. Native Americans smoked the dried leaves as a cure for lung ailments. Ironically, Indian tobacco contains a toxic substance used in gum and lozenges designed to appease smokers' craving for nicotine. This plant has been tied to human deaths and should never be used for self-medication. Bear left and descend gently. Sapling black birch have colonized the openings where imposing hemlocks once blotted out the sunlight. The thick growth is about six feet high on this rather steep slope.

Begin descending from the knoll, pass through another boulder field, and reach a low ledge cliff on the right. The rock wall is festooned with green moss, while small hemlocks protrude from their footholds in the wall's crevices. As the trees mature, their roots and the actions of ice will eventually help to cleave apart the cliff.

Walk down one long step and then level out. The first "cavelet"—a crevice in the wall in the form of a diagonally vertical fissure—comes into view. One can walk in a short distance. During an August visit, daddy long-legs with especially lengthy legs bounced along as they negotiated the moss-covered rocks. Evergreen wood fern grows on the rock as well. Pass through a narrow slot created by an uprooted hemlock. Liverwort—a tongue-shaped relative of mosses—thrives on moisture captured at the base of the cliff. Small pickerel frogs likewise find the cool, damp conditions to their liking. Continue along the cliff and pass a twin-trunked chestnut oak to your left, then a big hemlock to the right as the trail swings around it to the right and up over the outcrop. Proceed straight, not left, after the short climb to the level top. White pine make their first appearance among the hemlock.

The path bears left. A few Norway spruce, not native to the area, grow left of the trail. These are predominantly pine-oak-maple woods, with mountain laurel and witch hazel in the shrub layer. Witch hazel bark is the source of the astringent of the same name. While walking gently downhill a sunlit red maple stand—a sure sign of a swamp—comes into view. The white pine stand in rows and were no doubt planted. Their needles, growing five to a bundle, cushion the path. Sweet, or coast, pepperbush thrives in the damp soils, forming a thick growth. Beyond the pine to the right, the image is one of nearly total domination by red, or swamp, maple.

The trail bears right, crosses a rivulet which may be dry in summer, and enters dry oak forest. After an undulation the trail takes you to the top of a low ledge outcrop studded with silver mound and haircap mosses as well as blueberry. Reindeer lichen, an important winter staple of that caribou in the Arctic, grows on the rock too. There is even one red cedar. Pass between boulders, then along the edge of a rather level boulder field, and turn right. A profusion of seedling chestnut oak crowd and compete on the forest floor. More outcrops, then turn right and proceed up through and over angular rocks. Rusty-pink feldspar crystals are obvious in some. Negotiating a short portion of the trail here requires a few easy tree handholds. Reach the crest of the ledge vegetated with oak, black birch, red maple, and huckleberry. Note the shiny resin dots on the leaf surfaces of huckleberry.

Climb up another low ledge to where an oblong gray glacial erratic sits to the right. It rests on two much smaller stones. The melting glacier left this souvenir of the Ice Age perched on the ledge. Bear left and emerge into a sunny bedrock clearing where some views to the southwest are possible after leaf-fall. A red cedar (juniper) has shouldered up against the boulder, and clumps of little bluestem grass grow where soil exists. Quartz intrusions, harder than the rock that surrounds them, are visible in the ledge. This is a fine spot for a snack and a rest.

When ready to continue, turn right and walk around the erratic to enter the low tree growth. Proceed downward over boulders and through a small boulder field—another glacial reminder—and then up and over another low outcrop as the trail bears right. You'll find lowbush blueberry and huckleberry when you reach the top; in late summer both produce tasty blue-black fruits relished by mammals. Now swing left and descend along the other side of the outcrop. Ledge stone, stacked like a layer cake, rises on the left. Bear right and walk along a ten-foot-high gray ledge wall, then turn and go through a crevice between the ledge and boulders. At one point you are forced to bend over to fit through. Slabs of fine-grained, black-and-white-banded granitic gneiss have broken off to form an overhang or cave high enough to stand up under. The roof of the overhang shows pink feldspar, one of the three ingredients of granite.

Continue along the broken ledge face approximately 150 feet and make your way through a narrow cleft, this one requiring a short climb. Virginia creeper hangs off the overhang and Solomon's seal, with pendant

Chunks of gneiss rock, pried loose by the relentless forces of freezing and thawing, litter the floor of a 50-foot-long "cave."

pairs of deep-blue fruits in summer, grows on the rock. You are now looking down slightly into a larger cave roofed over by a 20-foot-wide ledge. This cave was created by the relentless actions of the elements as hunks of stone were pried loose from the overhang. Walk the overhang's 50-foot length. Sugar maple, beech, and oak grow in the adjacent forest. One beech, disfigured by a huge fungal canker, has fallen over and rests against the ledge. Quite a few beech have sprouted right along the outcrop wall, and beech roots spread like raised veins across the trail's surface. Far smaller are clumps of shining club moss, reminiscent of bottle brushes, which dot the outcrop.

The trail now diverges from the ledge and gradually bears left toward another, then turns left at the end of that outcrop and bears left again. A fascinating spiny-abdomened spider known as a spined micrathena had strung its silken threads across the trail; we paused to examine the creature. Come to a T intersection at a rocky old woods road. *Use caution here, as this can be a tricky intersection.* Stay straight on the blue trail and walk among oak, with some beech, laurel, and witch hazel. Shortly reach a junction with the Alternate Trail, marked by a sign, on the right. Both the Chatfield Trail and the Alternate are blazed blue. Turn right onto the Alternate Trail and descend among rocks under oak, blueberry, and huckleberry.

Swing right along the spine of a low ledge, then down to its base within beech and oak woodland and bear right. A second big black-and-yellow tiger swallowtail butterfly of the day caught our attention as it fluttered by. Later, another one would enable us to gain insight into its life cycle. Pass through a fern flat, cross a rivulet stream, go over more rock, and then turn left at the end of the outcrop, following the path just below it. Posted signs on the right indicate the edge of private property; to the left, state-forest signs border the trail. On lower-lying ground within the state forest, sweet pepperbush with spikes of frothy white flowers in summer and the canopies of skunk cabbage call attention to swampy ground. Descend gradually through oak woods punctuated by ledges and bear left at a low outcrop. You may need to duck under a fallen oak in the process.

At the edge of the swamp we inadvertently flushed a family of eight ruffed grouse. The young birds were nearly full grown. Their mother, all the while making odd mewing sounds, moved her offspring away, out of harm's way. Bear left, drop down over rocks, and turn right between outcrops. Cross a brook bed that carries water in spring and fall. Maple-leafed viburnum shrubs grow under its namesake tree as well as oak and hickory. The viburnums join a population of sugar maple seedlings and Christmas fern. Both maple and fern grow in rich limy, or neutral, soils. At the base of each leaflet of Christmas fern is a small lobe which imparts to it the appearance of a tiny Christmas stocking.

Continue your measured descent through another boulder field and cross a stream bed on rocks. Spicebush, which has incredibly fragrant foliage, thrives in such moist soils. Now bear right, then left, through lacy New York fern and climb gradually to a ledge face, the top of which is capped with common polypody fern. The name refers to its matted, spreading roots. Walk left along the ledge face and then turn right to climb up over it. We found a very vigorous jack-in-the-pulpit perched on a rock pedestal. In August its cluster of berries was still emerald green. Turn right and then immediately left after you gain the top, and climb gradually to another ledge you walk along.

The horizontal bedding planes of this twenty-five-foot-high formation are evident. The crevices had provided an eastern phoebe with a perfect shelf six feet up on which to construct her nest. Feldspar and a quartz vein are visible in the rock on the lower part of the cliff, and a gravel road is visible to your left. The trail bears left, rounds a huge boulder, passes a stone wall, and fords a brook which even in a dry season usually has pools occupied by green frogs. Forty feet beyond, reach gravel Champlin Road. Turn left onto the road and follow the blazes; to your right is posted, private land. The road crosses a brook, and then immediately a blue-blazed trail reenters the forest on the left. The path turns right, and then right again when it reaches a cliff face to follow along its base. A switchback to the left leads you to the top through a low crevice.

Turn right at the top. You're walking in open woods of chestnut and white oak, and then through greenbrier and huckleberry with a rock wall on the right. Hickory and oak have long ago overtopped red cedars which indicate a former usage of this former field for livestock grazing. Cross a stone wall and come to the right angle formed by the corner of the ledge cliff, bearing right along its base. Pass through boulders below the outcrop. False Solomon's seal, which has starry white flowers in a cluster all at the tip, in contrast to Solomon's seal, grows on the left.

Turn left at the T intersection to follow the blue blazes. The gneiss bedrock here is elephant gray. Begin climbing and bear left to cross the top of the ledge. Another spined micrathena had built its web across the trail, hoping to snare a meal that day. Perhaps the spider's prickly form camouflages it against predators and/or makes it tough to swallow. Climb rather steeply to gain the top of the ridge and follow along the crest. A screened view through cedar, hickory, and oak is possible in summer. We were charmed by an eastern chipmunk that retreated to a rock crevice—a protective cave of its own—then turned to watch our approach with some apprehension.

Leave the oak knoll, reenter taller oak woodland, and come to a Y intersection. Bear right and proceed uphill on an old roadway, with the slope dropping off to your left. Soon reach the junction with the Alternate Trail on the left. Keep straight and retrace your steps 1.5 miles back to the parking area; this involves clambering back over ledges. Be sure to turn right where the old woods road continues straight.

THE EGG AND US

As we passed back through the bedrock clearing marked by the glacial erratic, we watched another tiger swallowtail flying about in the sun. But this individual seemed to be moving with more purpose than usual. That purpose was soon apparent as the large, elegant insect fluttered above the leaves of a sapling black cherry in the clearing. We presumed it might be laying eggs as it gently touched the tip of its abdomen to the top of several leaves in turn.

Upon closer inspection we were delighted to find a tiny, round green egg adhering to the top of one leaf. No doubt the female butterfly had laid additional eggs on other leaves. We decided to try a little swallowtail husbandry by carefully removing a portion of the twig bearing the leaf and its attached egg and transporting it home. At home we placed the twig in a small jar of water to keep the leaf succulent and then put the jar in a small glass terrarium. We checked the egg more than once daily, and, to our delight, the egg hatched eight days later. An eighth-inch-long blackish caterpillar had emerged from the egg. It soon began to nibble on the cherry leaf.

From our butterfly field guides, we knew that black cherry was just one of the species' many preferred foods, and a number of young black cherry trees grew in our yard. The tiny larva grew and ate, grew and ate, and continued to do so. Twenty-two days after hatching, a molt reclothed the larva in a new green skin, and at its hind end it displayed a striking pair of "eyes." These feline orbs were actually just circles of orange and black pigment, but their role seems clearly to fool predators into thinking that this is the head of a more formidable creature. In reality, of course, the head is at the opposite end. Later, the caterpillar added to the illusory effect by holding up the rear end in such a way that its appearance as a head was enhanced further.

A week after its color change, it began visibly to react to sound. If we made a sudden sound, it responded with a quick movement, leading us to believe that it was capable of hearing. Over the course of the rest of the summer and into the fall, we continued to pick fresh fodder for the caterpillar while it continued to increase in size. On some days we could actually hear it chewing. From our reading we also realized that it would not form a chrysalis and emerge as a fully formed butterfly this year, as a monarch butterfly would have. Instead, as fall advanced we knew it would simply crawl down and pupate among the leaf litter that had accumulated at the bottom of the terrarium. Only next spring would it finally emerge as a gorgeous adult tiger swallowtail.

One day in late October, when the caterpillar had reached one inch in length, it disappeared as expected into the bottom of the terrarium, and under the dry leaves molted into a brown chrysalis. As I write these words, we await the spring and the miraculous ultimate transformation of the tiny green egg laid so many months before.

Getting There

From the north, take Route 9 to Route 81 (Exit 9). Drive south on Route 81 for 8.0 miles to its junction with Route 80 in Killingworth. Turn right from the rotary onto Route 80 (west) and follow it for 1.4 miles to the gravel parking area on the left, where there is room for a small number of vehicles; do not park along the highway. Watch for a blue sign for Chatfield Trail on the left here. The parking area is 0.3 mile beyond the entrance on the right for Chatfield Hollow State Park.

From the south, take Exit 63 off Interstate 95 for Route 81 (north). Drive north on Route 81 for approximately 5.3 miles to Killingworth. From the rotary in Killingworth, turn onto Route 80 (west) and follow the directions above.

—R.L.

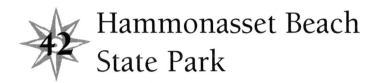

42 Hammonasset Beach State Park

Madison

- Willard's Island Nature Trail, Cedar Island Trail, Meig's Point Trail
- 3.0 miles
- 20-foot elevation gain
- 3.0 hours
- easy

For 1.5 million sun worshippers, bathers, anglers, and others each year, Hammonasset Beach State Park means fun in the sun and surf. But perhaps surprisingly to some, the 919-acre park is also one of the finest birding areas of the Connecticut coast.

Each fall thousands of hawks, shorebirds, and songbirds as well as monarch butterflies funnel through the park on their way south. The extensive salt marshes at the mouth of the Hammonasset River provide rich feeding grounds for these winged creatures as well as species that prey upon them.

One short loop and two out-and-back trails lead the walker and nature enthusiast through varied natural communities of salt marsh, rocky coastline, and isolated sandy uplands with a shrub and tree cover. Each offers pleasurable walking and wonderful opportunities for wildlife observation within some of the state's most threatened ecosystems.

Look Forward To

- extensive salt marshes
- diverse fauna and flora
- picturesque rocky shoreline
- fall migration spectacle

Hammonasset Beach State Park

The Trail

After parking near Meig's Point Nature Center, located on a knoll overlooking a salt marsh, walk past the nature center and down the one-lane paved road. The roadway is lined with tall common reed (*Phragmites*), bayberry, poison ivy, whose white berries are a favorite food of many birds, and goldenrod. Soon reach the Willard's Island Picnic area at the end of pavement, where you may alternatively park. The nature trail begins on the left. Interpretive leaflets may be available from a box at the trailhead as well as at the nature center when it is open.

Both sides of the wide, level macadam path are vegetated with a thick growth of red cedar (juniper), wild rose, shining sumac, bayberry, poison ivy, aromatic sweet fern—not a fern at all—*Phragmites*, and goldenrods. All but the last three produce nutritious fruits eagerly consumed by many species of birds and mammals. This relatively narrow strip of higher ground is surrounded by salt marsh. *Spartina* grasses grow along the water channels in the rich mud of the marsh, as do the odd, segmented spikes of glasswort, which in late summer take on a translucent reddish hue. The high salt content of this plant has given it a fitting nickname: pickleweed. You'll find blackgrass, meanwhile, on slightly higher ground near the edges of the marsh. Not a grass at all, it is actually a rush whose dark-brown fruiting capsules are the reason for its common name.

Reach a three-way split in the blacktopped path; follow the right branch. Virginia creeper (woodbine) twines up the pyramidal forms of red cedar, its crimson fall foliage contrasting with the supporting evergreens. Small flocks of perky, crested cedar waxwings give their high-pitched calls as they move about in search of fruit. The bluish berries of the cedars, which also give gin its distinctive taste, are among their favorites. A stately multibranched pear tree at the left of the path is a reminder that Willard's Island was once an orchard. In early autumn its remaining, fermenting fruit give off a noticeable but not unpleasant fragrance.

A trio of woody plants with Asian origins—autumn olive, Japanese honeysuckle, and Oriental bittersweet—find the sandy soils here to their liking. Autumn olive trees, planted years ago for erosion control and as food for wildlife, are numerous, their berries still green in late September. These are among the few nonleguminous plants that fix nitrogen in the soil by means of bacteria ensconced in root nodules. All three Oriental species are now more or less invasive in nature, to the detriment of native shrubs.

To the right of the path stands a big red maple, a species with wide moisture tolerances; the trail then curves left. Several apple trees with fruit in season appear surrounded by a dense thicket of rose, honeysuckle, sumac, dogwood, and young peach trees. Grape and Virginia creeper vines use the shrubs for support and to clamber up to the sunlight. Bumblebees crawl back and forth over the yellow flower masses of goldenrods, gathering pollen. A grove of spindly sassafras trees grows to the right. A screech owl nest box, the entrance hole of which has been enlarged by a gray squirrel, is mounted on one of the trees.

Come to a split in the trail; stay straight rather than going left. A very short distance farther along, reach a four-way intersection. Take the right branch, which forks again in thirty feet. Follow the right branch—a side loop to a salt marsh viewing platform. The treadway is now fine gray gravel. In addition to the tree, shrub, and vine species already mentioned, crab apple, white oak, and shad (Juneberry) now join the mix. The wooden viewing platform is located alongside salt marsh Dudley Creek at the far end of the loop on the right. Interpretive panels inform visitors about Willard's Island, salt marsh fishes, osprey, the heron family, and ducks. From here you are treated to expansive views of the Hammonasset River's biologically rich salt marsh and tidal-flat system.

If the tide is already low or falling, you can spot ribbed mussels protruding from the dark, peaty banks of the stream. The mussels are inundated twice daily by a salty broth which carries microscopic creatures to their waiting siphons. Gaze farther out and you'll notice masses of sun-bleached sticks on channel buoys and on top of tall tripods specially erected for the purpose. They are the nests of ospreys—large brown-and-white birds of prey which plunge feet first into salt or fresh water to gaff live fish. In summer osprey pairs raise two to three chicks to fledging in the structures. Once endangered by hard pesticides, habitat loss, and even shooting, these noble birds have made a heartening comeback. The ramped platform and a bench along the trail near it are wonderful places to relax and have a snack while you enjoy the scenery and wildlife passing by.

When ready to carry on, follow along the trail past tall grass and sunflowers back to the paved main trail. Gray catbirds hide and give their cat-like *meow* calls from the thickets, which now include bright-red-fruit-laden winterberry. Turn right at the main trail intersection. The trail continues through a dense growth of shrubs, sassafras, autumn olive, red cedar, grape, bittersweet, and Virginia creeper vines. Virginia creeper's stems and clusters of five leaflets add an attractive dash of red color to the scene. Grapes fermenting in the warm sunlight of late summer waft their aromatic vapors over the footpath. Welcome shade on hot days is provided by a large red maple on the right. A migrant Swainson's thrush, a denizen of dark, cool northern forests, plucked ripe black cherries in rapid succession as we watched.

The nature center comes into view as you continue along with the salt marsh to your right. Turn right when you reach the intersection to retrace your steps back to the trailhead. You can now turn right again to return to your vehicle or proceed through the picnic area to the beginning of the Cedar Island Trail.

The Cedar Island trailhead is not obvious. Cross the mowed picnic area to a dirt track at its far end and turn left. Walk to the far right corner of the mowed field and look for a small path that enters a strip of trees. Sassafras, pignut hickory, oak, black cherry, and basswood form a canopy over your head as granite boulders appear. Notice the cork-studded bark of a hackberry tree immediately left of the path. The view now opens up, enabling you to gain fine vistas of the salt marsh on both sides. Cross a wooden bridge; a vigorous stand of poison ivy, its foliage already rusty in late summer, grows tall on the right while patches of seaside goldenrod, a favorite nectaring plant of migrating monarch butterflies, show off their flower clusters at both ends of the bridge.

The path now gains ground gradually, and as a result the soil becomes drier. Shad, white oak, hickory, black cherry, huckleberry, lowbush blueberry, and azalea are common. The shad trees—so named because they bloom in April when the annual migration of shad fish up coastal rivers to spawn is underway—have multiple smooth, lithe gray trunks. Bracken fern, wild sarsaparilla, and striped wintergreen grow beneath the woody vegetation. The trail ends at a short boardwalk-surrounded salt marsh. Clinton Harbor is visible to the right from this unobstructed vantage point. Two large, pinkish granite boulders, dropped by the receding glacier of the last Ice Age, stand as mute evidence of its power. A clump of seaside goldenrod has colonized the top of one. High above it we watched an aerial ballet in the form of thirteen snowy egrets spiraling up into the cobalt-blue sky, perhaps to begin their autumnal migration.

The blue waters of Long Island Sound lie beyond the granite boulders and glacially deposited promontory of Meig's Point.

When ready, retrace your steps to the picnic area and your vehicle beyond, or continue on to the Meig's Point Trail. To reach Meig's Point, cross the main park road to the bathhouse, turn left, and walk over the sand along the beach to a boardwalk. Proceed up to a viewing platform atop the point. This mound is a glacial moraine created when the ice sheet dropped a load of debris during its slow and halting retreat. Seaside goldenrod, poison ivy, bayberry, shining sumac—whose leaf surfaces are highly reflective—and wild roses blanket the knoll. Take in a fine view over granite boulders of Long Island Sound from the wooden railing.

The gravel path descends the opposite side of the knoll. Continue straight after the dip past a number of side paths that intersect the main trail from the parking area on the left. Thickets of beach plum help to hold the glacial soil together. A picturesque view of the rocky point and beach lie ahead. Descend to the rock-and-sand beach and walk along the boulder-strewn shoreline, making your way between large chunks of 600-million-to-800-million-year-old granite and dark-green clumps of bayberry (wax myrtle). The wax-covered fruits of this aromatic shrub constitute important fuel for migrant tree swallows and wintering yellow-rumped (myrtle) warblers, among others. Just offshore big, black double-crested cormorants fly by low over the water. These common fish-eating relatives of pelicans also possess a pouched throat, albeit a much smaller one. A granite rock eighty feet out serves as a convenient loafing site for the birds.

At one point salt marsh vegetation advances right to the shoreline. The Cedar Island Trail boardwalk is visible out in the marsh to your left. Climb to another point of land thick with bayberry, sumac, greenbrier, wild roses, vines, grasses, and goldenrods. In September monarch butterflies wing by and alight on the goldenrods to take on fat-rich fuel for their perilous journey to central Mexico. The trail finally ends at the water's edge. Retrace your steps to the bathhouse and your vehicle.

AERIAL HIGHWAYS

Each autumn nature presents one of her most incredible and captivating spectacles—the long southward migration of birds and a few insects to areas where more clement weather and abundant food supplies enable these creatures to overwinter with relative ease prior to returning to breeding areas in the north.

As the multitudes move southward by day, hawks and monarch butterflies tend to follow time-honored corridors created by rivers and other landforms. Along submerging coastlines, such as along Connecticut's shore, where points of land jut out into the sea, the migrants tend to be funneled by such narrow appendages. Hammonasset is such a place. And when the winds are auspicious—that is, out of the northwest—thousands of hawks and even a few eagles may pass down to Meig's Point and thence along the shore of the Long Island Sound in a single day. These are the days birders wait for eagerly.

For each bird it is a significant expenditure and a great risk, but one which must be taken. Their form and behavior allows them to take advantage of certain atmospheric conditions. They float upward on the elevators of rising air currents created when the sun warms the earth, and ride the updrafts born of wind-powered air masses striking ridges. Incredibly keen vision enables these raptors to spot prey from high above the ground and (especially in the case of the pointy-winged falcons) to drop or swoop upon it with dizzying speed. The master of this art is the peregrine falcon. *Peregrine* means "traveler," and indeed each year of their lives these striking birds must make a round-trip journey of up to 18,000 miles!

Be sure to glance up occasionally, especially if you visit from late August to early November. In late September for instance, if the weather cooperates, you are sure to see long-tailed sharp-shinned and Cooper's hawks; dainty American kestrels, small relatives of the peregrine; ospreys; bulky red-tailed hawks; and perhaps even a bald eagle on flat, seven-foot wings. Sometimes the hawks pass by high overhead, and at other times they streak low over the grassy fields into the teeth of a brisk wind. It's definitely a spectacle worth seeing.

Nor are hawks, or, for that matter, shorebirds and songbirds, the only winged sojourners passing through the area each fall. Big orange monarch butterflies make an even more monumental journey (for an insect weighing less than a fraction of an ounce) of 2,000 or more miles to the transvolcanic mountain range of central Mexico. Although some of the birds have followed their migration routes before, none of the butterflies ever has —or ever will again. Covering 40 miles per day on the average, the monarchs take two months or more to complete the trip. The fat-rich nectar of goldenrods and asters provides the fuel for their wing muscles at stopover points such as this.

After spending the winter months in the cool, high-elevation evergreen forests of the Mexican mountains, the butterflies mate. The females fly back only a relatively short distance before laying their eggs on milkweed plants and then die. The hatching caterpillars feast, grow rapidly, pupate, and then as adults continue the northward odyssey. It is the third generation of butterflies we first see in New England fields in early summer. A later migrant generation, removed from the previous year's travelers by five generations, begins the long southward journey by the end of August.

Getting There

From Interstate 95, take Exit 62 for Hammonasset Beach State Park. Turn south at the end of the ramp (right if coming from the west, left if arriving from the east) onto the Hammonasset Beach State Park connector. Directional signs for the park are located at the end of both northbound and southbound ramps. Travel south on the connector and cross Route 1 at 1.3 miles. The park entrance is located 0.3 mile beyond Route 1.

From the entrance station (vehicle entry fee required from Memorial Day to Labor Day, and on weekends from late April to Memorial Day and from Labor Day to the end of September), follow the signs to Meig's Point for 1.7 miles, past a rotary, to a parking area on the left adjacent to the nature center. The park is open from 8 A.M. to sunset. The nature center is open from the end of June through Labor Day, Tuesday through Sunday, 10 A.M. to 5 P.M.

—R.L.

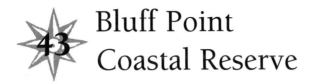

Bluff Point
Coastal Reserve

Groton

- unnamed trail
- 4.5-mile loop
- 100-foot elevation gain
- 3.0 hours
- easy

Farmland as recently as the 1950s, 778-acre Bluff Point State Park was designated a Coastal Reserve in 1975. Its long agricultural history extends back at least to the time of Governor John Winthrop, whose family farmed this peninsula during the eighteenth century. Winthrop served as governor from 1698 until his death in 1707. The foundation remnants of the family home and an extensive network of stone walls are all that remain from that era. Today the reserve represents one of Connecticut's largest and finest coastal natural areas open to the public.

At the western end of Bluff Point a mile-long barrier beach faces the ocean waves, which enabled a system of salt marshes to develop behind it. The salt marshes act as nurseries for many species of fin- and shellfish and provide rich feeding grounds for birds, mammals, amphibians, and other creatures. Once inhabited by people seeking the special charms of oceanfront property, the mammoth hurricane of 1938 destroyed the more than 100 vacation homes that once overlooked the Long Island Sound from the headland of Bluff Point.

A system of former horse-cart roads provides convenient access along the shore to the point at the southern tip of the peninsula and back across its now wooded spine. A day's outing at this popular park can easily combine the pleasures of beachcombing, birding, and woodland strolling.

Look Forward To

- rock-strewn coastline

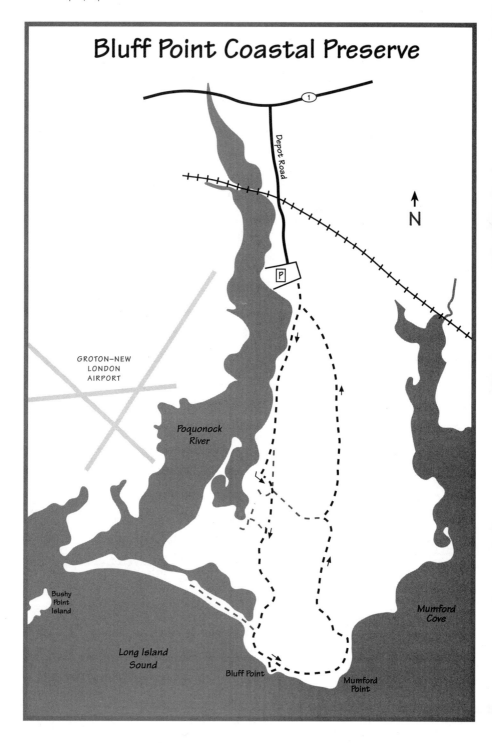

Bluff Point Coastal Preserve

- barrier beach and salt marsh system
- views of Fishers Island Sound and Long Island Sound
- fine birding

The Trail

After parking in the gravel lot, walk past the picnic area and by an iron gate across the gravel cart road, passing a sign on the left which enumerates park regulations. A self-guiding interpretive trail leaflet is available here. The old road is lined with mixed oaks, black cherry, greenbrier, shining sumac, and multiflora rose, and many trees are draped with Oriental bittersweet vines. In late summer goldenrod plants bloom profusely with heads of pollen-filled, yellow-orange blossoms.

Soon come to a short side path that leads to the water's edge. Windrows of dry, brown eelgrass have piled up along the river shore at your feet. It looks like masses of tangled recording tape. The living, green plant is an irreplaceable component of the estuary ecosystem. On the opposite shore of the Poquonock River is the Groton–New London Airport, often busy with aircraft landings and takeoffs. This is a pleasing vista nonetheless, as the back side of the barrier beach and the green mounds of Bushy Point Island are also visible.

Return to the cart road and continue south (right) for a short distance to a split; stay right. A grove of big-tooth aspen stands on the right. Their leaves turn golden in fall. Sassafras trees and huckleberry and arrowwood shrubs line the roadway. On warm late-summer days the air is filled with the mechanical buzzing of cicadas. Mockernut hickory joins the oak, while six-inch-high spotted (striped) wintergreen grows along the brushy edge. There are also poison ivy and bracken fern—one of the few ferns that tolerates dry, sterile soils. A slope rises up to your left covered primarily with immature trees.

Reach an open view of the river on the right. Bayberry shrubs, some with multiple clusters of wax-coated berries where the branches meet the shrub's main stem, do well in the sandy soils. The only large trees here are oak. Come to a clearing on the left where raspberry and sumac shrubs are overhung with masses of exotic and invasive Oriental bittersweet vines. Looking right reveals a pebbly beach and, beyond it, a wooden osprey nesting platform with a nest of sticks at the top, signifying it has been used by ospreys. Pass a gravel clearing on the left where little bluestem grass flourishes, and then walk by concrete slabs which indicate former settlement.

An open view of beach reveals people clamming in the rich mud of the flat when the tide is out. Hard- and soft-shell clams (actually the same animal during different parts of its shedding cycle) and oysters are still sought recreationally. Receding tides strand schools of small fish—mummichogs and Atlantic silversides—in tiny tide pools surrounded by salt marsh cord-grasses. Here they are easy prey for herons, egrets, greater yellowlegs in migration, and other long-legged predators. A bit farther along is a small enclave of salt marsh that was ditched years ago in an effort to control mosquito reproduction. Unfortunately ditching disrupts the salt marsh ecosystem and is detrimental to the small fish that eat the mosquito larvae.

Pass bayberry bushes heavy with fruit in late summer and then enter shaded forest. The trail now forks, with the cart road being the left tine and a less-traveled footpath constituting the right. Smooth-barked hickory, shad trees, and black birch grow between the parallel paths. To avoid the many bicyclists and joggers and even a few horseback riders who share the reserve with walkers, you may wish to take the right path. Here we witnessed a male downy woodpecker swallowing ripe blue-black arrowwood berries along the trail. Fruit makes up a relatively small but important percentage of this bird's diet, becoming more prominent in late summer and early fall. We also found the feather of a barred owl, a bird with a strictly meat diet.

A muddy dip in the path revealed the fresh imprints of nocturnal mammals—a raccoon and white-tailed deer. Deer are very numerous in the reserve, and that has had a negative impact on the area's plant diversity. Management efforts are underway to control the size of the deer population. Grapevines may have provided the impetus for the raccoon's passage. Another puddle proved to be the abode, at least for now, of a green frog. Green frogs resemble the larger bullfrog but possess two parallel pleats down their backs.

Reach an open area dotted with red cedar (juniper) trees. A plant with beautifully pink-purple, bell-shaped flowers and very slender leaves—gerardia—shows off its blossoms here in late summer. In this damp place you stand at the farthest reaches of the highest tides, which occur just twice each month. The glasswort and blackgrass growing in the salty soil likewise indicate the extent of ground inundated by the highest tides. Just beyond the clearing, the path becomes quite overgrown, so backtrack a short distance and cross over to the higher and drier cart road.

Continue south on the cart road, which is bordered on the right by an old stone wall, now in disrepair. Pass a big granite boulder that sits on the left. Some of the sassafras trees, with their deeply furrowed brown bark, are quite large. Their spicy leaves come in three shapes—single, mitten, and three-lobed. Come to a slight rise where bittersweet drapes the trees and shrubs; it spreads both by runners and by seed. The yellow fruit husks split open in fall to reveal orange-red berries, which are consumed and thereby dispersed by birds. At our feet on the path, a small black wasp was in the process of dragging a spider it had paralyzed back to its nest to become food for its developing young.

Reach a fork in the trail; the left branch leads uphill over a rougher woods road to join the high cart road you will walk later back to the start; stay straight. Come to a grassy track on the right which leads to the river, but stay straight here as well. Shiny-leaved common greenbrier with thorny green stems thrives in the sunlit clearing. The rotting hulk of a very large oak stands on the right. Japanese barberry, a low, prickly shrub with coral-red fruits, joins bittersweet in these disturbed soils. Reach a ditched salt marsh past which lies a finger of water, then one of sand, with the Long Island Sound beyond. The horizon may be studded with points of white canvas when wind conditions are favorable for sailing.

The roadway now winds under oak and hickory. In addition to the drone of cicadas, you may hear the measured explosive pops of a propane cannon coming from the airport runways—an effort to disperse flocks of birds. The cart road curves sharply right, while a rockier track goes straight and slightly uphill into the woods. Then curve left on the cart path and reach portable toilets on the right. A view of the water is just beyond. A few apple trees are holdovers from a former time and now provide food for wildlife. A tidal pond bordered by salt marsh vegetation is on your right. Access to Bluff Point Beach and Bushy Point Beach beyond it is possible on the right also. This pebble-and-sand strand is a mile-long barrier beach which shields the salt marsh behind it from the full storm force and saltier waters of Long Island Sound.

Great masses of empty slipper, or lamp, shells—more than I have seen anywhere else in New England—made up the wrack line on a day in early September. A small jellyfish lay among them. To the left, the beach below Bluff Point is composed of small, smooth granite pebbles with big angular granite boulders beyond. The plump red hips and dark-green foliage of salt-spray rose shrubs shone in the sunlight behind the rocks that provided seating for our lunch that day. The big blossoms can be either pink or white. As we ate, Forster's and common terns and predatory great black-backed gulls flew by in both directions, while monarch butterflies fluttered consistently westward along the shore. Some of the terns also plunge-dived into the sea for fish (something gulls don't do). The rocks at the low end of the tidal zone exhibit a blackish patina of life which the high-and-dry boulders do not possess. The big granite chunks above the tide line, however, graphically show their component minerals—pink feldspar, glassy quartz, and dark glistening mica crystals. Across the water to the west lies the verdant, tree-covered mound of Bushy Point Island.

You may want to explore the tidal pond behind the barrier beach by following a short trail on the backside of the sandy beach. Bushlike sea lavender adds its bouquet of tiny flowers to the scene along the edges of the salt marsh while hermit crabs, safely ensconced in their borrowed mollusk shells, crawl about in search of edible bits. Superbly camouflaged, their small dark shells resemble the myriad pebbles of the beach. Until they move, they remain virtually invisible! Some of their shells support a living fuzz known as snail fur which is actually made up of tiny microorganisms called hydroids. There are also small fish in the shallows and masses of snail-like periwinkles grazing algae off the mud in the brackish (mixed salt-fresh) water like a herd of tiny buffalo. A four-inch-diameter moon jellyfish lay stranded, dead in the pond.

The dune area separating the pond from the ocean is vegetated with beach grass, beach pea, and salt-spray (a.k.a. rugosa) rose. A wooden boardwalk connects both sides of the barrier beach; do not cross the thin strip except via the boardwalk, as it can lead to erosion. When the path narrows, return to the main trail, which then curves left. A rocky track goes right and up to the top of the Bluff Point, affording you a nice view of both the Fishers Island and Long Island Sounds. Goldenrod, huckleberry, sumac, greenbrier, and arrowwood crown this headland. The bluff is composed of easily eroded glacial till dropped by the receding glacier 20,000 years ago. Pinkish granite boulders litter the shore. A bench, installed in 1988 to commemorate the fiftieth anniversary of the great hurricane, is a convenient place to relax and enjoy the view.

Walk down the backside of the bluff to continue on the main trail. A fine view of Split Rock, a glacial erratic cracked by ice and storm waves, is visible a short distance away off Mumford Point. Anglers find the rock a convenient perch from which to cast. Northern porgy, or scup, was the catch of the day during an early-September visit. Follow the trail gradually uphill now through shrubbery, briars, and red cedar. Reach a point where a trail enters from the left; stay straight on the main dirt cartway. Small black cherry trees are full of ripe fruit in late summer—at least until birds and chipmunks strip the bounty. At this time of year the fragrance of ripening wild grapes is also in the air. Brown thrashers and gray catbirds feed on the fruit in the brushy tangles.

Come to a trail junction. A lesser path leads off to the right, but stay on the main trail and curve sharply to the left. The diets of many insectivorous birds change in late summer to include fruit, as was demonstrated by the black-capped chickadee we spied feeding upon the dark fruits of arrowwood. Another path goes right, toward the shore, and you may want to follow it to a different scenic vista. Back on the main trail you soon pass a fenced exclosure where the effects of deer browsing are being studied, and then curve left, walk down a gentle slope, and then bear right. A stone wall which once bordered pastureland now provides support for clinging vines and briars. Hay-scented, or boulder, fern grows along the rock fence, which you soon pass through.

The old cart road winds through more red cedar and black cherry, two trees whose seeds require lots of sunlight for germination. Black knot fungus disfigures the branches of the cherries. Numerous informal side paths lead off in both directions. Stay on the main trail and arrive at a large shrubby clearing where a smaller trail turns left as the main trail bears right. Eastern towhees and gray catbirds—thicket specialists—skulk in the thick cover of the shrubs. Another path goes off to the right as stone walls border both sides of the old roadway, which curves left. New York fern, Virginia creeper, and greenbrier all grow thickly along the roadside. Some rather sizable black birch appear as you enter woodland that also includes oak, hickory, and black cherry.

Gray squirrels are busy harvesting hickory nuts in late summer. The thud of falling nuts cut by the rodents is a soon familiar sound. Occasional granite boulders in the forest bespeak the ice sheet's legacy. The forest itself is rather open, with reduced underbrush. This may well be due to the large population of hungry deer in the reserve. Notice that you are walking downhill now. In the distance the water is visible through the trees. Black birch, characterized by smooth, dark bark, is the dominant tree and unpresumptuous, white-blooming woodland aster is the most abundant flowering plant in the late-summer woods.

The forest slopes downward to the left and up to your right. The roadway descends more noticeably now and curves left, passing through two concrete fence posts. Come to the junction with the low road and continue straight ahead back to the parking area and your vehicle.

SEA OF GRASS

Below the usually placid waters of coastal estuaries, where fresh water from the uplands mingles with the salt water of the sea to produce a growth medium rich in nutrients, flowing green grasslands of a different sort give rise to a highly diverse natural community. The major food-producing plant of these undersea pastures is eelgrass, which is really not a grass at all. It is a marine flowering plant which produces its flowers and seeds totally underwater. It spreads mostly by means of runners, however.

Fertile pastures of eelgrass, stimulated both by abundant sediments brought from far inland by rivers such as the Poquonock and by mineral-rich sea water, constitute the essential base of the life pyramid of estuaries. And when they decay, the organic material released provides nutrients for many other organisms. Even when lifeless and washed up on the beach, eelgrass continues to harbor small crustaceans and insects that shorebirds rely on for food. Eelgrass plays another important role in that its root systems anchor the sandy or muddy bottom soils of estuaries and coastal shallows and reduce wave erosion.

Eelgrass grows in vast dense beds which also harbor among their multitudinous blades a myriad of tiny creatures. The leaf surfaces themselves support a living film of algae and other microscopic life forms that nourish and sustain the higher animals that in turn become food for small fish and crustaceans—hermit crabs and pipefish, for example. These in their turn become food for still larger creatures, which then become food for ourselves. Thus estuaries are true nurseries for many of the shell- and finfish that humans harvest commercially. And eelgrass is the mother's milk of that nursery.

During the early 1930s a mysterious and fatal illness befell the eelgrass colonies of America's East Coast as well as those of Europe. Once vast beds of eelgrass were decimated. This, of course, had a domino effect upon the entire estuarine community dependent upon it. Wintering brant geese—smaller, darker relatives of the familiar Canada geese which graze almost exclusively upon the ribbonlike leaves of the plant when they winter in our estuaries—and bay scallops in particular were hard hit.

The cause of the plant's decline never has been fully explained, although a fungus and a slime mold were implicated. Changes in the temperature of sea water may have been a contributing factor. There has, however, been a marked increase in its production in marine ecosystems in most areas in recent decades, and brant geese and the other multitude of creatures that depend upon it directly or indirectly for sustenance and protection are the better off for it.

Getting There

Take Exit 88 (Route 117) off Interstate 95, and follow Route 117 south for 1.0 mile. Turn right onto Route 1 and drive 0.3 mile to the first traffic light, at Depot Road. Turn left onto Depot Road and follow it for 0.3 mile under the railroad overpass. Just beyond the overpass the road becomes dirt; continue on it for another 0.3 mile to the gravel parking area. Portable toilets are located here. The reserve is open 8:00 A.M. to sunset.

—R.L.

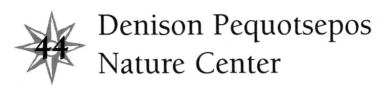

44 Denison Pequotsepos Nature Center

Mystic

- Red, White, and Orange Loop Trails
- 2.3 miles
- 70-foot elevation gain
- 2.0 hours
- easy

So close to the sea—just over a mile—but definitely an upland site. This 125-acre sanctuary, well known for its variety of bird life, rests on a granite ridge which extends south to Fishers Island Sound. One mile to the west is the Mystic River, and immediately southeast lies Quiambog Cove. Both are tidal, a characteristic attribute of Connecticut's "drowned" coastline.

The privately owned and operated sanctuary boasts a surprisingly diverse amalgam of natural communities—habitats, if you will—which keep the walker and naturalist intrigued with a corresponding assemblage of plants and animals. At least 169 species of birds have been identified on the property, and seven miles of well-marked and well-maintained trails lead through these attractive and wildlife-rich natural communities.

This is a fine place for a short but discovery-filled walk with children, as well as a longer jaunt for adults who want both to stretch their legs and to commune with nature. In addition the Nature Center, with its exhibits focused on the natural history of southeastern Connecticut and the rehabilitated owls and other raptors visible in the outdoor flight enclosures, will add to the charm and interest of your visit.

The trails are open dawn to dusk. Nature Center hours are Tuesday through Saturday, 9:00 A.M. to 5:00 P.M., year-round; Monday through Friday, 9:00 A.M. to 5:00 P.M., May through Labor Day; and Sunday, 1:00 to 5:00 P.M., May through December. Bikes are not allowed, and dogs must be leashed.

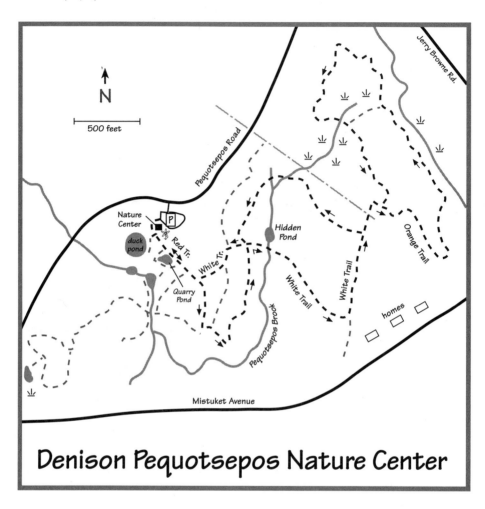

Denison Pequotsepos Nature Center

Look Forward To

- varied natural communities
- ledge outcrops
- nature center

The Trail

From the map kiosk immediately southwest of the Nature Center, turn left on the red-blazed trail and pass Quarry Pond to your right. Here submerged logs are often festooned with painted turtles out basking in the sun shell to shell. In late fall these reptiles retreat to the muddy pond bottom, surviving there in an amazing state of suspended animation. Continue past the pond and reach the Yellow Trail junction on the right. Walk straight ahead and pass another junction on the same side. Climb gradually for a brief distance to the first intersection with the White Trail on the left; continue on the Red Trail for now. Pass the first ledge outcrops in this forest of oak, birch, and hickory.

Soon reach the other end of the White Trail and turn left onto it. At the intersection with the Yellow Trail proceed straight ahead. The shrub layer of this otherwise open oak woodland is dominated by dense thickets of greenbrier. Sassafras, huckleberry, lowbush blueberry, and a few azalea also grow in the acidic granite soils, made even more acidic by tannins from the decaying oak leaf litter. A rounded granite outcrop, its former angularity softened by an overriding ice sheet more than 10,000 years ago, rises on the left. American chestnut roots continue to sprout here only to be killed back by the blight after they reach a certain size.

Follow the trail as it bends left and climbs to the top of the outcrop's rocky spine. Indian pipes and striped wintergreen poke up through last year's leaves, and beaked hazel bushes produce tasty nuts akin to filberts. The earth drops away in both directions. Watch your footing, as these rocks can be slippery when wet. That same moisture brings life to dormant lichens clinging to the rocks. Maple-leafed viburnum and huckleberry shrubs grow on top of the tough granite outcrop. Descend and continue straight on the White Trail through open woodland of black birch, red maple, oak, and hickory. As the trail climbs again gently, pass a granite boulder on the left.

Reach a short side trail, marked as overlook, which leads thirty-five feet to the edge of the cliff. No panoramas here, but instead a nice bird's-eye view into the forest below. The main trail continues through dry oak woods and over the top of another ledge. In fall the red and orange leaves of Virginia creeper, or woodbine, stand out against the somber-hued trunks up which they twine. White oak trees sprout profusely along their trunks, producing one- to two-foot-long limbs with leaves. I haven't seen this degree of trunk sprouting anywhere else; perhaps it follows the removal of limbs. Walk easily downhill and bear right.

More thick greenbrier and huckleberry are in evidence as you pass another low rock ledge on the right. White-breasted nuthatches hitch down the trunks of white oak looking for secure bark crevices to store tidbits for later retrieval. Come to the edge of an outcrop bordered by beech. The trail swings left where you gain a view of the damp woodland below, traversed by an intermittent brook. Fragments of green hickory nut husks left by industrious gray squirrels cap many of the rocks in fall. In addition to the ubiquitous greenbrier thickets, Solomon's seal, a member of the huge lily family, produces pairs of greenish yellow pendant flowers along its stalk in spring and blue-black berries in late summer.

Descend gradually from the ledges and bear right through oak, red maple, and greenbrier. Reach the intersection of the White and Yellow Trails; turn right onto the White Trail. Cross a small wooden bridge where Hidden Pond on the left may be without water during dry seasons. A post-mounted wood-duck box provides shelter for other creatures too. Tickseed sunflowers bloom profusely in fall in the black muck. Arrowwood, winterberry, nanny-berry, and abundant sweet pepperbush thrive in the damp woodland soil too. Leaving the damp spot, the path climbs gradually through rock-strewn woods of black birch. This appears to be an old woods road. Some of the densest greenbrier thickets yet flourish on either side of you.

Pass through an old stone wall and come to an unmarked T intersection; turn left. Houses are visible on the right. Red cedar growing here appear to have been planted. Cross a fallen stone wall; another continues on the left. Greenbrier has colonized these former pastures with a vengeance. Eastern towhees scratch for morsels within the relative safety of the thorny greenbrier patch. Come to a Y intersection of the Yellow and White Trails. Follow the right tine to join the Orange Loop. A white oak grows over the end of a boulder in a fashion reminiscent of an octopus tentacle clutching a clam, just before you come to a narrow power-line clearing. Cross it; reenter woods of white and red oak, hickory, and black birch (you are now on the Orange Loop); and turn right just before you reach a stone wall.

Turn left, pass through a stone wall, and come to an intersection of the Orange Loop; turn right. Hay-scented and New York ferns and tiny dark-green, treelike club mosses grace the forest floor shaded by red maple, as greenbrier is much reduced. Reach a split (both sides blazed orange) in the trail at a large American beech tree, its trunk blackened by graffiti scars. You will return to this tree later. Stay to the right and cross a boulder. A rock wall is at your right. Tall cinnamon fern require permanently moist ground, as at the point where the trail turns left, then right. You're walking through damp red maple woods with sweet pepperbush and azalea shrubs. Some of the trees are quite large.

On an early-October visit my wife, Chris, found a tiny, perhaps recently emerged, wood frog whose coloration enabled it to blend in perfectly with its surroundings. Hatched in temporary vernal pools, these frogs are often found far from water later in life, as their name implies. Bog bridges lead through the wettest sections, which may well be dry by late summer. Bear left and cross more such bridges through a swale, then climb gradually up the opposite slope. Curve right, toward a stone wall, and then left along it. Cross over the top of another outcropping. The cliff drops off steeply on the right to a small valley through which a part-time stream flows. One house is visible beyond. The path swings left.

While inch-long spring peepers called like chicks from the trees, we found another black-masked wood frog exactly the color of the decaying leaves. No telling how many others we might have missed. Pass another low rock outcrop on the right which has white wood asters blooming on it in fall; a higher ledge is visible on the other side of the small ravine. The path swings right and leads down into the ravine, across which a small stone wall runs diagonally. The wall even crosses the brook that flows near the base of the outcrop. On the far side of the ravine we discovered an eastern phoebe's old moss-covered nest under the overhang of a crevice in the outcrop. This bird is just one of at least 66 species that have nested in the sanctuary.

The trail goes left along the brook and reaches the border of the Mashantucket Land Trust Nature Preserve. Follow the orange blazes through a stone wall in the oak-maple woods and bear left. Princess pine and cinnamon fern are now common, and a few clumps of sphagnum moss appear. Come to a Y intersection. The left fork is a shortcut across the end of the Orange Trail; continue straight ahead through abundant hay-scented fern and scattered highbush blueberry, spicebush, and huckleberry shrubs. Princess pines, looking like miniature versions of their namesakes, bear candle-shaped strobules which produce the highly flammable spores once used by pioneering flash photographers. Pass through a stone wall in the mixed deciduous woodland, where greenbrier once again becomes abundant.

Follow the orange-blazed trail as it turns left while a side trail swings right. Pass through another stone wall and bear left at a low ledge. The path continues to curve left in a sort of hairpin turn, and then compensates somewhat in the other direction. As we passed by during our early-October visit, an eastern chipmunk watched our every action from its leaf-lined burrow entrance without moving so much as a single muscle or uttering a sound—a charming encounter. More small granite outcrops appear as the trail turns right. Black birch grow among the rocks. Striped wintergreen, which has thick, variegated green-and-white leaves and white flowers in spring, is common in these woods. Now descend easily to the right, around the end of the outcrop. This side of the ledge is higher, steeper, and more imposing than the other.

The trail curves left and bisects another stone wall. Agricultural fields in colonial times were generally small, usually only a couple of acres each, making for a lot of wall building. That is certainly evident here. The land is level now and black birch, oak, and a few small beech clothe it. Another stone wall is breached, and a depression on the forest floor on the right, a vernal pool, currently dry, provides essential breeding sites for salamanders and wood frogs in spring. Bear left and ignore the trail that leads off the property. At the fork, stay right and follow the orange blazes. Huckleberry, greenbrier, and pepperbush form a thick shrub layer. Note signs for the Mashantucket Land Trust. Cross a couple of bog-bridge sections, then reach a small trail junction on the right; stay left on the main trail.

Come to the now familiar graffiti-marred beech tree at a tricky inter-section. The trail ahead splits three ways; take the middle one and contin-ue straight to a T intersection. Both sides are blazed orange; turn left and pass through another stone wall. After a couple of turns, cross the power line right of way again (you're now on the Yellow Trail). Reach a junction with the White Trail on the right and turn onto it. Tufted titmice—pert, crested relatives of the smaller black-capped chickadee—sing their loud whistled *peter-peter-peter* in spring and summer. After another gap in a stone wall, curve right and gradually downhill through greenbrier thickets Uncle Remus's Br'er Rabbit would have been tickled to hide in. Spring peeper tree frogs pipe single shrill, high notes even in fall on mild days.

You are walking now amid oak and smooth-trunked black birch. The small seeds of black birch can germinate only on bare ground, so bare earth created by logging and by wind throws is essential for its reproduction. But black birch is also susceptible to fire, and its abundance in these woods indicates an absence of fire for some years. Amble downhill through a thick growth of huckleberry whose sweet blue-black fruits are highly sought after by mammals. As the soil moisture increases, sweet pepperbush, bear-ing spikes of small white flowers in summer; cinnamon fern, named after the color of its fertile fronds; and highbush blueberry line the path. Tread on wooden slabs strategically placed in a damp ferny spot, and cross a modest wooden bridge.

Now walk up a short hill with ledges to the right and come to a yel-low crossover trail on the right. A couple of red cedar, remnants of former pastureland, seem out of place now. Bear left on the White Trail, which takes you in about 150 feet to the Orange Trail T intersection. A house sits straight ahead beyond the T. Turn left; the path soon becomes the white-blazed trail. Walk gradually downslope with stone walls to your right, and come to an intersection on the left. Stay straight and continue through maple, birch, and oak woodland. Reach a Y split. Stay right, on the White Trail. Reach the Red Trail intersection and turn right onto it, retracing your steps to the Nature Center.

STRANGER THAN A FAIRY TALE

Wood frogs defy logic. They aren't the standard fairy-book characters that sit on lily pads. Instead, wood frogs roam the forest floor, snatching up insects and other tasty invertebrates. While most species of frogs are green like Kermit in order to blend in with their verdant aquatic surroundings, female wood frogs are usually a pinkish tan. In contrast, the skins of males are generally quite dark brown. In any event, a still wood frog is virtually invisible. Only sudden movement betrays it. Reaching three inches in length in the case of the larger female, wood frogs are also distinguished by their trademark dark-brown, raccoonlike masks.

In early spring, when the first "warm" rains and melting snows begin to penetrate the ground, the seemingly lifeless frogs emerge to create another generation. Instinctively they move to temporary pools of rain and meltwater which collect in woodland depressions. Wood frogs and several species of salamanders court and reproduce only in such vernal pools. Male wood frogs advertise for mates with uncanny, ducklike quaking calls. The larger females, heavy with unfertilized eggs, follow the sounds to the pools where the males are waiting. In a frenzy of mating activity, males tightly clutch the females' torsos with their forearms. As the female lays her mass of up to 1,000 jelly-covered eggs, usually at the site of a submerged twig, the male releases his sperm into the water. After she has deposited all her eggs, she leaves the pool.

The fertilized eggs, and the tadpoles from which they develop in about three weeks, must grow rapidly before the heat of summer dries the pond. The tiny larval frogs, sporting tails and breathing with gills, feed on the minute organisms of the pool for about two months. The basic energy source of vernal pools is created and fortified by the constant addition of organic matter—leaves, twigs and the like—that winds up in the depression. If they escape predators and the pool retains its water long enough, the tadpoles eventually absorb their tails, develop lungs, and crawl out of the primordial slime ready for a life on terra firma, a life which may last for at least three years after emergence.

When cold weather strikes, these frogs seek shelter under logs and leaf litter and within burrows. But they have an ace up their sleeves: an amazing ability to freeze solid and survive. Water is somehow shunted from within the animal's cells into its body cavity so that those same cells don't rupture due to the formation of ice crystals. The return of warmer temperatures in early spring provides the magic kiss that revives the torpid creature from its slumber. Indeed, this is how a "cold-blooded" animal that ranges north of the Arctic Circle—farther north than any other member of its kind—has mastered its frigid environment.

Thus the lowly wood frog, remarkable in so many ways, lives an existence far stranger than any that could have been imagined by the Brothers Grimm.

Getting There

From Interstate 95 take Exit 90 (note signs for Marinelife Aquarium/Mystic Seaport). Turn onto Route 27 south and drive for 0.1 mile. Turn left onto Coogan Boulevard and follow it for 0.7 mile, where it ends at Jerry Browne Road. Turn right onto Jerry Browne Road and follow it for 0.3 mile to Pequotsepos Road on the right at the top of the hill (just before the large water tower). Drive for 0.5 mile to the Nature Center entrance and parking lot on the left. The trailhead is located behind the Nature Center as approached from the parking area.

—R.L.

45 Barn Island Wildlife Management Area

Stonington

- unnamed trails
- 5.3 miles
- 65-foot elevation gain
- 3.5 hours
- moderate, because of length

Occupying 707 acres of salt marsh and adjacent uplands on the shores of Little Narragansett Bay, Barn Island Wildlife Management Area is situated in the extreme southeastern corner of the state virtually up against the Rhode Island border.

The extensive marshlands and impoundments here have long been a popular hunting ground for waterfowlers in fall, but the nutrient-rich tidal salt marshes also serve as veritable nurseries, spawning grounds, and feeding areas for a myriad of finfish, shellfish, and crustaceans.

Barn Island gives visitors easy access to some of the state's most extensive salt marsh communities. This biologically rich ecosystem is also endowed with great natural beauty. The trail system is overgrown and difficult to locate in some of the upland sections, but pleasing rambles that enable excellent wildlife observation are nevertheless very feasible by means of out-and-back walks. A visit to Barn Island is both fascinating and very enjoyable.

A salt marsh observation platform and portable toilets are located at the boat-launch parking lot a short distance down the road from the trailhead. Note that only vehicles with boat trailers may park there. Exercise caution during the hunting season, which extends from September 1 to the end of February; hunting is not permitted on Sundays. The major hunting season is October 15 to December 1. Barn Island Wildlife Management Area closes at sunset.

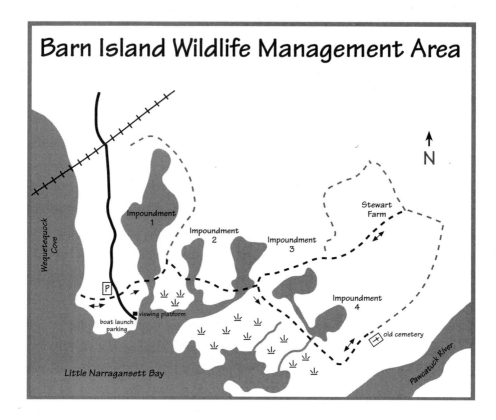

Barn Island Wildlife Management Area

Look Forward To

- Wequetequock Cove

- extensive salt marshes

- varied natural communities

- diverse wildlife

The Trail

You may want to begin by taking a side trail for a few hundred yards for a picturesque view of Wequetequock Cove, and a close look at the shore by following the grassy path from the pedestrian parking area through thickets of greenbrier, oriental bittersweet, and arrowwood. As you proceed, honeysuckle, sassafras, black cherry, black oak, and shining sumac also become abundant. Gray catbirds are common summertime residents who feel at home in this dense growth. Listen also for the sharply accented *chick-a-per-*

weeoo-chick of a skulking little white-eyed vireo. After walking in shade initially, emerge into sunlight where goldenrods bloom in late summer and
wild grapes ripen on vines draping the shrubs and small trees.

Soon emerge at the shore, where the smell of salt is in the air. At low
tide you can see that the shoreline is composed of tiny sand beaches interspersed with miniature islands of marsh peat, a sign of a sinking coastline.
Rocks draped with rockweed are also visible when the tide is out. The
wrack line of material left by the last high tide may contain slipper and
shiny jingle shells, various crabs, horseshoe crab (not a true crab at all)
carapaces, eelgrass, and the seaweeds codeum (green fleece) and Irish
moss.

Salt marsh cordgrass and the shrub marsh elder occupy the narrow
tidal zone between dry land and bay, while seaside goldenrod, groundsel
tree, wild rose, and poison ivy (away from the trail) thrive on terra firma.
Large, black double-crested cormorants often stand on rocks just offshore
with their wings extended for drying, and gray-and-white herring gulls are
ubiquitous. To your left are the beach and dunes. In late summer and early
fall, migrant monarch butterflies sip nectar from the feathery spikes of
goldenrod blossoms.

Backtrack to your vehicle. The main trailhead is on the opposite side
of the asphalt roadway at an iron gate. A memorial stone has been set here
and reads: In Appreciation Of Louis Bayer For His efforts In Preserving The
Barn Island Marshes. Follow the graveled path as it curves left and gently
downslope along a fringe of big bluestem grass (the indicator species of the
midwestern tall-grass prairie) and past a stand of skeletal red pines on the
right. Sassafras trees become more numerous and old man's beard lichen
hangs from a few branches. Mockernut hickory trees and some large red
oak up to two feet in diameter appear. Curve right to walk down a dike bordered on both sides by salt marsh. Eye-catching snowy egrets use their
sharp black bills to snatch fish stranded in small pools by a receding tide.

A few granite boulders dot the marsh, which 200 years ago was actually agricultural land. A steadily submerging coastline has inundated what
was once dry land. The leafless stems of glasswort, or pickleweed, take on
a reddish hue in late summer along the fringes of the marsh. At low tide
the mud flats of the tidal creek on the left are exposed to shorebirds and
other creatures seeking a meal. A big culvert channels the water under the
dike. Cormorants and other fish-eating birds frequent the channel as their
prey becomes easier to catch. Deciduous woodland rings the landward side
of the salt marsh, while on the right the marsh opens to the salty waters of
the bay.

Reenter woods after a few hundred yards. Among the trees are tupelo with shiny green leaves which change to red, yellow, and orange in autumn and pin oak; also moisture-loving cinnamon fern. Climb a few feet and oak, hickory, and sassafras appear. Nonnative autumn olive, once planted to provide wildlife food, and bracken fern also grow in the drier soil. Note the old apple trees, which hint at the land's former uses. Reach an intersection and stay straight. In late summer arrowwood offers blue-black fruits to birds and winterberry shrubs are heavy with bright red fruits; black cherry also provides a bounty for wildlife. The vine Oriental bittersweet and honeysuckle shrubs are ubiquitous alien exotics that are invasive. The seeds of both are dispersed by birds. This woodland also contains a few overtopped red cedar that began life in what was then a pasture.

Emerge onto another dike which has created another impoundment on the left. Great egrets, big white waders nearly the size of great blue herons and sporting impressive yellow-orange bills, stalk for frogs in the shallows. The sour odor of fermenting goldenrod nectar and the slightly sulfurous aroma of salt marsh decay mingle here in late summer. Cross drainage channels, and during low tides note the exposed clumps of ribbed mussels holding fast to the peaty banks. Well adapted for daily exposure to the drying effects of air, these animals retain some water within their shells after the tide recedes. By slightly opening their shells they are able to effect gas exchange (breathe) even when "high and dry." After about 100 yards enter black cherry, tupelo, red maple, and black oak woodland and curve right. Huckleberry and prickly greenbrier grow beneath the trees.

Come to a stone wall on the left at the edge of the next impoundment. The twisted and gnarled trunks of the tupelos are especially appealing visually. Tall, plumed common reed (*Phragmites*) lines this short dike. Cross the very modest drainageway and reenter woods. Tiny spring peeper tree frogs emit high-pitched peeps until cold weather silences them. A fast-flying sharp-shinned hawk disappeared into the trees as we entered the woodland during a mid-September visit. Patches of New York fern grow here and there between the oak, maple, and cherry as larger 600-million-to-800-million-year-old granite boulders dot the forest floor. Black locust trees, some of which are dead, appear. Bittersweet completely envelopes some trees.

Emerge at another impoundment as the path curves right. An osprey nesting platform is mounted on a pole out on the seaward side and northern harriers (marsh hawks) course low over the marshlands listening for rodents and other prey. Cross another flowage where long-legged shorebirds called greater yellowlegs catch fish in the shallows during migration. We glimpsed a beautiful buckeye butterfly here during our mid-September visit. Buckeyes display a series of eyespots on their upper wing surfaces which may fool predators. The dike curves left; a copse of white oak stands also on the left. The marsh is especially extensive on that side. Salt-spray rose and bayberry grow along the path.

Enter woodland once again as the land rises slightly. Granite boulders flecked with grayish green lichens lay in mounds under oak, tupelo, and Juneberry (shadbush) trees, and hay-scented, or boulder, fern and lots of greenbrier encircle the mounds, creating a dense shrub-vine layer. Come to a Y fork; remember it because you will be returning here later to strike off in another direction. Follow the right fork for now and reemerge into the open bordered by salt marsh. Visibility is limited as you make your way through common reed lining the roadway. Big green darner dragonflies patrol the marsh, snatching numerous salt marsh mosquitoes out of midair. Reach a large culvert and a view of the waterway on the left. A few barnacles encrust the rocks at the culvert's mouth. In late summer the numerous white-blooming groundsel trees along the dikes attract butterflies, while goldenrods attract bees, wasps, and butterflies.

Red cedar dots the higher ground adjacent to the marsh. Black locust trees rise above the rest of the trees, imparting a somewhat African savanna look to the scene, although here the tree islands are surrounded by salt marsh. Notice that the salt marsh on the bayside has been ditched. This was once done in an effort to eliminate the breeding grounds of pesky salt marsh mosquitoes, but in the process this alteration also reduced the population of mummichogs and other small mosquito-larvae-eating fish which acted as natural controls. In the long run, ditching has proven to be detrimental to salt marshes.

The dike curves left. Even when the path has not been recently mowed, it is easily passable on tracks. We found a black-and-yellow garden spider on its web in the tall grass in which a honeybee recently had been packaged in silk threads. Another osprey nesting platform, this one with old nesting material on it, stands on the right. On the left, migrating sandpipers probe the mud flats for edible morsels, fattening up for their long journeys. A stone wall out in the marsh on the right frames what were cornfields two centuries ago; these former agricultural fields are now inundated by tides, graphic evidence of the relatively recent rise in sea level. If you hear a crow giving a very nasal *ca*, you are hearing a fish crow, a smaller relative of the very familiar American crow, which is generally found only near tidal rivers.

Reenter woods of black locust, red maple, oak, flowering dogwood, and sassafras where red-orange wood lilies bloom in summer. Nonnative thicket-forming multiflora rose is abundant. Catbirds mew from the dense cover and eastern towhees scratch on the ground in forest openings. Curve left past scattered red cedar and between rock walls. Come to a cellar hole on the right, just below the wall, constructed of mortared granite blocks, now overgrown. Head gently downhill from the cellar hole under white pine, red maple, and oak that are once again of taller stature. Soon come to a half-acre clearing on the right occupied by a small cemetery. About two dozen headstones, apparently the oldest dating from 1795, are still standing. The old burying ground, bounded on all sides by stone walls, is being recolonized by sassafras, oak, cherry, and alder buckthorn.

In sharp contrast to the tranquillity of this spot, posted signs warn that Barn Island was once a bombing target range and may still contain old buried ordnance. While we were contemplating this a gray tree frog gave its trill from nearby. At the far end of the cemetery are imposing masonry gateposts. Beyond here the old roadway eventually becomes paved Stewart Road and leads to a residential area. When ready to move on from the cemetery, turn around and retrace your steps to the Y intersection located between the third and fourth impoundments.

Two hundred year old gravestones repose in a small cemetery slowly being reclaimed by sassafras, oak, cherry and buckthorn.

At the Y intersection you can continue back to your vehicle or turn right and walk through oak woodland as the road curves left. If you turned right, soon come to a trail junction on the left but continue straight on the old roadway under oak, tupelo, and red maple. Cinnamon fern, sweet pepperbush, azalea shrubs, and alder grow in the low-lying areas on both sides. Cross a drainageway where joe-pye weed and sedges thrive, then curve and "climb" to slightly higher ground occupied by white and black oaks, red maple, and black birch. Reach a trail intersection on the left, but curve right to enter a former pasture regenerating to white pine and red cedar where pretty American copper butterflies fly. Autumn olive, bearing translucent red berries is also common.

Arrive at lovely hayfields with blooming red clover which attracts hordes of cabbage white and sulfur butterflies in late summer. Continue your gradual climb through the hayfields of the Stewart Farm which afford nice, open vistas. Reach an iron gate as the track curves right and joins a gravel road going right. At this point turn around and retrace your steps to the Y intersection where you began this part of the excursion. When you reach the Y intersection, stay right to return eventually to the parking area.

THE JAWS OF DEATH

As we made our way back to an incoming tide, we were treated to quite a spectacle in the salt marsh—one we had never seen before. Dozens of small silvery fish were jumping en masse a few inches out of the water repeatedly as if fleeing the jaws of some formidable predator. The energy contained in that scene was remarkable and caused us to stare almost transfixed at the spectacle before us. Like a handful of skipping pebbles hurled across the water's surface, each jump took the school approximately one linear foot across the water before they fell once again into the watery realm they were attempting to escape. Sometimes we witnessed two quick jumps in immediate succession. A bit farther along in the tidal creek we saw smaller groups of the same species making three jumps in very rapid succession. It was really quite captivating.

Only later did we learn that our hunch had been correct: what was making these schools of Atlantic silversides fish act like jumping beans was that they were being hotly pursued by the highly predatory bluefish. Although hatched far offshore, by late summer young bluefish, known as "snappers," enter tidal marshes and feed voraciously upon the abundant small fish. It was this life-and-death struggle we were witnessing. No wonder, then, that small, vulnerable species like silversides travel in schools which reduce any one individual's chances of being slashed by a predator.

By the end of their first summer, snappers may reach twelve inches in length on a diet of Atlantic silversides and other bait fish. Eventually these large-mouthed tigers of the sea return to open water, where they may attain a length of three and a half feet. Here they are among the species most sought by anglers.

Getting There

From Interstate 95 take Exit 91, which is Route 234 and North Main Street in Stonington. Follow Route 234 west for 0.4 mile and turn left onto North Main Street. At 1.5 miles turn left onto Route 1 for 1.7 miles, and then turn right onto Greenhaven Road. Make an immediate right onto Palmer Neck Road and drive 1.5 miles to the trailhead off the pavement on the right.

—R.L.

Recommended References and Reading

Allport, Susan. *Sermons in Stone*. Norton: 1990. A fascinating treatise on New England's stone walls.

Bell, Michael. *The Face of Connecticut: People, Geology, and the Land*. The State Geological and Natural History Survey of Connecticut, Bulletin 110. 1985. Contains a wealth of information.

Cronon, William. *Changes in the Land: Indians, Colonists, and the Ecology of New England*. Hill and Wang. 1983. An interesting melding of human and natural history.

Godin, Alfred J. *Wild Mammals of New England*. Johns Hopkins University Press: 1977. The most complete book on the subject.

Golden Guides published by Golden Press. Titles include: *Pond Life, Insects, Butterflies and Moths, Mammals, Birds, Nonflowering Plants, Trees, Reptiles and Amphibians, and Rocks and Minerals*. Excellent introductory identification series for children.

Jorgensen, Neil. *A Guide to New England's Landscape*. Globe Pequot Press: 1977. A geological perspective.

Jorgensen, Neil. *A Sierra Club Naturalist's Guide to Southern New England*. Sierra Club Books: 1978. An ecological examination of natural communities and their characteristic plants and animals.

Morgan, Ann Haven. *Field Book of Ponds and Streams: An Introduction to the Life of Fresh Water*. G. P. Putnam's Sons: 1930. Still one of the best works on the subject.

Newcomb, Lawrence. *Newcomb's Wildflower Guide*. Little, Brown and Company: 1977. Utilizes easy-to-use keys; wonderful illustrations.

Peterson Field Guides. published by Houghton Mifflin Company. Titles include *Eastern Birds, Mammals, Animal Tracks, Eastern and Central Reptiles and Amphibians, Eastern Butterflies, Trees and Shrubs, Wildflowers, Ferns, Freshwater Fishes, Atlantic Seashore,* and *Eastern Forests.* All are excellent.

Rupp, Rebecca. *Red Oaks & Black Birches: The Science and Lore of Trees.* Garden Way Publishing: 1990. Full of interesting information about our common native trees.

Stokes Nature Guides published by Little, Brown and Company. Titles include: *Nature in Winter; Bird Behavior I, II,* and *III; Animal Tracking and Behavior; Observing Insect Lives;* and *Amphibians and Reptiles.* These are behavior oriented and excellent.

Teale, Edwin Way. *A Naturalist Buys An Old Farm.* Dodd, Mead & Company: 1974. An intimate portrait of Connecticut Audubon Society's Trail Wood Sanctuary.

Thomson, Betty Flanders. *The Changing Face of New England.* Houghton Mifflin Company: 1977. An ecological and land-use perspective.

Walton, Richard K., and Robert W. Lawson. *Birding by Ear: Guide to Bird Song Identification,* and *More Birding by Ear: Eastern and Central,* three CDs or cassettes. Peterson Field Guides: Houghton Mifflin Company. 1989, 1994. Both teach songs of common species by comparison method.

About the Authors

RENÉ LAUBACH has been director of Massachusetts Audubon Society's Berkshire Wildlife Sanctuaries since 1985. Growing up in Michigan, he spent fourteen years in museum work before assuming his current position.

Laubach has authored articles for Massachusetts Audubon Society's *Sanctuary* magazine and for several scientific journals dealing with birds. With his wife, Christyna, and John B. Bowles, he wrote *A Guide to the Bats of Iowa,* published by the Iowa Department of Natural Resources. He is also author of *A Guide to Natural Places in the Berkshire Hills* and, with Michael Tougias, *Nature Walks in Central Massachusetts,* an AMC Nature Walks Book. He also coauthored his most recent work, *The Backyard Bird House Book: Building Nestboxes and Creating Natural Habitats,* with his wife.

René counts traveling among his favorite pursuits. When not exploring New England, he enjoys leading natural history tours for the Massachusetts Audubon Society to the American Southwest and Latin America.

CHARLES W. G. SMITH is horticulture editor of Storey Communications in Williamstown, Massachusetts. He is the author of the gardening book *The Big Book of Garden Secrets* and the hiking book *Nature Walks in the Berkshire Hills.* In addition to authoring books, Smith has written articles for a number of magazines, including *Fine Gardening, Country Journal,* and *Harrowsmith Country Life.* He regularly lectures on hiking and gardening throughout New England.

Smith grew up in central Connecticut within sight of the Hanging Hills of Meriden and received his Bachelor of Science degree in Environmental Horticulture from the University of Connecticut. He presently lives in a log cabin in the Berkshire Hills with his son, Nathaniel, and his fiancee, Christine.

About the AMC

Begin a new adventure!

Join the Appalachian Mountain Club, the oldest and largest outdoor recreation club in the United States. Since 1876, the Appalachian Mountain Club has helped people experience the majesty and solitude of the Northeast outdoors. Our mission is to promote the protection, enjoyment, and wise use of the mountains, rivers, and trails of the Northeast.

Members enjoy discounts on all AMC programs, facilities, and books:

Outdoor Adventure Programs

We offer more than 100 workshops on hiking, canoeing, cross-country skiing, biking, and rock climbing, as well as guided trips for hikers, canoeists, and skiers.

Mountain Huts and Visitor Centers

The AMC maintains backcountry huts in the White Mountains of New Hampshire and visitor centers throughout the Northeast, from Maine to New Jersey.

Books and Maps

Guides and maps to the mountains, streams, and forests of the Northeast—from Maine to North Carolina—and outdoors skill books from backcountry experts on topics from winter camping to fly-fishing.

Appalachian Mountain Club
5 Joy Street
Boston, MA 02108
617-523-0636

Find us on the Web at www.outdoors.org.

Recommended Reading
from AMC Books

Visit the AMC Bookstore at www.outdoors.org.

Nature Walks in Northern Vermont
Nature Hikes in the White Mountains
Nature Walks in the Berkshire Hills
Nature Walks in and around New York City
Nature Walks in Southern New Hampshire
Nature Walks in the New Hampshire Lakes Region
Nature Walks in Southern Maine
Nature Walks in Central Massachusetts
Nature Walks near Philadelphia

Quiet Water Canoe Guide: New York
Quiet Water Canoe Guide: New Hampshire/Vermont
Quiet Water Canoe Guide: Maine
Quiet Water Canoe Guide: Massachusetts/Connecticut/Rhode Island

AMC Guide to Freshwater Fishing in New England:
    How and Where to Fish in All Six New England States
Watercolor Painting on the Trail: A Hiking Artist's Handbook
Seashells in My Pocket: A Child's Guide to Exploring the Atlantic Coast
Into the Mountains: Stories of New England's Most Celebrated Peaks
The Complete Guide to Trail Building and Maintenance

Alphabetical Listing of Areas

NOTES

NOTES